MODELS
OF GOD

MODELS OF GOD

Theology for
an Ecological,
Nuclear Age

SALLIE McFAGUE

SCM PRESS LTD

copyright © Fortress Press 1987

Biblical quotations, unless otherwise noted, are from
the Revised Standard Version of the Bible, copyright
1946, 1952, © 1971, 1973 by the Division of Christian
Education of the National Council of the Churches
of Christ in the USA, and are used by permission.

British Library Cataloguing in Publication Data

McFague, Sallie
Models of God: theology for an ecological
nuclear age.
1. God
I. Title
231   BT102
ISBN 0–334–01039–X

First British edition published 1987
by SCM Press Ltd
26–30 Tottenham Road London N1 4BZ

Printed in Great Britain by
Richard Clay Ltd, Bungay, Suffolk

To Mary Ann Tolbert

Contents

Preface   ix

Part One
Theology for an Ecological, Nuclear Age

1. A New Sensibility   3

    A Holistic View of Reality   6
    The Nuclear Nightmare   14
    Theological Construction   21

2. Metaphorical Theology   29

    Metaphors, Models, and Concepts   31
    Sources and Resources: Scripture, Tradition,   40
      and Experience
    The Christian Paradigm   45

3. God and the World   59

    The Monarchical Model   63
    The World as God's Body   69
    God as Mother, Lover, Friend   78

Part Two
Models of God for an Ecological, Nuclear Age

Introduction   91

4. God as Mother   97

The Love of God as Mother: Agape   101

The Activity of God as Mother: Creating   109

The Ethic of God as Mother: Justice   116

5. God as Lover   125

The Love of God as Lover: Eros   130

The Activity of God as Lover: Saving   137

The Ethic of God as Lover: Healing   146

6. God as Friend   157

The Love of God as Friend: Philia   159

The Activity of God as Friend: Sustaining   167

The Ethic of God as Friend: Companionship   174

Conclusion   181

Note to the British Edition   188

Notes   189

Preface

In the closing pages of my last book, *Metaphorical Theology*, I experimented with the model of God as friend in an attempt to address the issues of idolatry and irrelevance leveled against the patriarchal imagery of the Christian tradition. The dominance of the patriarchal model, I felt, excluded the emergence of other models to express the relationship between God and the world, and so the model had become idolatrous and had rendered the tradition's imagery anachronistic. Since writing that book I have come to see patriarchal as well as imperialistic, triumphalist metaphors for God in an increasingly grim light: this language is not only idolatrous and irrelevant—besides being oppressive to many who do not identify with it—but it may also work against the continuation of life on our planet. Our nuclear capability places human beings of the late twentieth century on the verge of eliminating not only themselves but also most if not all other forms of life on earth. In this unprecedented danger, we must ask whether the Judeo-Christian tradition's triumphalist imagery for the relationship between God and the world is helpful or harmful. Does it support human responsibility for the fate of the earth, or does it, by looking to either divine power or providence, shift the burden to God? If a case can be made, as I believe it can, that traditional imperialistic imagery for God is opposed to life, its continuation and fulfillment, then we must give serious attention to alternatives. It is this I propose to do in these pages.

The nuclear issue is, however, part of a larger picture. I see the threat of a nuclear holocaust as epitomizing the genuinely novel context in which all constructive work in our time, including theology, must take place. To be sure, other eras undoubtedly considered their times as unprecedented as we find ours. But the crux for those of us who find our time exceptional is that the "old ways," the old solutions, will not do for us. The nuclear threat is but the most extreme example of what some call the postmodern sensibility. If the Enlightenment was the first watershed, thrusting us into the modern world, then the contemporary era must be called the second watershed, for its assumptions differ from those of the Enlightenment that created the modern world. Any listing of these assumptions will vary but will probably include some of the following: a greater appreciation of nature, linked with a chastened admiration for technology; the recognition of the importance of language (and hence interpretation and construction) in human existence; the acceptance of the challenge that other religious options present to the Judeo-Christian tradition; a sense of the displacement of the white, Western male and the rise of those dispossessed because of gender, race, or class; an apocalyptic sensibility, fueled in part by the awareness that we exist between two holocausts, the Jewish and the nuclear; and perhaps most significant, a growing appreciation of the thoroughgoing, radical interdependence of life at all levels and in every imaginable way. These assumptions, I believe, form the context for theology *if it is to be theology for our time.* The sorts of theological tasks that can be undertaken within this context are, of course, many, and the kind of reflection I will attempt in the present book is a modest, but I believe essential, one. It takes place at the level of the religious and theological imagination.

Let me try a sketch of what I am doing and then I will say a few words about the way I will do it. I begin with the assumption that what we can say with any assurance about the character of Christian faith is very little and that even that will be highly contested. Christian faith is, it seems to me, most basically a claim that the universe is neither indifferent nor malevolent but that there is a power (and a personal power at that) which is on the side of life and its fulfillment. Moreover, the Christian believes that we have some clues for fleshing out this claim in the life, death, and appearances of Jesus of Nazareth. Nevertheless, each generation must venture, through an analysis of what fulfillment could and must mean for its own time, the best way to express that claim. A critical dimension of this expression is the imaginative picture, the metaphors and models, that underlie the conceptual systems of theology. One cannot hope to interpret Christian faith for one's own time if one remains indifferent to the basic images that are the lifeblood of interpretation and that greatly influence people's perceptions and behavior. One of the serious deficiencies in contemporary theology is that though theologians have attempted to interpret the faith in new concepts appropriate to our time, the basic metaphors and models have remained relatively constant: they are triumphalist, monarchical, patriarchal. Much *deconstruction* of the traditional imagery has taken place, but little *construction*. If, however, metaphor and concept are, as I believe, inextricably and symbiotically related in theology, there is no way to do theology for our time with outmoded or oppressive metaphors and models. The refusal to deal with the constructive task results in either a return to anachronistic models—a conservative retreat—or a move away from all images toward abstract language. The first ghettoizes Christianity; the other renders it sterile. In this situation, one thing that is needed—and which I attempt in these pages—is a *remythologizing* of the relationship between God and the world. I will experiment with the models of God as mother, lover, and friend of the world, and with the image of the world as God's body. I will try to show that these metaphors are credible candidates for theology today from both a Christian and a postmodern perspective.

Although the bare statement of such a project makes it sound presumptuous at the very least, I wish to be clear at the outset concerning the nature of the project. The kind of theology being advanced here is what I call metaphorical or heuristic theology; that is, it experiments with metaphors and models, and the claims it makes are small. As I mentioned earlier, what can be said with certainty about Christian faith is very little; theology, at any rate my kind of theology, is principally an elaboration of a few basic metaphors and models in an attempt to express the claim of Christianity in a powerful, comprehensive, and contemporary way. As remythologization, such theology acknowledges that it is, as it were, painting a picture. The picture may be full and rich, but it *is* a picture. What this sort of enterprise makes very clear is that theology is *mostly* fiction: it is the elaboration of key metaphors and models. It insists that we do not know very much and that we should not camouflage our ignorance by either petrifying our metaphors or forgetting that our concepts derive from metaphors. We must not forget the crack in the foundation beneath all our imaginings and the conceptual schemes we build upon them. That crack is exemplified in the "is not" of metaphor which denies any identity in its assertions. Nonetheless, admitting that theology is mainly fiction, mainly elaboration, we claim that some fictions are better than others, both for human habitation and as expressions of the gospel of Christian faith at a particular time. So we try out different models and metaphors in an attempt to talk about what we do not know how to talk about: the relationship between God and the world, from a Christian perspective, for our time. We flesh out these metaphors and models sufficiently for seeing their implications and the case that can be made for them. This elaboration of a few models is the principal focus of the present essay. Although this sort of theology "says much," it "means little." That is, metaphorical theology is a postmodern, highly skeptical, heuristic enterprise, which claims that in order to be faithful to the God of its tradition—the God on the side of life and its fulfillment—we must try out new pictures that will bring the reality of God's love into the imaginations of the women and men of today. That task must be attempted and attempted again. My contribution is a modest experiment with a few metaphors; other experiments with other metaphors are appropriate and needed.

I have structured this experiment in two main parts: the first sets the context for the experiment and the other carries it out in detail. Chapter 1 suggests some crucial aspects of the sensibility needed in contemporary theology: a holistic or ecological, evolutionary view of reality; acceptance of human responsibility for nuclear knowledge; and an awareness of the constructive character of all human enterprises. Chapter 2 spells out the implications of this sensibility for theology and, in particular, addresses the nature of metaphorical, heuristic theology, as well as its use of traditional sources. It ends with a reading of the Christian faith as a destabilizing, inclusive, nonhierarchical vision of fulfillment for all, especially for the outcast and outsider. In chapter 3 a sketch is attempted of the all-embracing context within which the particular models of God as mother, lover, and friend will be considered: this context is modeled on the world as God's body, which is contrasted with the traditional model of the world as the king's realm. In the chapters constituting the second half of the book, the models of God as mother, lover, and friend are investigated in detail in relation to three main questions: What sort of divine love is suggested by each? What activity, work, or doctrine is associated with each? And what does each imply concerning the conduct of human existence? In these chapters we will consider the following: the problematic nature of these models from a traditional Christian perspective; a construal of agape, eros, and philia as various forms of both divine and human love; an interpretation of the doctrines of the creating, saving, and sustaining activities of God; and in light of our models, the nature of sin and evil, and the character of church and sacraments. Finally, we will consider the implications of these models for the conduct of human existence: the demand of justice for all; participation in healing the divisions among beings; and the offer of companionship to others, especially the outsider. The assumption of the experiment is that the models of God as mother, lover, and friend in the context of the world as God's body is a credible, appropriate, and helpful imaginative picture of the relationship between God and the world from a Christian perspective for our time, and that it is preferable in a number of ways to traditional alternatives. This sounds like a big claim, but I would recall once again that it is the same kind of claim as that presented by the models of God as lord, king, and patriarch, with the world as his realm. Both are imaginative pictures (although the latter, because conventional, does not appear to be) attempting to spell out, on the basis of a few metaphors, the salvific power of God. The question we must ask is not whether one is true and the other false, but which one is a better portrait of Christian faith *for our day*.

This book, like all books, is written by a particular author for a particular readership: I am white and middle-class, writing to a mainstream Christian audience. What joins author and readers is that the ecological and nuclear issues are peculiarly ours; that is, as mainstream, middle-class Christians we have the leisure and the power to attend to these basic but semiremote threats to life as our sisters and brothers oppressed by more immediate and daily threats to survival do not. It has been decisions of those with power and money that have created our ecological crisis as well as escalated the possibility of nuclear war; hence, the "oppression of life" which has resulted is the peculiar responsibility of the white middle class and especially of white middle-class American Christianity, which in significant ways has contributed heavily to the present situation. This essay, then, is a "liberation theology" for life and its continuation, written out of and to the social context of those who control the resources—the money and power—necessary to liberate life. It is admittedly, therefore, middle-class and mainstream. Its radical character lies not primarily in programs for revolutionary action but in changes in consciousness, the assumption being that a new imaginative picture of the relationship between God and the world must precede action. The action that eventuates may well be revolutionary, but blueprints for action are not the central concern here. Finally, though this essay is not a feminist theology in the sense that its guiding principle is the liberation of women, the fact that I am female is relevant to my perspective as author, for it is the form of oppression that has provided me with sufficient disorientation from middle-class, mainstream Christianity both to question it and to risk alternative formulations of Christian faith.

In closing this preface, I would like to thank the people and institutions that have helped me with the manuscript. I am grateful to Vanderbilt Divinity School and to its Office of Women's Concerns for appointing me the Antoinette Brown Lecturer in 1983, for it was in that lecture, entitled "A New Way of Seeing, A New Way of Being: Feminist Theology, the Nuclear Threat, and Images of God," that I began to think through the issues in the present book. Also of special importance in germinating ideas for the project were two classes of a course that I taught under the title of "Models of God" at Vanderbilt Divinity School for both professional and doctoral students. Billed as "an experimental course in constructive, revisionist theology, focusing on additions and alternatives to the classical, hierarchical, monarchical model of God for an ecological, nuclear age," it investigated models of God as mother, liberator, lover, healer, judge, and friend, as well as naturalistic and impersonal models, for their appropriateness as Christian images of God and their implications for the relationship between God and the world. The course required students to be well versed in the history of theology as well as able to think imaginatively and boldly. I learned a great deal from these students, who in groups of three or four worked concretely and in depth with a model, sharing their findings with the rest of the class. In appreciation, I would like to list their names here: Lori Adams, Sally Ahner, Kelly Boyte, Anna Case-Winters, Jody Combs, Alix Evans, Wendy Farley, Mark Forrester, Bill Friskics, Douglas Gastelum, Melissa Harrison, Carolyn Higginbotham, James Howard, Bill Johnston, Joy Kraft, John Kay, Karen Knodt, Peter Larson, Don Makin, Viki Matson, Michael Petty, Janet Pierce, Michael Rice-Sauer, Philip Roberson, Mary Schertz, Tara Seeley, Paul Shupe, Nancy Victorin, Sandra Ward-Angell.

I am also very grateful indeed to some colleagues who read and commented on the manuscript: Ian Barbour, John B. Cobb, Jr., Peter Hodgson, Gordon Kaufman, Rosemary Radford Ruether, Mary Ann Tolbert, Sharon Welch, and Maurice Wiles. The generosity of their time and the thoughtfulness of their reflections have meant a great deal to me.

I am indebted to the Vanderbilt University Research Council as well as to the Association of Theological Schools for grants that made it possible for me to spend a year in Cambridge, England, working on the manuscript. I wish to single out for special appreciation one institution in Cambridge, Clare Hall, for appointing me a Visiting Fellow of the college and providing me with a study. I am extremely fortunate in my editor at Fortress Press, Davis Perkins, who has ably overseen all aspects of producing the book, and am grateful also to other members of the Press, especially Barry Blose and Stephanie Egnotovich. Finally, I am dedicating the book to Mary Ann Tolbert, colleague and friend, with whom I shared a memorable sabbatical year in England and whose companionship while I was writing this book made all the difference.

PART ONE | *Theology for an Ecological, Nuclear Age*

1
A New Sensibility

"Sticks and stones may break my bones, but names can never hurt me." This taunt from childhood is haunting in its lying bravado. It *is* the "names" that hurt; one would prefer the sticks and stones. Names matter because what we call something, how we name it, is to a great extent what it is to us. We are the preeminent creatures of language, and though language does not exhaust human reality, it qualifies it in profound ways. It follows, then, that naming can be hurtful, and that it can also be healing or helpful. The ways we name ourselves, one another, and the world cannot be taken for granted; we must look at them carefully to see if they heal or hurt.

How are we naming reality in the twilight years of the twentieth century? I would suggest that we live most of the time and in most ways by outmoded, anachronistic names. We are not naming ourselves, one another, and our earth in ways commensurate *with our own times* but are using names from a bygone time. However helpful and healing these names may have been once upon a time, they are hurtful now. And Christian theology that is done on the basis of anachronistic naming is also hurtful.

We live in our imaginations and our feelings in a bygone world, one under the guidance of a benevolent but absolute deity, a world that is populated by independent individuals (mainly human beings) who relate to one another and to other forms of life in hierarchical patterns. But this is not *our* world, and to continue doing theology on its assumptions is hurtful, for it undermines our ability to accept the new sensibility of our time, one that is holistic and responsible, that is inclusive of all forms of life, and that acknowledges the interdependence of all life.

3

We can approach the issue of the difference between the bygone
world and our world by evoking some images that may help us feel
our world from the inside. The first is a passage from an early essay
by Pierre Teilhard de Chardin called "Cosmic Life," which, despite
being more lyrical than his later writings, is characteristic of his
mature position. The essay, as he himself says, presents the "fire in
his vision." In the passage he is attempting to *feel* "matter."

> . . . and I allowed my consciousness to sweep back to the farthest
> limit of my body, to ascertain whether I might not extend outside
> myself. I stepped down into the most hidden depths of my being,
> lamp in hand and ears alert, to discover whether, in the deepest
> recesses of the blackness within me, I might not see the glint of the
> waters of the current that flows on, whether I might not hear the
> murmur of their mysterious waters that rise from the uttermost
> depths and will burst forth no man knows where. With terror and
> intoxicating emotion, I realized that my own poor trifling existence
> was one with the immensity of all that is and all that is still in process
> of becoming.[1]

He takes a journey into the unknown, the mystery of his own body,
and with lamp in hand tries to see and hear what he is not usually
aware of: his connection with everything else that has been, is, and
will be. The atoms, molecules, and cells that constitute his organic
structure connect him in profound ways to everything else in the
universe. As he remarks, "My life is not my own," for although he
appears to be an individual to his own consciousness, there lies
hidden within him the dense multitude of beings "whose infinitely
patient and lengthy labour" has resulted in "the *phylum*" of which,
as he put it, he is "for the moment the extreme bud."[2]

The world that Teilhard helps us to feel is one whose heartbeat is
relationship and interdependence. The poet Wallace Stevens expresses it precisely: "Nothing is itself taken alone. Things are because of interrelations or interconnections."[3] Moreover, in this
world the absolute divisions between human beings and other beings and even between the organic and the inorganic are softened,
as are many of the hierarchical dualisms that have accompanied
those divisions: spirit/flesh, subject/object, male/female, mind/
body. The holistic paradigm suggested in place of the atomistic
paradigm has, I believe, revolutionary consequences for Christian

theology. Not simply to accept this paradigm but to feel it, to incorporate it into our imaginations, is a necessary dimension of the new sensibility required of Christian theology in our time.

The second image I would like to evoke comes from Jonathan Schell's book *The Fate of the Earth*. In this passage he speaks of extinction—the power to extinguish ourselves and perhaps all life—that is the consequence of nuclear knowledge.

> Death cuts off life; extinction cuts off birth. Death dispatches into the nothingness after life each person who has been born; extinction in one stroke locks up in the nothingness before life all the people who have not yet been born. For we are finite beings at both ends of our existence—natal as well as mortal—and it is the natality of our kind that extinction threatens. We have always been able to send people to their death, but only now has it become possible to prevent all birth and so doom all future human beings to un-creation.[4]

We have never before been in the position of potential "un-creators" of life, of being able to prohibit birth, but it is precisely imagining the extent of this power and feeling deeply what it means to live in a world where this is possible that is part of the new sensibility required for Christian theology. In such a world the future is not simply given to us, as it has always been, but must be achieved.[5] Humanity cannot assume that benevolent forces will take care of the future, for we know—and shall always know—that we have the power to extinguish it. The permanence of this knowledge means that disarmament alone is not sufficient; we must, as Schell says, "learn to live politically in the world in which we already live scientifically."[6] It is also true, I believe, that we must learn to live theologically in the world in which nuclear knowledge is a permanent possession and responsibility.

The third image for a new sensibility comes from a famous passage by Nietzsche:

> What then is truth? A mobile army of metaphors, metonymics, anthropomorphisms: in short, a sum of human relations which become poetically and rhetorically intensified, metamorphosed, adorned, and after long usage, seem to a nation fixed, canonic and binding; truths are illusions of which one has forgotten that they *are* illusions; worn-out metaphors which have become powerless to affect the senses, coins which have their obverse effaced and now are no longer of account as coins but merely as metal.[7]

Nietzsche is saying not only that we construct the worlds we inhabit but also that we forget we have done so. The works of the
imagination, the world views in which we live, were once valuable
currency for the conduct of life. But what we call truth, says Nietzsche, are worn-out metaphors, coins that have their stated value
erased and hence are worthless metal. He presents a challenge—a
double-edged one—that Christian theology must take seriously.
No longer is it possible to insist without question on the "fixed,
canonic and binding" character of metaphors and the concepts built
upon them that have come to us "after long usage." The constructive character of theology must be acknowledged, and this becomes
of critical importance when the world in which we live is profoundly different from the world in which many of the traditional
metaphors and concepts gained currency. Theologians must think
experimentally, must risk novel constructions in order to be theologians *for our time.*

The other challenge raised by Nietzsche involves the question
whether, if theology (as well as all other constructive thought) is
profoundly metaphorical, it is only "illusion." Is it only the play of
fantasy, with one construction as good (or as bad) as another?
Nietzsche does not in this passage explicitly address the question of
the status of metaphor; he addresses only the status of worn-out
metaphor. Yet he raises the former question implicitly with his
contrast between metaphors that once were powerful and those
which have lost their currency. The question of truth with which
Nietzsche sharply challenges us cannot be avoided, for the
metaphors, the constructions, we accept and live by may well control the future—may help determine both whether we have one
and what it will be.

We need to look carefully at each of the aspects of our world
suggested by Teilhard de Chardin, Schell, and Nietzsche, and at the
implications of those aspects for Christian theology.

A Holistic View of Reality

During the last twenty years, feminist Christian theologians
have made a strong case against the androcentric, hierarchical
character of the Western religious tradition. They have insisted that
the humanity of women be given equal status and that the divisions

that separate people—male/female, rich/poor, old/young, white/
colored, straight/gay, Christian/non-Christian—be minimized in
order to create an inclusive vision. As Elisabeth Schüssler Fiorenza
puts it, "Not the holiness of the elect but the wholeness *of all* is the
central vision of Jesus."[8] But only in a few instances has this vision
been extended to the nonhuman world.[9] The feminist theologians
who have given attention to the nonhuman world have been, for
the most part, those involved in Goddess traditions and witchcraft,
for whom the body, the earth, and nature's cycles are of critical
importance.[10] Those of us within the Christian tradition have much
to learn from these sources,[11] but even these feminists have not, I
believe, focused primarily on the intrinsic value of the nonhuman
in a way sufficient to bring about the needed change of consciousness. Nor have other forms of liberation theology, which generally
speaking are more anthropocentric than is feminist theology. All
forms of liberation theology insist on the "deprivatizing" of theology,[12] but to date this has been for the most part limited to human
beings and has not included the destiny of the cosmos. The principal insight of liberation theologies—that redemption is not the
rescue of certain individuals for eternal life in another world but
the fulfillment of all humanity in the political and social realities of
this world—must be further deprivatized to include the well-being
of all life. This is the case not only because unless we adopt an
ecological perspective recognizing human dependence on its envi-
ronment, we may well not survive, but also, of equal theological if
not pragmatic importance, because such a perspective is the dominant paradigm of our time and theology that is not done in conversation with this paradigm is not theology *for our time.*

What is at stake here is not a sentimental love of nature or a
leveling of all distinctions between human beings and other forms
of life but the realization, as Teilhard de Chardin says, that his and
everyone else's "poor trifling existence" is "one with the immensity
of all that is and all that is still in the process of becoming." We are
not separate, static, substantial individuals relating in external
ways—and in ways of our choice—to other individuals, mainly
human ones, and in minor ways to other forms of life. On the
contrary, the evolutionary, ecological perspective insists that we
are, in the most profound ways, "not our own": we belong, from the

cells of our bodies to the finest creations of our minds, to the intricate, constantly changing cosmos. The ecosystem of which we are part is a whole: the rocks and waters, atmosphere and soil, plants, animals, and human beings interact in dynamic, mutually supportive ways that make all talk of atomistic individualism indefensible. Relationship and interdependence, change and transformation, not substance, changelessness, and perfection, are the categories within which a theology for our day must function.

To appreciate the extent to which we are embedded in the evolutionary ecosystem requires an act of imagination, since the Western sensibility has traditionally been nurtured by an atomistic, reductionistic perspective that separates human beings from other beings and reduces all that is not human to objects for human use. But the example of the human mind shows that human development is both culture- and nature-dependent. Infants have brains, but the human mind depends not only on other human beings in order to develop the distinctive characteristics of human existence but also on the stimuli of nature such as light, sound, smell, and heat: without the "warbling birds, blossoming cherry trees, sighing wind, and speaking humans, there would be no sources of signals—and thus no intellects."[13] We do not ordinarily feel indebted to birds and trees for our minds, but recognizing and appreciating that debt is an aspect of the new sensibility necessary for today's theology.

All of this is a poetic way of expressing the most fundamental tenet of the evolutionary, ecological perspective: that the question of what an entity is most basically is answered in terms of its relationships.[14] Thus, for instance, electrons, protons, and neutrons are viewed not as substantial entities but on the models of waves and particles. It is how they behave within the system of which they are a part that determines, on any particular occasion, which model will be used to describe them. What is the case at the subatomic level becomes even clearer at the level of life: each living organism is part of a system, a system with levels.

> The life of the cell is best understood in terms of ecological relationships among molecules. The living organism is best seen in terms of its ecological relationship with its environment. The interdependence of each living organism with other living organisms and with other components of its environment is the principle of population ecology.[15]

To feel in the depths of our being that we are part and parcel of the evolutionary ecosystem of our cosmos is a prerequisite for contemporary Christian theology. It is the beginning of a turn from the anthropocentrism and individualism so deeply embedded in the Western religious tradition, which is nowhere more precisely put than in Augustine's statement in the *Confessions:* "God and the soul, nothing more, nothing at all." That tradition, with its stress on the human individual, continued in much of Protestantism, flowering in the existentialism of the twentieth century. To be sure, another more political context for theology, with deep roots in the Hebrew Scriptures and certainly also in Augustine's two cities, as well as in Calvin's insistence that God is sovereign over the secular state, emerges in our time in the liberation theologies. But what has received less attention—and that largely from the Greek cosmological rather than the Hebraic historical tradition—is the creation which also "groans" for fulfillment.[16] Such lack of attention leads at the very least to an attitude of unconcern for the earth that is not only our home but, if we accept the evolutionary, ecological paradigm, also the giver and sustainer of our lives in basic and concrete ways. It has created a mentality of human domination and ruthlessness aptly captured in a remark by Huston Smith contrasting Western and Eastern attitudes toward nature:

> When Mount Everest was scaled the phrase commonly used in the West to describe the feat was "the conquest of Everest." An Oriental whose writings have been deeply influenced by Taoism remarked, "We would put the matter differently. We would speak of 'the befriending of Everest.'"[17]

One is reminded of Oriental nature paintings, in which human beings are often depicted not only as diminutive in comparison with the surrounding water and trees but also in a pose of mutual deference with a mountain—each bent, as it were, toward the other.

The evolutionary, ecological perspective perhaps comes across most clearly by contrast with the picture of the world it is replacing: the mechanical model. The mechanical model, bequeathed to us by Newtonian physics and Leibnizian philosophy, informs not only our daily common-sense assumptions and values in the West but also much of traditional Christian theology. Darwin, in the life

sciences, and Einstein, in physics, were to overturn this model, but
many of its characteristics, sketched here by A. R. Peacocke, remain
part of our sensibility:

> By the end of the nineteenth century the absolutes of space, time,
> object, and determinism were apparently securely enthroned in an
> unmysterious, mechanically determined world, basically simple in
> structure at the atomic level and, statistically at least, unchanging in
> form—for even geological and biological transformations operated
> under fixed laws.[18]

This picture, though based in the physical rather than the biological sciences, was assumed to cover both, so that life—and not only
the most fundamental physical processes of the universe—was
understood on the model of a machine. In the early years of the
twentieth century there was a movement toward a model more
aptly described as organic, even for the constituents with which
physics deals, for there occurred a profound realization of the
deep relations between space, time, and matter, which relativized
them all. In other words, relationships and relativity, as well as
process and openness, characterize reality as it is understood at
present in all branches of science. It is a considerably more complex picture than the old view, with a hierarchy of levels of organi-
zation from the microworld of the subatomic through the
macroworld of the biosphere to the megaworld of intergalactic
space.[19] But the characteristics of all levels of reality in this picture
are similar: the play of chance and necessity replaces determinism;
events appear to be more basic than substances, or to phrase it
differently, individuals or entities always exist within structures
of relationship; process, change, transformation, and openness
replace stasis, changelessness, and completeness as basic descriptive concepts. Whereas with the model of the machine, life is
patterned on the nonliving, with the organic model the nonliving
takes on characteristics of life. The model is most appropriate
to life, and hence the qualities of life—openness, relationship,
interdependence, change, novelty, and even mystery—become
the basic ones for interpreting all reality.

It is obvious how this perspective breaks through the old dualisms generated by the mechanical model—spirit/flesh, human/
nonhuman, objective/subjective, reason/passion, supernatural/

natural—for in the organic model hard lines cannot be drawn between matter and energy, the organic and the inorganic, the mind and the body, human beings and other forms of life.[20] In addition, the organic or evolutionary, ecological model is one that unites entities in a way basically different from the mechanistic model: instead of bringing entities together by means of common laws that govern all, creating a pattern of external relations, it unites by symbiotic, mutual interdependencies, creating a pattern of internal relations. In the organic model, one does not "enter into relations" with others but finds oneself in such relationships as the most basic given of existence. What separates entities differs as well: whereas in the mechanistic model entities are separated dualistically and hierarchically, in the organic model (or "mutualistic" model—a term that avoids the suggestion of reducing life to bodies which is implied in "organic") all entities are considered to be subjects as well as objects, to have intrinsic value as well as instrumental worth. "The ecological model is a model of living things which are acted upon and which respond by acting in their turn. They are patients and agents. In short they are subjects."[21] To take this perspective does not mean granting consciousness to amoebas, let alone to rocks, but it is to relativize the differences that have in the past been viewed as absolutes. It is to adopt the view toward the world so well captured in Martin Buber's famous distinction between I-Thou and I-It. It is the difference between an aesthetic and a utilitarian perspective, between one that appreciates the other (*all* others) and one that merely uses the other. An aesthetic sensibility toward the cosmos is one that values what is unselfishly, with a sense of delight in others for their own sakes. Such appreciation and delight are a necessary step in turning from an anthropocentric to an ecological sensibility. Thus, in the evolutionary, mutualistic model, all entities are united symbiotically and internally in levels of interdependence but are also separated as centers of action and response, each valuable in its own "beingness," however minimal or momentary that may appear to us. The symbol of the mountain and the human being bent toward each other, if allowing more agency and response to the mountain than can be empirically defended, does express an attitude of respect for otherness rare in the traditional Western sensibility.

Moreover, such an attitude is a basic ingredient in the development of the kind of global consciousness and conscience in relation to human solidarity and solidarity with other levels of life which is the required sensibility for the twenty-first century. Although it is manifestly utopian to imagine that the appreciation of otherness, whether human or nonhuman, will revolutionize our national and international behavior, it is surely folly to continue to encourage in ourselves and those whom we influence individualistic, hierarchical, dualistic, and utilitarian ways of thinking that are outmoded and have proved to be destructive of life at all levels.

The evolutionary, ecological, mutualistic model suggests an ethic toward others, both human and nonhuman, characterized by both justice and care. Carol Gilligan in her work on male- and female-oriented studies of moral development contrasts the pattern of "competing rights," in which one assumes that self and other should be treated fairly in spite of differences in power, and that of "responsibility and care," in which one assumes that everyone will be responded to and included.[22] The first pattern, characteristic of Western male development, begins from a position of separation and works toward connection; the second, characteristic of Western female development, begins from a position of relationship and works toward independence. The ethical pattern of the West has been principally the first, a logic of justice with emphasis on rights and rules and respect for the other. It is a noble ethic in many ways and underlies both the Western regard for the individual and the democratic form of government. But it is an "unfair" ethic, for it has been applied only to human beings—and even here, selectively. An ethic of justice in the evolutionary, ecological, mutualistic model would include the competing rights of other levels of life and would insist on these rights not simply from a utilitarian but also from an aesthetic point of view. That is to say, other levels of life deserve just treatment because of their intrinsic worth. Sorting out the rights of competing levels of life is, needless to say, a complex task, but to include the cosmos in the justice enterprise is essential. The second ethical pattern, that of care, has had a much slighter impact on Western thought. It has, as Gilligan points out, been seen as a weakness when individuals, usually women, understand moral response to focus on sensitivity to the needs of others, responsibility for including and caring for others, rather than on autonomous thinking and clear decision making in regard to the conflicting rights of separate parties.[23] But the model of reality we have sketched clearly demands not only the logic of justice but also the ethic of care. In fact, when the logic of justice is extended to include the nonhuman world, it moves naturally into such a mode, for appreciation for the cosmos *in our time* means responsibility for what is weaker and more vulnerable than human beings.

This is an important point and signals a significant change from the past. Until a few generations ago, nature appeared more power- ⁄ ful than we are. But this is no longer the case. Our ability to diminish if not destroy life through nuclear energy is perhaps the clearest proof of our power, but damage to other species and the ecosphere through a variety of pollutants and practices makes the point as well. In other words, the logic of justice, the acceptance of the rights of others, if applied (with meaningful distinctions and relativities) in our time to all others, does inevitably move into an ethic of care, for there is no way that such justice can be accorded except through care. It is for this reason that we need to imagine new models for the relationship between ourselves and our earth. We can no longer see ourselves as namers of and rulers over nature but must think of ourselves as gardeners, caretakers, mothers and fathers, stewards, trustees, lovers, priests, co-creators, and friends of a world that, while giving us life and sustenance, also depends increasingly on us in order to continue both for itself and for us.

If one were to do Christian theology from the holistic perspective, it is evident that some significant changes from traditional models and concepts would be necessary for expressing the relationships between God and the world and between ourselves and the world. Language that supports hierarchical, dualistic, external, unchanging, atomistic, anthropocentric, and deterministic ways of understanding these relationships is not appropriate *for our time*, whatever its appropriateness might have been for other times. It would appear that the appropriate language for our time, in the sense of being true to the paradigm of reality in which we actually live, would support ways of understanding the God-world and human-world relationships as open, caring, inclusive, interdependent, changing, mutual, and creative.

Needless to say, I am not proposing that the only criterion for theology is its fit with the reigning understanding of reality. But for theology to do *less* than fit our present understanding—for it to accept basic assumptions about reality from a very different time— seems blatantly wrongheaded. Nor am I suggesting that the holistic perspective and the guidelines it suggests for interpreting the rela- tionships between God and the world and between ourselves and the world will necessarily be more permanent than earlier par- adigms and guidelines. The evolutionary, ecological model insists above all else that the only permanence is change and hence that a theology appropriate to the holistic model will, at the very least, have to overcome what Rosemary Radford Ruether calls the "tyranny of the absolutizing imagination," which supposes that revolutions, theological or any other kind, are for all time.[24] What is needed is attention to the needs of one's own time. It is my con- tention that a theology that does not work within the context of the holistic view of reality cannot address the needs of our time.

The Nuclear Nightmare

"The question now before the human species . . . is whether life or death will prevail on the earth. This is not metaphorical language but a literal description of the present state of affairs."[25] But Jonathan Schell's statement has not sunk in. It has not sunk in because we do not want it to, because we do not want to live in the nuclear age, an age in which we must exist with the knowledge that we can destroy ourselves and other forms of life. We prefer to live in the bygone prenuclear age, when God, the mighty King and benev- olent Father, was in charge of the world. The thought that we are in charge is too terrifying to contemplate, for we know the evil in our own hearts and in the hearts of others. The thought threatens us with despair for the future: it raises doubts about whether there will be one and about what it will be. So the nuclear issue becomes the unspoken, unacknowledged terror that shadows all we do. Like sex in the Victorian era, it is the unmentionable of our time. Strate- gies for avoiding it are many: nuclear protesters are characterized as crazy peaceniks with apocalyptic imaginations; the commercial and other benefits of nuclear energy are expounded; the nuclear issue is accused of diverting concern from political and social forms of oppression. And yet scientists on both sides of the East-West divide concur on the likelihood of a "nuclear winter," and a high percentage of young people in study after study believe there will be a nuclear holocaust in their lifetime.

Why is the nuclear issue, which is certainly a strong candidate to be *the* issue of our time, ignored, ridiculed, and repressed? The reasons undoubtedly lie deep within us and are beyond easy understanding, but surely one reason is that as a threat rather than a reality, nuclear doom requires an act of the imagination if it is to become part of our reality, part of our "world." Nuclear consciousness, an essential part of the sensibility needed in our time, must come about as an act of consciousness-raising. This is the case because the world that we could destroy is not destroyed. What we see when we look about us is not postholocaust wreckage but preholocaust order and beauty. The aftermath of Hiroshima and Nagasaki is our principal aid to imagining postholocaust destruction, but even that picture does not help a great deal since there are approximately twenty thousand megatons of nuclear explosives now in existence and one megaton equals the explosive yield of eighty Hiroshimas.[26] A lesser leap of the imagination is needed in regard to many of the other pressing issues of our time, or rather, more ready means are available to raise consciousness on the issues of starvation, sexism, political oppression, poverty, and racism.[27] But nuclear war has not happened, and in this sense it will always be an "unreality" (so long as it does not happen), in contrast to the other terrible, oppressive realities of our time.

What is real, however, as Schell and others have pointed out, is *the knowledge that we have the power to destroy ourselves and other forms of life.* And it is the acceptance of this knowledge and of the responsibilities that come with it which is essential, I believe, to a new sensibility. Accepting this knowledge and understanding the changes it implies for our ways of thinking about the world and for relating to others in the world do not, however, involve seeing the nuclear nightmare as the issue that dwarfs or eliminates all others. On the contrary, the nuclear issue and issues of political and social oppression are intrinsically related, for at the heart of all these issues is the question of power: who wields it and what sort it is. It is, nonetheless, more immediately clear how the ecological and nuclear issues are related, for since the ecosystem is a whole of which we are a part, a major disturbance such as a nuclear war would undermine the entire system. Thus, the holistic vision and the nuclear nightmare are tightly knit: the former is a prerequisite for avoiding the latter. The awareness of our power over the ecosystem implies, as I suggested, the necessity for changing our images of our relationship to it from ones of domination to ones of care and nurture. But the nuclear issue is also intrinsically related to other issues of domination: of rich over poor, white over black, men over women. For the pattern in each case involves *an understanding of power as domination.* The question posed in each case is whether the only kind of pertinent relations between beings is of domination? Is power always domination? Is there another way to effect change, to bring something about, apart from domination?

The answer that immediately comes to mind invokes of course the "power of love." But one is reluctant to move too quickly in that direction, fearing sentimentality, or worse, ineffectiveness. If the issue is power, the power to destroy life, how dare one speak of "mere" love? Let us keep the answer to that question in abeyance while we look more closely at the nuclear issue and current understandings of power.

If our situation is one in which we know that we have the power to destroy ourselves and other forms of life, then power understood as domination and control, as absolute mastery and sovereignty, is counterproductive. For the political realities are such that the exercise of that kind of power raises rather than lowers international tensions and thus contributes to the likelihood of a nuclear holocaust. If in a nuclear age war is outmoded as a form of settling disputes, because there can be no victors, only losers, then the understanding of power which accompanies nationalism and military solutions is not only anachronistic but harmful.

But—and here Christian theology must take its part in the discussion—power as domination has been and still is a central feature of the Western view of God. One of the most distinctive adjectives describing the Judeo-Christian view of God is "almighty": this God is the creator, redeemer, and sustainer of all that is, the high and holy One who is in control, who is to be worshiped and glorified as the sole power in the universe. Such a view of God does not necessarily move in the direction of domination: the almighty can be seen as providential and loving. But whether the understanding of "almighty" moves in the direction of domination or providence, the power is still all God's—it is not shared. As Gordon Kaufman points out in *Theology for a Nuclear Age*, divine sovereignty is the issue with which theologians in the nuclear age must deal.[28] In cruder versions of the traditional view, God is the king who fights on the side of his chosen ones to bring their enemies down; in more refined versions, God is the father who will not let his children suffer.[29] The first way of thinking supports militarism; the second, escapism. As Kaufman states, two groups of American Christians currently rely on these images of God in their responses to the nuclear situation: one group claims that if a nuclear holocaust comes, it will be God's will—the Armageddon—and America should arm itself to fight the devil's agent, communist Russia; the other group passively relies on the all-powerful father to take care of the situation.[30] What neither version supports is *human* responsibility for the world, nor does the tradition supply us with much material for envisioning what power that is not domination or providence might be. If power as domination supports militarism and thus feeds the tensions that could lead to a nuclear holocaust, and power as providence supports escapism and thus lulls us into passivity, what kind of power does the situation call for? Quite obviously it calls, at the outset, for acceptance of our power, the power of human beings, over life and death. We have become, willy-nilly, co-creators in the sense that we have the power to "let life continue." But the acceptance of that power involves a radical change in the very understanding of power, for in order to exercise that power, power must be conceived differently than in the past. Kaufman makes a very important proposal at this juncture when he says that the relationship between God and the world—in other words, between God's power and ours—has in the past been "dualistic" and "asymmetrical" and now needs to become "unified" and "interdependent."[31] The evolutionary, ecological perspective, the holistic vision that is basic to a new sensibility, renders untenable any understanding of the God-world relationship in which God is viewed as a being externally related to the world as the power that totally controls it. It is, for those who accept the basic assumptions of our world (and not a bygone one), incredible. And yet this view of the God-world relationship still largely domi- nates the common understanding as well as our liturgies—and of- ten even theology. As Langdon Gilkey writes, attempting to sum up the "classic formulation" of God in Western culture,

> . . . the word or symbol "God" has generally referred to one, supreme, or holy being, the unity of ultimate reality and ultimate goodness. So conceived, God is believed to have created the entire universe, to rule over it, and to intend to bring it to its fulfillment or realization, to "save" it.[32]

The relationship between God and the world envisioned in this passage is neither unified nor interdependent. On the contrary, the stress is on the separation of God from the world and on God's control of it: God is the supreme and holy being who rules and saves the world.

The question arises whether the problem lies with the *personal* God of this tradition. Does a view of God as personal entail the ideas of separation, dualism, and control? Sometimes the attempt to relate God and the world in more unified, interdependent ways is thought to require a sacrifice of the personal dimension of the divine. Kaufman, for instance, questions the viability of the per- sonalistic tradition of the West, opting to understand God as the "unifying symbol of those powers and dimensions of the ecological and historical feedback network which create and sustain and work to further enhance life."[33] One of the most distinctive aspects of the Judeo-Christian tradition is that in its kind of theism the deity is appropriately addressed as Thou, not It. One could credit this to the strongly agential Hebraic roots of the tradition—to the under- standing of God as one who wills, loves, acts, and responds. But this conception of God has persisted as highly characteristic of the Judeo-Christian tradition in spite of the contributions of Platonic and Aristotelian views of the divine which are more impersonal and abstract. The stress on the dynamic, loving action of God is clearly seen in liberation theologies today, especially black and Third World theologies. God is the liberator who will free the op- pressed. God as Thou also figures in various kinds of process the- ologies, which, by taking the relationship of the self to the body as the analogy for understanding the relationship between God and the world, have a basis for underscoring both the personal and the radically interdependent character of the divine in relation to the world. Process theologies, however, have not focused much attention on the kind of personal metaphors and models most appropriate *for our time;* or to put it differently, in criticizing (as Kaufman also does) the monarchical, triumphalist models that support asymmetrical dualism, process theologians have not moved boldly to suggest other models more suited to a view of God as intrinsically and radically relational. And though black and Third World theologies fully retain the agential aspects of the Western concept, they do so in a way that limits God to the realm of persons and history, leaving much of the cosmos unaddressed. Too, they have not experimented with new models, apart from that of liberator, which has been limited to freeing oppressed humanity.

The question, then, is this: In what metaphors and models should we conceive of God as Thou who is related to the world in a unified and interdependent way? To understand God as Thou, it seems to me, is basic for our relating to all reality in the mode of mutuality, respect, care, and responsibility. The qualities of personal relationship are needed in our time not only in the God-world relation but in the human-world relation as well. The problem, I believe, is not that personal metaphors and concepts have been used for God; it is not the personal aspect that has brought about the asymmetrical dualism. The problem lies, rather, in the particular metaphors and concepts chosen. The primary metaphors in the tradition are hierarchical, imperialistic, and dualistic, stressing the distance between God and the world and the total reliance of the world on God. Thus, the metaphors of God as king, ruler, lord, master, and governor, and the concepts that accompany them of God as absolute, complete, transcendent, and omnipotent permit no sense of mutuality, shared responsibility, reciprocity, and love (except in the sense of gratitude). Even the one primary metaphor for God that would allow for a more unified, interdependent view, that of father, has been so qualified by being associated with the metaphors of king and lord (as, for instance, in the phrase, *almighty Father*) that its potential as an expression of a unified, interdependent view of God and the world is undercut.

It has become increasingly and painfully evident to many Westerners, both those within the Judeo-Christian tradition and those
outside who nonetheless are influenced by its imagery, values, and
concepts, that the language used to express the relationship between God and the world needs revision. It is my contention that
this revision must begin at the level of the imagination, in a
"thought experiment" with metaphors and their accompanying
concepts that, unlike the principal ones in the tradition, express a
unified, interdependent framework for understanding God-world
and human-world relations. I see this experiment in part as a response to Kaufman's call to students of religion to combat the ways
the traditional imagery for God supports either militarism or escapism in this nuclear age, by entering "into the most radical kind
of deconstruction and reconstruction of the traditions they have
inherited, including especially the most central and precious symbols of these traditions, *God* and *Jesus Christ* and *Torah.*"[34] There
are, undoubtedly, many ways to respond to this call, but *one* critical
aspect of the deconstruction and reconstruction of religious symbols involves both a critique of the triumphalist, imperialistic, patriarchal model and a "thought experiment" with some alternative
models that are, I believe, commensurate with the evolutionary,
ecological sensibility and with the Christian faith. No one, of
course, can create images of God; religious symbols are born and
die in a culture for complex reasons. At most, one can try to attend
carefully to the images in the culture and church which appear to
be emerging and to experiment imaginatively with them, reflecting
on their implications for life with God and with others.

The models of God as mother, lover, and friend offer possibilities for envisioning power in unified, interdependent ways quite
different from the view of power as either domination or benevolence. I believe these models are uniquely suited for theology in a
nuclear age and could serve as well to recontextualize the present
dominant metaphor of father in a parental rather than patriarchal
direction. We asked earlier about power that is not domination or
benevolence and suggested that we hold in abeyance a consideration of the "power of love." The kind of power associated with the
models of mother (and father), lover, and friend is indeed love, and
love that is unified and interdependent. That is, if one reflects on

the characteristics of the love shown by parents, lovers, and friends, the words that come to mind include "fidelity," "nurture," "attraction," "self-sacrifice," "passion," "responsibility," "care," "affection," "respect," and "mutuality." In fact, all the qualities of love so neatly demarcated in the ancient divisions of agape, eros, and philia come into play. These words suggest power but a very different kind of power from that associated with the models of lord, king, and patriarch.

If theologians and students of religion are to be part of the solution to the problem posed by the unprecedented nuclear knowledge that human beings now possess, they must, I believe, answer the call to deconstruct and reconstruct the traditional symbols of Christian faith. This task suggests that Christian theology, in our time at least, cannot be merely or mainly hermeneutics, that is, interpretation of the tradition, a translation of ancient creeds and concepts to make them relevant for contemporary culture. Rather, theology must be self-consciously constructive, willing to think differently than in the past. If one reflects on the contrasts between the theologies of Paul, Augustine, Luther, Schleiermacher, and Barth (just to take a sampling of the tradition) as to their basic images, root metaphors, concepts, and assumptions about reality, one has to acknowledge an enormous variety, all of it, however, capable of being accommodated within the Christian paradigm. Theology in our day needs to be self-consciously constructive in order to free itself from traditional notions of divine sovereignty sufficiently to be able to experiment with other and more appropriate metaphors and models that may help us cope with the "question now before the human species . . . whether life or death will prevail on earth."

Theological Construction

In addition to the holistic vision and acceptance of responsibility for nuclear knowledge, a third aspect of the new sensibility for doing theology in our time is consciousness of the constructive character of all human activities, especially of those within which we live and therefore of which we are least aware: our world views, including our religions. One of the distinctive features of the twentieth century, evident in all fields including science, is increasing

awareness of the creative, interpretive character of human existence. But it is important that our interpretive creations not be
reified or petrified. Paul de Man, the deconstructionist literary
critic, makes the point vividly with his comment that the story of
language is "like the plot of a Gothic novel in which someone com-
pulsively manufactures a monster" on which one "then becomes
totally dependent" and which one "does not have the power to
kill."[35] We are reminded of Nietzsche's description of truth as
worn-out metaphors that have become "fixed, canonic and binding"
so that we forget that they are "illusions." The double-edged allega-
tion of Nietzsche concerning the constructive as well as the illusory
character of human language—in our case, the language of theology—must be squarely faced. I do not believe that recognition of,
even celebration of, the constructive character of theology necessarily involves the admission that all construction is merely play
and that hence one construction is no better than another. At this
point, the absolutism of fundamentalism and the absolutism of
deconstruction are similar: the first insists that only one construction (which is not admitted to be a construction) is true, right, and
good, and the second insists that all constructions (which are solely
the products of aesthetic playfulness) are equally illusory, with
none more true, more right, or better than any of the others.[36] What
links these positions, in my view, is related to metaphor: fundamentalism fails to appreciate that the language of theology is
metaphorical, and deconstruction refuses to acknowledge that
there is anything but metaphor.

It is evident that fundamentalism does not accept the metaphorical character of religious and theological language, for its basic
tenet is the identification of the Word of God with human words,
notably those human words in the canonical Scriptures of the
church. The essence of metaphorical theology, however, is precisely the refusal to identify human constructions with divine reality.[37] Since a metaphor is a word or phrase appropriate to one
context but used in another, no metaphorical construction can be
univocally applied, that is, applied in the form of identity. To say
that "God is mother" is not to identify God with mother, but to
understand God in light of some of the characteristics associated

with mothering. It is, then, also to say, "God is not mother," or, to combine the positive and negative aspects of metaphorical assertion, "God is/is not mother," or yet again, "God *as* mother" (which underscores the comparative nature of metaphor: God viewed in the capacity, character, or role of mother). In other words, the constructive character of metaphor is self-evident, since the appropriate, literal, or conventional context for applying the title of mother is obviously not the divine. Yet much if not all religious language and a great deal of theological language is of this type; that is, language that is literally appropriate to personal, social, or political human relationships or to the natural world is applied metaphorically to God. Thus, the fundamentalist's assertion of univocity between human language about God and God or "God's Word" fails to appreciate the most basic characteristic of religious and theological language: its iconoclastic character, what the tradition calls the *via negativa.* All language about God is human construction and as such perforce "misses the mark."

On the other hand, deconstruction, in many ways a highly perceptive critique of Western metaphysics, focuses on metaphor, for one way of describing deconstruction is as an insistence that there is nothing but metaphor.[38] As the latest stage of a journey beginning with Nietzsche—who saw how language deceives us into believing it is fixed and definite, referring to something outside ourselves, when in fact it is nothing but the play of metaphors— deconstruction concludes that the root metaphor of human existence is writing and interprets writing literally as metaphoricity itself.[39] The increasing realization of the power of language as the most distinctive attribute of human existence, and the realization of the ways in which we construct the worlds we inhabit through it, have during this century come to the point of claiming with the French deconstructionist Jacques Derrida that "there is nothing outside the text"—and this statement includes author and referent.[40] If there is only text, or writing, this means there is only the play of words, interpretation upon interpretation, referring to nothing but other words, an endless spiral with no beginning or end. This is language as "metaphoricity itself." There is nothing but metaphor; metaphor is the ultimate metaphor, for all words miss the mark, are inappropriate, and out of context, because there is no mark, there is no way to judge appropriateness, there is no conventional or literal context for a word or phrase.

I disagree with this understanding of metaphor, but before going into that, I would first underscore the value of deconstruction's critique of Western metaphysics for the new sensibility needed to do Christian theology in our time. Its extreme position gives it a base for launching a full-scale attack on what it calls the "metaphysics of presence" in Western thought. This metaphysics takes many forms, but in essence it is an attempt to cover up the absence, emptiness, and uncertainty we sense (and fear) may be at the heart of things. What metaphor does, say the deconstructionists, is to insist on absence, for if metaphor is a word or sign standing for another word or sign in endless repetition with no reference outside itself, then there is no possibility of words conveying "presence": not our presence to one another, or the world's presence to us, or God's to us. The metaphysics of presence is most evident in the desire for completeness and totality, full presence, in the Judeo-Christian tradition, and especially in the orthodox christological assertion that God is present, fully and completely, in one human being. Jesus Christ, fully God and fully man, is the ultimate assurance that the universe is not blank emptiness: on the contrary, full and unmediated presence, not just of other selves or the reality of the world but of Presence itself is ours in the Christ, and through him we are assured of the return of what we have lost, the garden of Eden, as well as of even greater fulfillment in the paradise to come.[41] And, says deconstruction, Western theology claims also to have assurance of this Presence in the Book, the Text of texts, in which human words truly refer to the Word itself. Hence, in our language about this Presence we need not take *aporia*, absence, seriously into account nor acknowledge the uncertainty, incompleteness, or relativity of our interpretations so long as we stay close to the Book. But, deconstruction continues, the history of Western metaphysics is one of massive forgetfulness, forgetfulness that metaphor lies at the base of all our constructions, including that most sacred Text: it too is but the play of words, interpretation upon interpretation, creating a shimmering surface that has no author and no referent.

One need not agree with all this to see its value for informing the sensibility of late twentieth-century theology. Deconstruction is not a new method or theory; rather, as its name itself suggests, it is a calling to attention of what could be called the underside of all our constructions, the "is not," the incompleteness, the partiality, the uncertainty, that must accompany all our creations lest we reify them into absolutes. Deconstruction cautions us against trying to save ourselves through our constructions. The temptation is to seek security, in a vast number of complex ways, against the abyss, the chaos, the different, the other, the unknown—whatever threatens us. By seeking security through our constructions, we refuse to step outside the houses of language we have erected to protect us from the emptiness and the terror we cannot control. Our safe havens, called dogmas and orthodoxy, become absolutes, giving the illusion of being certain, being "on the inside," having the truth.

Deconstruction criticizes as childish our nostalgia for Presence. It calls Christian theology (and all other constructions or world views) to adulthood. In this it makes a major contribution to adjusting the sensibility of our time. The desire for full presence, whether in the form of nostalgia for the garden of Eden, or the quest for the historical Jesus, or the myth of God incarnate, is a denial of what we know as adults to be the case in human existence: such innocence, certainty, and absoluteness are not possible. What deconstruction, with its denial of all presence, brings out powerfully even for nondeconstructionists is that absence is at least more prevalent than presence: the world in which we live is one in which we create structures to protect us against the chaos, absence, death, oppression, and exclusion that surround us—a negativity symbolized by the ultimate absence, a nuclear holocaust. It is by no means a completely new insight when deconstruction speaks of the absence of presence, for a long tradition of negative theology has accompanied the tradition of presence and is vividly encapsulated in H. Richard Niebuhr's statement that faith as the attitude of fundamental trust in being itself comes about only when one becomes "suspicious" of one's own "deep suspicion of the Determiner of Destiny."[42] But deconstruction's critique makes clear the necessity of developing "negative capability"—the ability to endure absence, uncertainty, partiality, relativity, and to hold at bay the desire for

closure, coherence, identity, totality. It is a call "to put away childish things" and grow up.

What deconstruction does not do, however, is offer any assistance on the question of *which* constructions are better than others.
It deals eloquently with the "is not" of metaphor, but it refuses to
deal with the "is." I agree with the deconstructionists that all constructions are metaphorical and hence miss the mark; I nevertheless disagree with them when they say that language (writing) is
about only itself and that no construction is any better than any
other. To claim that all constructions are metaphorical is to insist
that one never experiences reality "raw"; it does not follow from
this, however, that there is nothing outside language. All that follows is that our access to reality is in every case mediated and hence
partial and relative. Nor is the admission of the metaphoricity of
our constructions a denial that interpretations can genuinely conflict. In fact, the opposite is the case, for the presence of many
constructions, many metaphors, assumes conflict and the need for
criteria.

There is indeed no way behind our constructions to test them for
their correspondence with the reality they presume to represent,
but the constructions do, I believe, have a twofold relationship with
reality which deconstruction ignores. First, they are productive of
reality; that is, our metaphorical constructions are redescriptions or
new readings of what lies outside them, in place of old or conventional descriptions or readings. All renderings of reality are
metaphorical (that is, none is literal), but in our novel constructions
we offer new possibilities in place of others. In this sense we create
the reality in which we live; we do not copy it, or to put it more
pointedly, there are no copies, only creations. The assumption here,
however, is that there is a reality to which our constructions refer,
even though the only way we have of reaching it is by creating
versions of it.[43] This is altogether different from the deconstructionist's position that there is nothing to which the text refers.

Second, our constructions are intended to be better than the ones
they refute or replace. This is of course a very difficult issue, because if one admits that all are readings, with the new replacing the
old, on what basis can some be better than others? They certainly
cannot claim to be better absolutely, or from all perspectives, or for

all time.[44] At the most, they might be better relatively (to other constructions) from a particular perspective, and for a particular time. And this is the claim I would make: that a construction of the Christian faith in the context of a holistic vision and the nuclear threat is from our particular perspective and for our particular time relatively better than constructions that ignore these issues. It is relatively better in part because of what Christian faith at base is about. The claim is that to understand the Christian faith in terms of the holistic vision and in response to the nuclear threat is in continuity with the basic Christian paradigm as well as being an appropriate construction of that faith for our time. I will attempt to make that case, but it cannot be proved. As with any construction, the most one can do is to "live within" it, testing it for its disclosive power, its ability to address and cope with the most pressing issues of one's day, its comprehensiveness and coherence, its potential for dealing with anomalies, and so forth. Theological constructions are "houses" to live in for a while, with windows partly open and doors ajar; they become prisons when they no longer allow us to come and go, to add a room or take one away—or if necessary, to move out and build a new house.

In this chapter, I have been searching for a standpoint from which to do Christian theology in our time. I have suggested that a new sensibility is required, one characterized by the felt awareness of our intrinsic interdependence with all that lives, a holistic, evolutionary, ecological vision that overcomes ancient and oppressive dualisms and hierarchies, that encourages change and novelty, and that promotes an ethic of justice and care; one characterized as well by a profound acceptance of human responsibility for the fate of the earth, especially in view of a possible nuclear holocaust, and therefore by the willingness to think differently, to think in metaphors and models that support a unified, interdependent understanding of God-world and human-world relationships; and finally, one characterized by the recognition that although all constructive thought is metaphorical and hence necessarily risky, partial, and uncertain, implying an end to dogmatism and absolutism, it is not thereby fantasy, illusion, or play.

I believe that the supposition that theology is a verbal game is as dangerous as the refusal to admit the role of imagination in theology. There is something outside language, or to phrase it differently, the "games" we play with language make a difference in what we understand reality to be and how we conduct our lives in relation to other beings, both human and nonhuman. A person who is starving, imprisoned, discriminated against, tortured, or homeless can scarcely be expected to believe that the ideology that permits such oppression is a mere game, no worse than any other. Nor would such a person believe that language is the totality of reality: hunger, fear, and suffering unite beings, both human and nonhuman, in a wordless community where a cry of pain is the universal word. Language is nonetheless a serious matter; it is our window, albeit not a transparent one, onto the world. We live our lives according to our constructions of the world; as Erich Heller said, "Be careful how you interpret the world; it *is* like that." There is no retreat from the conflict of interpretations, because life is not a game—or if one chooses to think that it is, then it should be said that the game may be up unless the rules by which we have been playing are changed.

2
*M*etaphorical Theology

Is the theology needed for our age so different from the Christian theology of the past that we must step outside that tradition for our sources and resources? Is our time so unprecedented that nothing from the past, including the Christian faith, has relevance to it? Are we, as the deconstructionists and some radical feminist theologians would claim, in a post-Christian world? My answer to these questions is complex and involves both agreement and disagreement.

It involves agreement in that I believe our time is sufficiently different and sufficiently dire that theologians must not shrink from the task of thinking boldly and imaginatively. If one accepts the portrait of our contemporary situation which I have tried to draw, one must ask, What understanding of the relationship between God and the world can address *that* situation? If, to portray the Christian faith in the broadest strokes, it affirms the underlying direction of the universe to be on the side of life and its fulfillment—if, in other words, faith in the God of the Judeo-Christian tradition is faith in the ultimate trustworthiness of things—then how, in our time and in metaphors and concepts appropriate to our time, can that faith be expressed with persuasive power? This task will necessarily involve significant departures from past metaphors and concepts, since many of the traditional ones were themselves "significant departures" made in order to address precisely and powerfully the salvific love of God for their own times. In an era when evil powers were understood to be palpable principalities in contest with God for control of human beings and the cosmos, the metaphor of Christ as the victorious king and lord, crushing the evil spirits and thereby freeing the world from their

control, was indeed a powerful one. In our situation, however, to
envision evil as separate from human beings rather than as the
outcome of human decisions and actions, and to see the solution to
evil as totally a divine responsibility, would be not only irrelevant
to our time and its needs but harmful to them, for that would run
counter to one of the central insights of the new sensibility: the
need for human responsibility in the nuclear age.

In other words, in order to do theology, one must in each epoch
do it differently. To refuse this task is to settle for a theology appropriate to some time other than one's own. To be sure, this understanding of theology involves a somewhat different view of the
founding (i.e., scriptural) images and concepts than is often held. It
sees the rich and diverse metaphors and concepts of the Bible as
models or exemplars *of* theology, rather than as dictums *for* theology. On my view, what we have in Paul's letters and in the Gospel
of John are two highly imaginative (and very different) attempts to
express the salvific love of God in metaphors and concepts appropriate to their time—in the one case, in a missionary, proselytizing
context, and in the other, in a sectarian, otherworldly one. Is one
right and the other not? That is not the way to ask the question;
evidently, they were both right for their time. The question we must
ask is, Are they right *for our time?* or to phrase it differently and
more to the point, What should we be doing for our time that would
be comparable to what Paul and John did for theirs? Does Christian
theology involve, either through translation or through interpretation, using the metaphors and concepts of Scripture (and the tradition), or does it involve taking scriptural texts as a model of how to
do it, that is, of how to do it in the language of one's own time? I
believe the second option is the necessary and appropriate one, and
this will, quite obviously, involve significant departures.

As radical as this suggestion may sound, it is mainly radical for our
self-consciousness of what we are doing rather than for our doing of
it. I am not saying that our time is *totally* unprecedented and that
theology must be done in a fashion entirely different from that of the
past. For examples of relatively unselfconscious radical theological
recontextualizing, we need only think of Augustine's Neoplatonism
or Thomas's Aristotelianism, both of which are considered nonetheless to be in continuity with the very different theologies of Paul and

John. What are needed in our time, I believe, are attempts at new exemplars, new models, of the Christian faith. These will involve, as theologies of the past have involved, new metaphors and concepts for expressing the salvific power of God. Many such efforts are needed, and what I am attempting in these pages is a modest "thought experiment" concerning a few metaphors and their accompanying concepts. This thought experiment, if it is not to be merely a covert translation of a theology for another time, must be bold and constructive, willing to follow out the associations and implications of these metaphors and not to see them merely as another way to express the same thing as traditional metaphors.

So my answer to the question is that we are in an unprecedented situation, a post-Christian world, in that we cannot accept currency from former times as our truth. Another way to answer the question, however, is to say that Christians are always in a post-Christian world if "post-Christian" means the refusal simply to accept as Christian what is received from another time. The remainder of this chapter will attempt to look more carefully at the character of the theological experiment I am proposing: What sort of construction is it? What are its sources and resources? How can it claim continuity with the Christian paradigm? The first question will involve metaphors, models, and concepts; and the second will treat Scripture, tradition, and experience; the third will attempt a sketch of "demonstrable continuities" within the Christian paradigm.[1]

Metaphors, Models, and Concepts

Dennis Nineham, in the epilogue to *The Myth of God Incarnate*, writes that it is "at the level of the *imagination* that contemporary Christianity is most weak." He goes on to say that people

> find it hard to believe in God because they do not have available to them any lively imaginative picture of the way God and the world as they know it are related. What they need most is a story, a picture, a myth, that will capture their imagination, while meshing in with the rest of their sensibility in the way that messianic terms linked with the sensibility of first-century Jews, or Nicene symbolism with the sensibility of philosophically-minded fourth-century Greeks.[2]

An important point is made in this comment: belief is related to an imaginative and credible picture or myth of the relationship between God and the world. What our time lacks, and hence a task that theology must address, is an imaginative construal of the God-world relationship that is credible to us. I have attempted to suggest that a credible theology for our time must be characterized by a sense of our intrinsic interdependence with all forms of life, an inclusive vision that demolishes oppressive hierarchies, accepts responsibility for nurturing and fulfilling life in its many forms, and is open to change and novelty as a given of existence. But it is perhaps less clear what an imaginative construal of the God-world relationship might be. The last chapter proposed theology to be a constructive, metaphorical enterprise, but more needs to be said about its character.

The first thing to say is that theology, as constructive and metaphorical, does not "demythologize" but "remythologizes." To envision theology as metaphorical means, at the outset, to refuse the attempt to denude religious language of its concrete, poetic, imagistic, and hence inevitably anthropomorphic, character, in the search for presumably more enlightened (and usually more abstract) terminology. It is to accept as one of theology's primary tasks remythologizing for our time: identifying and elucidating primary metaphors and models from contemporary experience which will express Christian faith for our day in powerful, illuminating ways. Theologians are not poets, but neither are they philosophers (as, in the Christian tradition, they have often become). Their place, as understood by metaphorical theology, is an anomalous one that partakes of both poetry and philosophy: they are poets insofar as they must be sensitive to the metaphors and models that are at once consonant with the Christian faith and appropriate for expressing that faith in their own time, and they are philosophers insofar as they must elucidate in a coherent, comprehensive, and systematic way the implications of these metaphors and models. Thus, to suggest, as I do, that the metaphors of mother (and father), lover, and friend, and of the world as God's body, are appropriate for remythologizing Christianity in our time means making a case for them at both the imagistic and conceptual levels. My first point, then, is that a constructive, metaphorical theology insists on a continuum and a symbiotic relationship between image and concept, between the language of prayer and liturgy and the language of theory and doctrine. There is nothing distinctive about this statement except the emphasis on the theologian's contribution to remythologizing. The theologian ought not merely interpret biblical and traditional metaphors and models but ought to remythologize, to search in contemporary life and its sensibility for images more appropriate to the expression of Christian faith in our time.

A second and more complex issue in regard to theology, as constructive and metaphorical, concerns metaphor and model. What are they, and why call theology metaphorical?[3] A metaphor is a word or phrase used *in*appropriately. It belongs properly in one context but is being used in another: the arm of the chair, war as a chess game, God the father.[4] From Aristotle until recently, metaphor has been seen mainly as a poetic device to embellish or decorate. The idea was that in metaphor one used a word or phrase inappropriately but one need not have: whatever was being expressed could be said directly without the metaphor. Increasingly, however, the idea of metaphor as unsubstitutable is winning acceptance: what a metaphor expresses cannot be said directly or apart from it, for if it could be, one would have said it directly. Here, metaphor is a strategy of desperation, not decoration; it is an attempt to say something about the unfamiliar in terms of the familiar, an attempt to speak about what we do not know in terms of what we do know. Not all metaphors fit this definition, for many are so enmeshed in conventional language (the arm of the chair) that we do not notice them and some have become so familiar that we do not recognize them as attempting to express the unfamiliar (God the father). But a fresh metaphor, such as in the remark that "war is a chess game," immediately sparks our imaginations to think of war, a very complex phenomenon, as viewed through a concrete grid or screen, the game of chess.[5] Needless to say, war is not a chess game; hence, a description of war in terms of chess is a partial, relative, inadequate account that, in illuminating certain aspects of war (such as strategizing), filters out other aspects (such as violence and death).

Metaphor always has the character of "is" and "is not": an assertion is made but as a likely account rather than a definition.[6] That is, to say, "God is mother," is not to define God as mother, not to assert identity between the terms "God" and "mother," but to suggest that

we consider what we do not know how to talk about—relating to
God—through the metaphor of mother. The assumption here is
that all talk of God is indirect: no words or phrases refer directly to
God, for God-language can refer only through the detour of a description that properly belongs elsewhere. To speak of God as
mother is to invite us to consider some qualities associated with
mothering as one partial but perhaps illuminating way of speaking
of certain aspects of God's relationship to us. It also assumes, however, that many other metaphors may qualify as partial but illuminating grids or screens for this purpose. The point that metaphor
underscores is that in certain matters there can be no direct description. It used to be that poetry and religion were thought to be
distinctive in their reliance on metaphor, but more recently the use
of metaphors and models in the natural and social sciences has
widened the scope of metaphorical thinking considerably.[7]

The differences between a metaphor and a model can for our
purpose be simply stated: a model is a metaphor with "staying
power."[8] A model is a metaphor that has gained sufficient stability
and scope so as to present a pattern for relatively comprehensive
and coherent explanation. The metaphor of God the father is an
excellent example of this. In becoming a model, it has permitted an
understanding of many things. If God is seen as father, human
beings become children, sin can be understood as rebellious behavior, and redemption can be thought of as a restoration to the
status of favored offspring. As the creeds of the church amply
illustrate, models approach the status of concepts: Father, Son, and
Holy Spirit are models of the divine life that inform the tradition's
most central concept, the trinity.

It should be evident that a theology that describes itself as
metaphorical is a theology "at risk." Jacques Derrida, in defining
metaphor, writes, "If metaphor, which is *mimesis* trying its chance,
mimesis at risk, may always fail to attain truth, this is because it has
to reckon with a definite absence."[9] As Derrida puts it, metaphor
lies somewhere between "nonsense" and "truth," and a theology
based on metaphor will be open to the charge that it is closer to the
first than the second. This, I believe, is a risk that theology in our
time must be willing to run. Theology has usually had a high stake
in truth, so high that it has refused all play of the imagination:

through creedal control and the formulations of orthodoxy, it has refused all attempts at new metaphors "trying their chance." But a metaphorical theology is necessarily a heuristic venture: it insists that new metaphors and models be given a chance, be tried out as likely accounts of the God-world relationship, be allowed to make a case for themselves. A metaphorical theology is, therefore, destabilizing: since no language about God is adequate and all of it is improper, new metaphors are not necessarily less inadequate or improper than old ones. All are in the same situation and no authority—not scriptural status, liturgical longevity, nor ecclesiastical fiat—can decree that some types of language, or some images, refer literally to God while others do not.[10] None do. Hence, the criteria for preferring some to others must be other than authority, however defined. We will deal with this issue later in the chapter, but at this point I am emphasizing that metaphorical theology encourages nontraditional, unconventional, novel ways of expressing the relationship between God and the world not because such ways are necessarily better than received ways but because they cannot be ruled out as *not* better unless tried. Since metaphors are imaginative leaps across a distance—the best metaphors always giving both a shock and a shock of recognition—a metaphorical theology will dare to take risks as well, for the recognition does not come without the shock. A metaphor that has lost its shock (its "is not" quality) loses as well its recognition possibilities (its "is" quality), for the metaphor is no longer "heard": it is taken to be a definition, not a likely account. Thus, a metaphorical theology is open to change, willing to risk the disorientation of new "truths," as well as the possibility that the leap across the abyss will be unsuccessful.[11]

The course I am recommending for theology is not that of theology as "hermeneutics" or of theology as "construction."[12] This is the third point to make about theology as metaphorical construction. I have claimed that it remythologizes in the sense that the theologian as poet-philosopher attempts to identify primary metaphors and models from contemporary experience and elucidate their conceptual implications in order to express Christian faith for our day in powerful, persuasive ways. I have further claimed that, as metaphorical, such theology is always dealing with improper language, language that refers only through a detour, and hence that since it can always miss the mark, there can be no sacred, authoritative, or proper metaphors and models (nor concepts associated with them). I now wish to add a third characteristic of metaphorical theology by suggesting that it is best described as neither hermeneutics nor construction but heuristics. The *Shorter Oxford English Dictionary* defines "heuristic" adjectivally as "serving to find out" and, when employed as a noun related to learning, as "a system of education under which pupils are trained to find out for themselves." Thus heuristic theology will be one that experiments and tests, that thinks in an as-if fashion, that imagines possibilities that are novel, that dares to think differently. It will not accept on the basis of authority but will acknowledge only what it finds convincing and persuasive; it will not, however, be fantasy or mere play but will assume that there is something to find out and that if some imagined possibilities fail, others may succeed. The mention of failure and success, and of the persuasive and the convincing, indicates that although I wish to distinguish heuristic theology from both hermeneutical and constructive theology, it bears similarities to both.

If the characteristic mark of hermeneutical theology is its interpretive stance, especially in regard to texts—both the classic text of the Judeo-Christian tradition (the Hebrew Scriptures and the New Testament) and the exemplary theologies that build on the classic text—then heuristic theology is also interpretive, for it claims that its successful unconventional metaphors are not only in continuity with the paradigmatic events and their significance expressed in this classic text but are also appropriate expressions of these matters for the present time. Heuristic theology, though not bound to the images and concepts in Scripture, is constrained to show that its proposed models are an appropriate, persuasive expression of Christian faith for our time. Making this case involves, of course, some determination of the Christian paradigm, some statement of interpretation concerning how it should be conceived in our time— and this will be forthcoming. The point I am making here, however, is that although a heuristic theology is not limited to interpreting texts—neither the classic text nor texts of the tradition—it is concerned with the same "matter" as those texts and that tradition, namely, the salvific power of God. Its claim, however, will be that that reality is not limited to its biblical or traditional metaphors, models, and concepts, though these do provide "case studies," previously successful metaphors and models that give invaluable assistance in the attempt to characterize "demonstrable continuities" within the Christian paradigm.

If, on the other hand, the distinctive mark of constructive theology is that it does not rely principally on classical sources but attempts its articulation of the concepts of God, world, and human being with the help of a variety of sources, including material from the natural, physical, and social sciences as well as from philosophy, literature, and the arts, then heuristic theology is also constructive in that it claims that a valid understanding of God and the world for a particular time is an imaginative construal built up from a variety of sources, many of them outside religious traditions. Like theology as construction, theology as heuristics supports the assertion that our concept of God is precisely that—*our concept* of God—and not God. Different theologians have expressed this in a variety of ways: Paul Tillich draws the distinction between the symbol God and God as Being-itself, and Gordon Kaufman offers the contrast of the "available" God of our constructs and the "real" God.[13] But a metaphorical, constructive theology has a distinctive emphasis: it will be more experimental, imagistic, and pluralistic than most theologies that fall into the constructive category.[14]

To say that metaphorical theology is experimental is to emphasize its as-if quality, its heuristic quality of finding out for itself. It is a kind of theology especially well suited for times of uncertainty and change, when systematic, comprehensive construction seems inappropriate if not impossible. Many constructive theologies of the past, such as the great systems of Augustine and Thomas, give the appearance of being finished and closed, even though their creators renounced such claims, as in Thomas's famous statement that all he had written was but "straw." But the sort of constructive theology recommended here could be called "free theology,"[15] for it must be willing to play with possibilities and, as a consequence, not take itself too seriously. Though the situation it addresses, the salvific power of God for its time, is a matter of ultimate seriousness, theology's contribution is not. Or to put it more positively, theology is but one way to address that situation, a way that demands risk and novelty. Theologians are placed among many workers in the vineyard; their task is a peculiar and, I believe, limited one, with special responsibility for the language used to express the relationship between God and the world. The kind of theology I am recommending, then, focuses on the images and concepts that have been used in classical formulations of the Judeo-Christian tradition to express that relationship as well as on alternatives one might consider. This is a different view of constructive theology from what is usual within the Christian tradition and one with greater emphasis on its tentative, relative, partial, and hypothetical character.

To say that metaphorical theology is imagistic is to state the obvious, since a metaphor is a kind of image, a verbal one. But emphasizing this is important because of the bias of constructive theology toward conceptual clarity, often at the price of imagistic richness.[16] The kind of theology, or at least *one* kind of theology, needed to address the ecological, nuclear sensibility of our time, focuses on the construction of new metaphors and models. Although it would be insufficient to rest in new images and to refuse to spell out conceptually their implications in as comprehensive a way as possible, the more critical task is to propose what Dennis Nineham calls a "lively imaginative picture" of the way God and the world as we know it are related. Metaphorical theology will chiefly focus on trying to establish the persuasive appropriateness of the metaphors for our situation, though it will, of course, also undertake the task of showing the conceptual implications and comprehensiveness of its proposed models of God and the world. The assumption here is that belief and behavior are more influenced by images than by concepts, or to phrase it in a less disjunctive way, that concepts without images are sterile. It is no coincidence that most religious traditions turn to personal and public human relationships to serve as metaphors and models of the relationship between God and the world: God as father, mother, lover, friend, king, lord, governor. These metaphors give a precision and persuasive power to the construct of God which concepts alone cannot. Because religions, including Christianity, are not incidentally imagistic but centrally and necessarily so, theology must also be an affair of the imagination.

To say that metaphorical theology is pluralistic is to make two points. First, since no metaphor or model refers properly or directly to God, many are necessary. All are inappropriate, partial, and inadequate; the most that can be said is that some aspect or aspects of the God-world relationship are illuminated by this or that model in a fashion relevant to a particular time and place. One of the classic difficulties with metaphors that become models, such as that of God the father, is that they are often reified, petrified, and expanded so as not only to exclude other models but also to pretend to the status of definitions.[17] I would insist, however, that models of God are not definitions of God but likely accounts of experiences of relating to God with the help of relationships we know and understand. We speak of relating to God as one would to a companion or lover; or a king or master; or the sun or ocean; or a rock or mountain; or a mother or sister. Obviously, we are not here defining the nature of God, nor could we do so if we used less anthropomorphic and naturalistic language. Predicates such as omniscience, infinity, omnipotence, and omnipresence do not properly apply to God either, for the meaning of all such language—knowledge, finitude, power, presence—applies properly only to our existence, not God's. All that such predicates represent is an attempt to make human qualities limitless. In other words, how language, any language, applies to God we do not know; what religious and theological language is at most is metaphorical forays attempting to express experiences of relating to God. It is like the experience of relating to a mother, or a mountain, or a king, or a comrade, or an ocean, or a liberator—or to use the more abstract language, to One who is limitlessly good, powerful, knowledgeable, and present. In other words, if one accepts that metaphors (and all language about God) are principally adverbial, having to do with how we relate to God rather than defining the nature of God, then no metaphors or models can be reified, petrified, or expanded so as to exclude all others. One can, for instance, include many possibilities: we can envision relating to God as to a father and a mother, to a healer and a liberator, to the sun and a mountain. As definitions of God, these possibilities are mutually exclusive; as models expressing experiences of relating to God, they are mutually enriching. Thus, metaphorical theology is pluralistic, welcoming many models of God.

The second way that metaphorical theology is pluralistic is that, as a partial account focused especially on the imagistic foundation of theology, it is but *one kind* of theology, not the only or proper kind. Since metaphorical theology, as I have envisioned it, is hypothetical, tentative, partial, open-ended, skeptical, and heuristic, it would be contradictory to claim that such theology is anything more than one of many needed kinds of reflective enterprises. To propose and elucidate metaphors and models of the relationship between God and the world appropriate for an ecological, nuclear age is not to reject other theological projects. Nor does a metaphorical theology, which sees itself focused principally at the level of the imagination, denounce kinds of theology that propose to reflect on Christian faith in other ways. I am not merely suggesting that theological tolerance is a good thing; rather, my own position within a metaphorical theology demands it. The kind of theology that seems essential to me in our time, one that works at the foundational level of the imagination, where the images that form our concepts are grounded, is necessarily partial and hypothetical. It can in no way claim comprehensiveness or closure; hence, it must be open to other attempts, other methods, other routes. Metaphorical theology is necessarily tolerant or pluralistic, aware that, just as the particular metaphors and models it proposes are but relative, heuristic ones, so also the project as such, this kind of theology as a whole, is a tentative affair and can advance few solid claims in its own behalf. In this sense, it is, I believe, in the tradition of the *via negativa:* finding little to say of God with certainty, it boldly makes its case hypothetically and lets it rest.

In summary, metaphorical theology is a kind of heuristic construction that in focusing on the imaginative construal of the God-world relationship, attempts to remythologize Christian faith through metaphors and models appropriate for an ecological, nuclear age.

Sources and Resources: Scripture, Tradition, and Experience

If we now ask concerning the sources and resources for metaphorical theology as described, it is evident that the answer will be a complex one. David Tracy claims that what unites all contemporary theologies, in spite of vast differences, is the "agreed-upon need for each theologian to interpret both situation and tradition."

The two "constants," he claims, are an analysis of the situation that theology must address and an "understanding of the ultimate norm of the Christian tradition" from which to address the situation.[18] This so-called method of correlation might be seen as just one theological method among many, but the case can be made that, if broadly enough interpreted, it will cover most recognizably Christian theologies, because of a peculiarity of the Christian religion: its claim to be both historical and contemporary. As historical faith, one that claims in some sense an illumination, revelation, or rendering explicit of divine reality in history, specifically, in the paradigmatic figure of Jesus of Nazareth and the subsequent witness to that event in Scripture, Christianity must always deal with the constant of its tradition. Hence, there will always be a hermeneutical task: how does one interpret the Christian pole?[19] This is a very complex enterprise because of the many possibilities not only within the foundational text of Scripture but also within the long and rich tradition built upon it. But the Christian religion, although historical, claims as well to be contemporary; that is, the significance of the story of Jesus is its present relevance, not its description of the past, although—and here is the difficult part—the story of the past gives a clue, at least a clue, to its present relevance. The point is that one cannot, in this tradition, distill some eternal truths from the "story of Jesus" and then cast the story aside; on the contrary, the events of and surrounding the life, death, and appearances of Jesus of Nazareth are claimed at the very least to be paradigmatic, that is, exemplars, models, parables of the God-world relationship, *for today*. Interpreting that constant, therefore, is a perennial task. The Christian theologian is constrained by the constant of the tradition, however interpreted in attempting to deal with the other constant, that of the contemporary situation.

The previous chapter attempted a sketch of the first constant, that of our present crisis and its need for both a holistic sensibility and a nuclear responsibility. We now must turn to the Christian pole by asking two questions: First, how does a metaphorical theology understand its Christian norm; in other words, what does it say about the authority of Scripture, tradition, and experience? And second, how does a metaphorical theology interpret the "demonstrable continuities" within the Christian paradigm for our time?

The tripartite division of Scripture, tradition, and experience is an artificial and deceptive one, for not only is it false to draw a sharp line between Scripture and tradition, inasmuch as Scripture is the earliest written record of the tradition's interpreting process and many classics of the tradition approach the status of Scripture. What is more, both Scripture and tradition fall under experience insofar as both are witnesses to experiences of the salvific power of God. As difficult as it is to deal with Scripture and tradition in the context of experience, it is necessary to do so, in order to make the case that both are interpretations in metaphors and concepts appropriate to particular times and places of the transforming love of God for the world. To claim that experience is the primary category is not, however, to say that religious experience is the basic criterion for a Christian theology or that we experience apart from or outside formative, linguistic communities: it is only to say that all our texts, including Scripture and the classics of the theological tradition, are "sedimentations" of interpreted experience.[20] To say, then, that Scripture and tradition fall within the realm of experience and that all experience is interpreted means that we are always involved in a hermeneutical spiral that has no clear entrance or exit. We are born into particular circumstances and communities that form us at the most basic levels and interpret our experience for us in ways we cannot control and, in significant ways, do not even recognize. Yet we also participate in and add to the spiral of interpretation, making claims that our experience is or is not adequately interpreted by these formative communities—and when it is not, advancing novel frameworks that are more persuasive.

If one accepts this model of the relationship between Scripture, tradition, and experience, one will see a continuum among the three, rather than sharp divisions separating them. Scripture (both the Hebrew Scriptures and early Christian literature) is the sedimentation of experiences of the salvific power of God in persuasive, powerful metaphors, models, and concepts, contemporary to the various times of interpretation. In the New Testament the interpretation of this salvific power is focused on the paradigmatic life and death of Jesus of Nazareth, and experiences of that transformative event are expressed in metaphors, models, and concepts of the first-century Mediterranean world. The tradition continues the

process of expressing experiences of God's saving love by interpreting them in contemporary terms, with the difference being
reliance on the earliest interpretation as normative.

It is at this point that difficulties arise, for instead of Scripture's
being understood as case studies, or a prime Christian classic, or a
prototype, it has too often been seen as the authoritative text, the
only norm for subsequent theology.[21] As such, the language (metaphors, models, and concepts) of two thousand years ago has become
sacralized and made normative. The consequences of this process
are far-reaching: not only has Christian faith been interpreted for
most of its history in anachronistic, irrelevant ways but it has also
become a "book religion"—as seen most clearly in Protestantism's
sola scriptura—although it is evident in the book Christianity wor-
ships that it is the transformative power of God's love, not a text, that
is the focus of Christian faith.[22]

If one looks at Scripture as a case study, classic, or prototype, one
sees what it is itself rather than what the church has wanted to
make of it. That is, what constitutes this book are a number—and a
vast number, if one includes the Hebrew Scriptures—of experiences of persons and communities witnessing to the transforming
power of God in their lives, interpreted in terms not of some past
time but of their own time. If we wish to take Scripture seriously
and see it as normative, we should take it on its own terms as a
model of how theology should be done, rather than as the authority
dictating the terms in which it is done. For example, it is sometimes
a cause for consternation that the pluralism of the New Testament—the different perspectives of the three Synoptic Gospels as
well as the great differences between the theologies of Paul and
John, not to mention the pastoral letters and the Book of Revelation—makes it difficult if not impossible to base theology on the
Bible. Which perspective should one choose? But that question is
the wrong one if one sees the Bible as case study or prototype. It is
not so much an interpretation that one looks for in the Bible as a
process, not so much a content as a form.

As I will attempt to show soon, there is a paradigmatic content of
"demonstrable continuities" within Christianity, but of such gener-
alizability that it can and must take many different forms. It is not
primarily what one can say in a general way about Christian faith

that is interesting or important; what are interesting and important
are the particular metaphors, models, and concepts which make
God's saving power a concrete reality for particular peoples in
particular times and places. Our primary datum is not a Christian
message for all time which becomes concretized in different contexts; rather, it is experiences of women and men witnessing to the
transforming love of God interpreted in a myriad of ways. If what
can be said in a general way is something like "To believe in the
God of the Judeo-Christian tradition is to believe in the trustworthiness of things or that the power in the universe is gracious," that
is something important but very imprecise. What are more significant are the ways this faith is interpreted and expressed; but to
elevate one way of interpreting it (the "historical Jesus," Pauline or
Johannine Christology, Augustinian or Thomistic metaphysics,
Luther's "justification by faith," Barth's notion of election) as the
one and only way is to reify and petrify certain metaphors, models,
and concepts that although appropriate to some people in certain
times, may be no longer. If we take the form of Scripture seriously,
the plurality of interpretive perspectives that it is, we will have to
do the same risky, adventuresome thing that it does: interpret the
salvific love of God in ways that can address our crises most persuasively and powerfully. And this will not, cannot, mean using the
terminology of two thousand years ago.

The first thing to say, then, from the perspective of a metaphorical theology, is that the Christian pole or constant gives us a clue for
how to do theology. It is precisely the patchwork, potpourri character of the Hebraic and Christian Scriptures with their rich flood of
images, stories, and themes—some interweaving and mutually
supportive, and others disparate, presenting alternative possibilities—that gives Christian theologians "authority" to experiment, to
find grids or screens with which to interpret God's transforming
love within the givens of their own time. These givens include both
the portrait of the situation to be addressed and the ways in which
it can be most persuasively addressed. Thus, Scripture as case
study, classic, or prototype implies that a theologian in the closing
years of the twentieth century should delineate the situation to be
addressed in terms of the need for an ecological, nuclear sensibility.
To depict our situation in terms of another time—of Luther's, for

instance, with the need in the late Middle Ages for people to win righteous status before God (a need Luther's theology addressed through "justification by grace through faith")—is to take the question and the answer from another time. One way to ask the question in our time (although not the only way) is to ask it in terms of the need for a holistic vision that accepts human responsibility in a nuclear age. If we ask that question, the answer must surely be in metaphors, models, and concepts appropriate to it. We cannot depict the contemporary situation to which Christian faith should speak (the first constant) in the way we have done—as an evolutionary, ecological vision of interdependence with human beings possessing the ability to end life—and then depict the Christian pole (the second constant), which should address *this* situation, in the language of dying and rising gods, personal guilt and sacrificial atonement, eternal life and so forth. Such metaphors and concepts do not address the contemporary situation as depicted.

The formal criterion for theology, then, is that it reflect, in tough-minded, concrete ways and in the language and thought forms of one's own time, about what salvation could, would, mean now, to us. Different people and communities will spell this out in different ways: thus it was in scriptural times, and thus it should be in other times as well. In our time, we have competing interpretations of the two "constants," and this is as it should be. What the formal criterion does not allow, however, is resting in an interpretation of God's salvific love from some bygone time, for this will invariably be escapist and, finally, destructive: that gospel will be good news not for our time but for another.

In addition to the formal criterion of the Christian constant, there is also a material one, which I have alluded to with the phrase "demonstrable continuities," and to this we now turn.

The Christian Paradigm

The material norm of Christian faith involves a specification of what distinguishes this faith. It involves risking an interpretation of what, most basically, Christian faith is about. Such interpretation is, of course, not done in general or for all time; it is always a partial, limited account of the contours of the salvific power of God in a particular time in light of the paradigmatic figure Jesus of

Nazareth. To see the story of Jesus as paradigmatic means to see it as illuminative and illustrative of basic characteristics of the Christian understanding of the God-world relationship. These characteristics are not known solely from that story nor exemplified only in it, but that story is a classic instance, embodying critical dimensions of the relationship between God and the world. A metaphorical theology, as I have suggested, does not take the Christian constant, in either its formal or material mode, as the only source and resource for theology. The question as we approach the issue of the paradigmatic figure Jesus of Nazareth is not whether everything we need in order to do theology in our time can be generated from that figure but whether there are clues or hints here for an interpretation of salvation in our time. That is to say, are there distinguishing marks of the story of Jesus that are relevant to a holistic, nuclear age? If one understands the life and death of Jesus of Nazareth as a parable of God's relation to the world, and if to be a Christian means to be willing to look "God-wards" through his story, then one is constrained to say in what ways that story is significant now.[23]

This will involve understanding the story differently from in the past, but, I believe, in a way that has "demonstrable continuities" with the past. My perspective on that story is similar to that of the so-called liberation theologies. Each of these theologies, from the standpoint of race, gender, class, or another basic human distinction, claims that the Christian gospel is opposed to oppression of some by others, opposed to hierarchies and dualisms, opposed to the domination of the weak by the powerful. These theologies, however, unlike the short-lived death-of-God or play theologies, are not just another fad; like other major revisions of the Christian paradigm, they are a new way of understanding the relationship between God and the world, a new way of interpreting what salvation means. These theologies are not marginal, strange, or even particularly novel enterprises, relevant only to the groups from which they emerge. Rather, they are in the classical tradition of fundamental reformulations of Christian faith, just like the theologies of Augustine, Luther, and Schleiermacher. In the case of each of these writers, something about the writer's own experience did not fit with current understandings of Christianity: his experience presented an anomaly that could not be contained in the contemporary paradigm. A changed interpretation was imperative if the writer was to continue to identify himself as a Christian—and if Christian faith was to speak to the critical issues of the times. These theologians, however, believed they were interpreting Christianity not just for themselves or their own kind but for all. From a particular perspective came a universal claim.

These two notes of fundamental revisionist interpretation—experience and universality—are present also in the liberation theologies. The experience of being oppressed by gender, race, or poverty does not limit the theology that emerges to women, people of color, or the poor. Rather, the particular experiences of oppression serve as glasses bringing into sharper focus what one asserts the heart of the gospel truly to be for one's own time. There are important differences among the liberation theologies, but there are common notes as well, and they stand in significant contrast to some other readings of Christianity. But such theologies, and the material norm of Christianity that they suggest, should be judged in the same way and with the same criteria as other theologies. Here I am echoing Letty Russell's objection that feminist, black, and Third World theologies need to be qualified by an adjective, whereas white, male, Western theologies are called just theology.[24] These other theologies are also just theology. As with all theology, they emerge out of a concrete, social context; they identify what they believe the central vision of Christianity to be; they offer particular insights, insights that emerge in part because of special perspectives—insights that ought to be seen as illuminating to all people, if they are indeed in continuity with the Christianity paradigm and an appropriate rendering of it for our time. The crucial difference between these new theologies and classical theology is that for the first time they are coming from women, from people of color, and from the poor.

These theologies share a common reading of the material norm of Christianity in certain respects. First, Christian faith is seen as destabilizing conventional expectations and worldly standards. At the very least, it is a disorienting perspective that upsets usual divisions and dualisms. Second, Christian faith is inclusive, reaching out to the weak, to the outsider, to the stranger, to the outcast.

Third, Christian faith is antihierarchical and antitriumphalist, epitomized in the metaphor of the king who became a servant, one who
suffers for and alongside the oppressed. These points are general
ones (and different liberation theologies would orient them differently—toward, especially, the oppressive situation of women, people of color, or the poor); nonetheless, they constitute a significantly
different rendering of Christian faith from that found in other interpretations. It is not the traditional and still-popular message that
Jesus Christ, fully God and fully man, died for the sins of all humanity and was resurrected to new life, as his followers shall be also.
Nor is it the more recent so-called liberal interpretation that Jesus is
the power by which the individual can overcome alienation, mean-
inglessness, and despair. In the first case, the issue to which the
gospel speaks is death from sin; hence, the good news is eternal life.
In the second case, the issue to which the gospel speaks is personal,
existential anguish; hence, the answer is new meaning. Liberation
theologies claim (in different ways) that the issue to which the
gospel speaks is the destructive, oppressive domination of some over
others; hence, the answer is a new way of being in the world free of
all hierarchies. If one were to identify the heart of the gospel for
these theologies—their material norm—it would be the surprising
invitation to all, especially to the outcast and oppressed. It is a destabilizing, inclusive, nonhierarchical vision of Christian faith, the
claim that the gospel of Christianity is a new creation for all of
creation—a life of freedom and fulfillment for all.

But is this vision in continuity with the Christian paradigm? Is it
a revision, a reseeing of that vision, or is it a substitution for it? Can
a claim be advanced that it is one credible, strong candidate for
interpreting salvation in our time within the Christian paradigm, or
is it a marginal or even bogus view? To answer these questions, we
will first look briefly at the story of Jesus as a destabilizing, inclusive, nonhierarchical vision. Second, we will go beyond most of the
liberation theologies to extend this vision to the cosmos and our
responsibility for it.[25] That is, we will look at the paradigmatic story
of Jesus for clues and hints concerning the kind of metaphors most
appropriate for modeling the relationship between God and the
world, and hence between human beings and the world, in an
ecological, nuclear era.

It is clear that the story of Jesus is a resource, but not the only source, for the material norm of the liberation theologies, that Christian faith gives a destabilizing, inclusive, nonhierarchical vision of fulfillment for all of creation.[26] For although that vision is compatible with and illuminated by the paradigmatic story of Jesus, it is generated as much by the social, economic, political, and ecological realities of the late twentieth century. Nonetheless, if the paradigmatic story is revelatory of God's "way with the world," then it will be relevant to our world and can, without misrepresentation or distortion, be shown to be. Does this mean that each age reads into the story what it needs to, what it must, in order to make it speak to the deepest crises of its own time? Perhaps. Still, each theology—and liberation theologies are no exception—claims that its interpretation is a truer, less distorted interpretation of the story. Interpretations can and must change from age to age, and often they change substantially in order to address radically new situations; nevertheless, the theologian is constrained to return to the paradigmatic story of Jesus for validation and illumination.[27]

What case can be made that the paradigmatic Christian story is a destabilizing, inclusive, nonhierarchical vision of fulfillment for all of creation? Can a portrait—though not necessarily the only portrait—be sketched along these lines? Nothing more than a "cartoon," in the sense of a preliminary draft, is possible here, but that is sufficient, for what we seek are the chief features or characteristics of that story, not its historical basis or subsequent interpretation. Three aspects that appear to be characteristic of the story of Jesus are his speaking in parables, his table fellowship with outcasts, and his death on a cross. Each is suggestive, and much has been made of each. The parables have been interpreted as moral imperatives; the table fellowship as a symbol of the eucharistic sacrifice; the death on the cross as God's triumph over sin, death, and the devil. But whatever the interpretations, few dispute that these three features are part of the story. A liberation theologian would interpret them differently: the parables illuminate the destabilizing aspect of the good news of Christianity; the table fellowship its inclusive character; and the death on the cross its nonhierarchical emphasis. As we look at each of these in more detail, what is being sought is not primarily validation of the story of Jesus as having these characteristics but illumination of our situation by that paradigmatic story.

The interpretation of the parables of Jesus in the last quarter century makes the case that they are a destabilizing, disorienting inversion of expectations and conventional standards.[28] The parables, brief stories told in the secular language of Jesus' time, are extended metaphors that say something about the unfamiliar, the "kingdom of God," in terms of the familiar, a narrative of ordinary people doing ordinary things. They work, however, on a pattern of orientation, disorientation, and reorientation: the parable begins in the ordinary world with its conventional standards and expectations, but in the course of the story a radically different perspective is introduced, often by means of a surrealistic extravagance, that disorients the listener, and finally, through the interaction of the two competing viewpoints tension is created that results in a reorientation, a redescription of life in the world.[29] A parable is, in this analysis, an assault on the accepted conventions, including the social, economic, and mythic structures that people build for their own comfort and security. A parable is a story meant to invert and subvert these structures and to suggest that the way of the kingdom is not the way of the world. In Jesus' parables we see an elder son who does not get what he deserves and a younger son who gets what he does not deserve; late workers being paid the same as those who have labored all day; a feast that is given for the poor and the outcasts when the prominent guests decline; a foreigner who comes to the aid of a Jew when his own religious leaders walk by on the other side. Throughout the parables two standards are in permanent tension with each other, and the effect of their interaction is disorientation for the listener. As John Dominic Crossan points out, not "liking" the parables is the appropriate reaction to them, for they undermine efforts at conventional security: "You have built a lovely home, myth assures us: but, whispers parable, you are right above an earthquake fault."[30]

At the very least the parables suggest that attempts at separating the "worthy" from the "unworthy," dualisms such as rich/poor, Jew/Gentile, elder/younger son, etc.—and by implication, male/female, white/colored, straight/gay, Christian/non-Christian—are without basis in the vision of existence alluded to by the phrase "the kingdom of God." What is suggested is a radically egalitarian, nondualistic way of being in the world. Liberation theologies make the case that Scripture is on the side of the poor and oppressed, but what is distinctive in the parables is not primarily a reversal that elevates the "unworthy" but a destabilization of *all* dualisms. Such destabilization is far more radical than an inversion, for it means refusing all categorizations of insider/outsider, though human beings appear naturally and deeply to desire such distinctions. But the parables, as one aspect of the portrait of our paradigmatic story, sketch a world in which such categorizations are disrupted and overturned.

Is it appropriate to extend this disruption beyond the human dualisms to those of spirit/flesh, mind/matter, soul/body, human/nonhuman, sky/earth? Flesh, matter, body, the nonhuman, and the earth are conventionally, perhaps even "naturally," considered inferior, and notably in the Christian tradition they have been so considered. But if the destabilization of the parables is to support the holistic sensibility needed in our time, then the oppression of flesh, matter, body, the nonhuman, and the earth must also be ended. If sin from the perspective of parabolic destabilization is the "natural" desire of human beings to separate themselves, in superior/inferior dualisms, from one another and from the earth, then salvation from this perspective would be an overturning of those patterns—a making whole or healing of the divisions. What is needed for a holistic sensibility to become a reality in our time is a change of consciousness in the way we see our world and ourselves in relation to the world. The destabilization of the parables is a necessary radical first step: when extended to the cosmos, it proclaims the end of the conventional, hierarchical, oppressive dualism of human/nonhuman.

What we see in Jesus' parables becomes more explicit in his table fellowship: the destabilization of the parables becomes an "enacted parable" as Jesus invites the outcasts of society to eat with him. Some scholars argue that Jesus' practice of eating with "tax collectors and sinners" was both the central feature of his ministry and its major scandal.[31] Like the parables, Jesus' table fellowship is destabilizing, but it goes further than the disruption of conventional dualisms, for as a friend of outcasts (Matt. 11:19), inviting them to eat with him, he epitomizes the scandal of inclusiveness for his time. What is proclaimed in Luke 4 as the heart of Jesus' ministry— good news to the poor, release to the captives, liberty for the op- pressed—and what is manifested as well by his healings of the sick is pushed to an extreme in his invitation to the ritually unclean to eat with him. Jesus offended by inviting the outsiders to come in, to join with him not merely as needy outcasts but as his friends in joyful feasting. The central symbol of the new vision of life, the kingdom of God, is a community joined together in a festive meal where the bread that sustains life and the joy that sustains the spirit are shared with all.[32] The radical inclusiveness of this vision is eloquently summarized by Elisabeth Schüssler Fiorenza: "Since the reality of the *basileia* for Jesus spells not primarily holiness but wholeness, the salvation of God's *basileia* is present and experien- tially available whenever Jesus casts out demons (Luke 11:20), heals the sick and the ritually unclean, tells stories about the lost who are found, of the uninvited who are invited, of the last who will be first. . . . Not the holiness of the elect but the wholeness *of all* is the central vision of Jesus."[33]

The emphasis here is on inclusiveness: all are invited and what they are invited to is a feast, fulfillment, joy. The invitation is not to chosen individuals but to all. But unless we envision this feast as merely an allegory of a spiritual feast in another world—as solely an eschatological, mythological feast—it has implications for the holistic sensibility needed in our time. That is, the insistence of liberation theologies that salvation must be a social, political, eco- nomic reality in history, since oppression is precisely that kind of reality, means that in order for all to be invited, an ecological atti- tude must emerge. Without enough bread, some cannot be invited. An ecological sensibility that cares for the earth that "cares for us" must accompany a vision of social, political, economic justice if that vision is to become anything other than rhetoric.[34] Only a sensibil- ity that accepts our intrinsic interdependence not only with all other people but also with the earth will be able to create the conditions necessary to help bring about the fulfillment of all as salvation for our time.

An ecological sensibility is not only an aesthetic appreciation for the intrinsic value of all forms of life—an attitude of "bending toward the mountain"—though it includes such appreciation; it is also a different way of thinking, a change to thinking the way nature itself works in terms of interdependence, relationality, reciprocity. As Rosemary Radford Ruether puts it, we must "convert our minds to the earth," turn away from linear, dichotomized, dualistic thinking that gives the human desire for short-term gains predominance over the long-term well-being of the earth and its ability to support us.[35] The aesthetic and utilitarian (in the sense of ecologically wise) attitudes are intrinsically related: we cannot be supported by an earth we do not support. Hence, political and economic liberation and the ecological, holistic sensibility are not two projects but one. The inclusiveness of the gospel—the invitation to fulfillment for all—must extend to the cosmos as well as to all peoples. The feast of joy, the invitation to share the bread and wine that symbolize both life itself and the good life, cannot be accepted unless we become caretakers of the earth. In our time, salvation must be understood to extend to all, or it will apply to none.

Nowhere is this fact more evident, of course, than in the threat of a nuclear holocaust. It stands as the ultimate challenge to accept the global village as our model of reality as we approach the twenty-first century. If political and economic liberation are intrinsically related to an ecological sensibility, so also is the acceptance of human responsibility for nuclear knowledge, for here also, and with chilling exactitude, salvation must be seen as extending to all people and to our earth: if we do not learn to live together, we will die together.

The parables, the table fellowship, and now the cross—they form a pattern in the sketch we are attempting of an interpretation of the story of Jesus for an ecological, nuclear age. The destabilization of the parables that is fleshed out in the invitation to all, especially to the "unworthy" and the outcast to share in the feast of life, is radicalized further in the cross. Here the way necessary to bring about this new mode of being is suggested. The way is radical identification with all others. In a world in which hierarchies and dualisms are fiercely defended, such identification will bring punishment, often swift and brutal punishment. The cross epitomizes the retribution that comes to those who give up controlling and triumphalist postures in order to relate to others in mutual love.

As many have noted, there are ambiguous if not contradictory interpretations of the cross in Christianity, some seeing it as the critique of triumphalism epitomized in the king who becomes a servant, and others as but the prelude to the resurrection, when the king will reign in glory, as shall his loyal subjects.[36] The first interpretation is consonant with the parables and the table fellowship, for it continues and sharpens the distinction between two ways of being in the world, one of which is destabilizing, inclusive, and nonhierarchical and the other of which is conventional, exclusive, and triumphalist. That is to say, the first interpretation is a direct assault on the second; in fact, if one accepts it, one must criticize the second as a perversion of the gospel. If one accepts the interpretation of the parables and the table fellowship of Jesus advanced here, then a triumphalist christology and atonement must be rejected. The mythology in which the cross and especially the resurrection have been interpreted is not only anachronistic but harmful, for the destabilizing, inclusive, nonhierarchical vision of salvation needed in a holistic, nuclear age is undermined by it. For instance, if we see Jesus as "fully God and fully man," the substitutionary sacrifice who atoned for the sins of the world two thousand years ago and who now reigns triumphant along with all who loyally accept his kingly, gracious forgiveness of their sins, we not only accept a salvation we do not need but weaken if not destroy our ability to understand and accept the salvation we do need. The triumphalist mythology makes impossible the interpretation of the way to our salvation on several points.

First, it insists that salvation rests with one individual and in one past act. In first-century Palestine and throughout many centuries of Christian history, the notion of a representative human being in whose act and existence others, even centuries removed, could participate made sense in terms of Platonic and Aristotelian philosophies. It does not any longer. Both the individualism and the remoteness of this view, from our perspective, are contrary to the idea that salvation in our time must be the task of all human beings working in concert with the loving power of God as a present and future activity. It is not what one individual did two thousand years ago that is critical but what we, with God, do now.

Second, the classical mythology assumes that sin is against God—

that it is traitorous or rebellious behavior against the King, Lord, or Father—whereas in the interpretation of the parables and table fellowship we have suggested, sin is against other people and the earth: it is exclusivistic, dualistic, hierarchical separation of insiders from outsiders. The classical mythology supports escapism of the worst sort; it is a misplaced religiosity that provides comfortable, personal assurance while undermining the will to work to overcome the oppression and domination of some by others—to overcome, that is, sin as it needs to be viewed in our time.

Third, the classical mythology supports metaphors and models of God contrary to those needed for imagining the God-world relationship in our time. It encourages us to think of God in triumphalist, royalist, highly individualistic, "distant" political imagery that is counterproductive to the kind of metaphors in which *we* need to think of God. In the classical imagery the King "empties" himself, becoming a servant only for the duration of Jesus' brief ministry and the sacrifice of the cross, but his true being is as almighty King, Lord, and Father, and he returns in the resurrection to his power and glory. If, however, one sees the cross not as the King's sacrifice, in the mode of his Son, for the sins of the world, but as a paradigm of God's way with the world always, other possibilities emerge. If one sees the cross as revealing God's distinctive way of being in and with the world, one will have a significantly different understanding both of God and of the way to speak to God—and an understanding more relevant to *our* salvation. In other words, if Jesus of Nazareth as paradigmatic of God is not just a "phase" of God but is genuinely revelatory of God, then the mode of the cross, the way of radical identification with all, which will inevitably bring punishment, sometimes to the point of death, becomes a permanent reality. It becomes the way of the destabilizing, inclusive, nonhierarchical vision.

Jesus of Nazareth, then, does not "do something on our behalf" but, far more important, manifests in his own life and death that the heart of the universe is unqualified love working to befriend the needy, the outcast, the oppressed. This we never would have guessed; it can scarcely be believed; and mostly, it is not. But if one takes clues from the parables, Jesus' table fellowship, and the cross, to believe in Jesus as a paradigm of God means that or something like that. It means that God is "like Jesus" and if Jesus is not a king but a servant, then God should be spoken of in "servant" language in relation to the world.

At this point, however, metaphorical theology should step in. That is to say, although the inclusive way of the cross and the triumphalist way of resurrection were in Jesus' time powerfully and appropriately contrasted by the metaphors of servant and king, they can be no longer. The language of servitude is no longer current, acceptable, or significant for expressing the distinctive and unconventional kind of love epitomized in the cross. There are, I believe, other metaphors, such as those of mother, lover, and friend, that express dimensions of that love more fully and appropriately for our time. If one accepts that salvation in our time needs to be understood as a destabilizing, inclusive, nonhierarchical vision, these metaphors with their associations of caring, mutuality, attraction, nurturing, supporting, empathy, responsibility, service, self-sacrifice, forgiveness, and creativity are highly suggestive. They not only underscore self-sacrifice and radical self-giving to others, as does the servant metaphor, but also suggest dimensions of salvation for our time that the servant metaphor cannot: the interdependence of all life, including the life of God with the world, and reciprocity, including our responsibility to work with God for the fulfillment of all that lives. To see God's relationship to the world through the paradigm of the cross of Jesus is illuminating of salvation for our time if neither the servant nor the king is a major model but some other highly significant and very rich metaphors are investigated for their potential as expressions of the destabilizing, inclusive, nonhierarchical vision in an ecological, nuclear age. That is my thesis.

If, in other words, Jesus of Nazareth in his parables, table fellowship, and cross is a paradigm of God's relationship to the world, if he is a model or parable through which we can grasp something of God as well as discover a way to speak of God, then we have to ask how this can and should be expressed in different times and places. Metaphorical theology says it always has to be interpreted differently. We circle back, then, to an opening question of this chapter: What should we be doing for our time that would be comparable to what Paul and John did for theirs? One task is to conduct a thought experiment with new metaphors (and their accompanying concepts) that appear to have potential to express the trustworthiness and graciousness of the power of the universe *for our time.* The first step in this thought experiment is to attend to a fourth distinctive feature of the story of Jesus—the appearance stories—and to what the feature might suggest for a contemporary way to imagine the relationship between God and the world. How can we understand the resurrection in a way that emphasizes the destabilizing, inclusive, nonhierarchical vision of fulfillment? Is the relation of a risen king to his realm the appropriate construct? I think not, and in the next chapter I will propose another way of imagining the God-world relationship. This will afford us the context for a detailed treatment in subsequent chapters of the models of God as mother, lover, and friend.

3

*G*od and the World

Then he appeared to more than five hundred brethren at one time, most of whom are still alive, though some have fallen asleep. Then he appeared to James, then to all the apostles. Last of all, as to one untimely born, he appeared also to me. (1 Cor. 15:6–8)

The appearance stories are a fourth distinctive feature of the paradigmatic story of Jesus of Nazareth. Some scholars now claim that the "appearance" of Jesus, the awareness of his continuing presence and empowerment, is what "really happened" in the resurrection: ". . . lo, I am with you always, to the close of the age" (Matt. 28:20b).[1] That is to say, a critical aspect of Jesus' story as paradigmatic of God's relationship with the world is that it continues. The permanency of the way of the cross, the way of self-sacrificial, befriending love inviting all to fulfillment, is the permanency not just of an example but of an empowerment. The resurrection is a way of speaking about an awareness that the presence of God in Jesus is a permanent presence in our present. The appearance stories capture this awareness better than do the empty-tomb narratives with the associated interpretation of the bodily resurrection of Jesus and his ascension to glory. The empty-tomb narratives have been elaborated to suggest that personal, bodily translation into another world to join the Savior is the way divine presence becomes permanent to us and that until that time of full presence we live in the between-time, sustained by symbolic moments of the presence of God in the sacraments and the preaching of the Word. But on such a view, most times and most places are empty of God: God is not, on this reading, a permanent presence in our present—not "omnipresent," present in all places at all times, but partially, fitfully, selectively present. The appearance stories suggest, however, as Paul's narration implies, that God in Christ will be present even to the last and the least. Whatever the resurrection is, if interpreted in light of the appearance narratives, it is inclusive; it takes place in every present; it is the presence of God to us, not our translation into God's presence.

Like other aspects of the paradigmatic story of Jesus, the resurrection has been interpreted in many different ways. The interpretation suggested here is in keeping with an understanding of the Christian gospel as a destabilizing, inclusive, nonhierarchical vision of fulfillment for all of creation. It asks, How should one understand the presence of God to the world in order to empower that vision? In some way, the surprising invitation to the oppressed, to the last and the least, expressed in the parables, the table fellowship, and the cross needs to be imaginatively perceived as permanently present in every present and every space: it needs to be grasped, in the most profound sense, as a worldly reality. It is obvious that the traditional view of the resurrection does not fulfill these criteria, for in that view some, not all, are included; salvation occurs principally in the past (Jesus' resurrection) and the future (the resurrection of elected individuals), not in the present, every present—and such redemption is otherworldly, not worldly.

But what if we were to understand the resurrection and ascension not as the bodily translation of some individuals to another world—a mythology no longer credible to us—but as the promise of God to be permanently present, "bodily" present to us, in all places and times of our world?[2] In what ways would we think of the relationship between God and the world were we to experiment with the metaphor of the universe as God's "body," God's palpable presence in all space and time? If what is needed in our ecological, nuclear age is an imaginative vision of the relationship between God and the world that underscores their interdependence and mutuality, empowering a sensibility of care and responsibility toward all life, how would it help to see the world as the body of God?

In making this suggestion, we must always keep in mind its *metaphorical* character: we are not slipping back into the search for unmediated divine presence (which the deconstructionists have criticized so thoroughly). There is no way behind this metaphor or any other construal of the God-world relationship; at most, a metaphor fits with some interpretation of the Christian gospel and is illuminating and fruitful when lived in for a while. Hence, to imagine the world as God's body is to do precisely that: to imagine it that way. It is not to say that the world is God's body or that God is present to us in the world. Those things we do not know; all that resurrection faith can do is imagine the most significant ways to speak of God's presence in one's own time. And the metaphor of the world as God's body presents itself as a promising candidate.

This image, radical as it may seem (in light of the dominant metaphor of a king to his realm) for imagining the relationship between God and the world, is a very old one with roots in Stoicism and elliptically in the Hebrew Scriptures. The notion has tantalized many, including Tertullian and Irenaeus, and though it received little assistance from either Platonism or Aristotelianism because of their denigration of matter and body (and hence did not enter the mainstream of either Augustinian or Thomistic theology), it surfaced powerfully in Hegel as well as in twentieth-century process theologies.[3] The mystical tradition within Christianity has carried the notion implicitly, even though the metaphor of body may not appear: "The world is charged with the grandeur of God" (Gerard Manley Hopkins); "There is communion with God, and a communion with the earth, and a communion with God through earth" (Pierre Teilhard de Chardin).[4]

We are asking whether one way to remythologize the gospel for our time might not be through the metaphor of the world as God's "body" rather than as the king's "realm." If we experiment with this metaphor, it becomes obvious that royalist, triumphalist images for God—God as king, lord, ruler, patriarch—will be inappropriate. Other metaphors, suggesting mutuality, interdependence, caring, and responsiveness, will be needed. I will suggest God as mother (father), lover, and friend. If the world is imagined as self-expressive of God, if it is a "sacrament"—the outward and visible presence or body—of God, if it is not an alien other over against God but expressive of God's very being, then, how would God respond to it and how should we? Would not the metaphors of parents, lovers, and friends be suggestive, with their implications of creation, nurture, passionate concern, attraction, respect, support, cooperation,

mutuality? If the entire universe is expressive of God's very being—*the* "incarnation," if you will—do we not have the beginnings
of an imaginative picture of the relationship between God and the
world peculiarly appropriate as a context for interpreting the salvific love of God *for our time?*

It is this picture we will be investigating in as much detail as
possible in these pages. The issue is how to remythologize the Christian's cry of affirmation "Christ is risen!"—the promise of God's
saving presence always—for our space and time. We will first look at
the tradition's monarchical mythology for imaging God's relationship to the world. The classical picture, an imaginatively powerful
one, employs royalist, triumphalist metaphors, depicting God as
king, lord, and patriarch who rules the world and human beings,
usually with benevolence. Is this understanding of God's presence
in and to the world, and hence, by implication, our presence in and
to the world, one that is appropriate and helpful for a holistic, nuclear time? I believe it is not and will suggest below that we consider
the world as God's body. In what ways is this metaphor an appropriate context for interpreting the destabilizing, nonhierarchical, inclusive vision of fulfillment for all of creation? How would we feel and
act differently in a world that we perceived as the body of God?

Finally, if we accept the imaginative picture of the world as
God's body, it is obvious that the triumphalist, imperialistic
metaphors of God will no longer be appropriate. I have suggested
the metaphors of God as parent, lover, and friend of the earth that
is expressive of God's very self. We will in subsequent chapters be
investigating these metaphors in detail, but some general issues
concerning these images need to be considered first.

For instance, the question arises whether any personal metaphors should be employed for imaging God's presence. Are not
more abstract, impersonal, or naturalistic metaphors better for
encouraging an ecological sensibility? In the final section of this
chapter we will consider the viability of metaphors of personal
presence such as mother (and father), lover, and friend. Are these
metaphors too intimate, too personal, and indeed, perhaps too
individualistic? What defense can be given for imaging God on
analogy with human beings and in metaphors expressive of our
most important relationships?

As we begin this exercise of the deconstruction and reconstruction of metaphors in which we imagine the saving power of God in our contemporary world, it is necessary to remind ourselves of the nature of our project. We will not be defining or describing the world or universe as God's body nor God's relationship to it as that of mother, lover, or friend. Rather, we will be using descriptions that properly apply elsewhere and letting them try their chance at the difficult task of expressing some significant aspects of the Godworld relationship in our time. That they will miss the mark or be nonsense some of the time will come as no surprise. A heuristic theology plays with ideas in order to find out, searches for likely accounts rather than definitions. The object of this kind of theology is to suggest metaphors that create a shock of recognition. Does "the world as God's body" or "God as lover" have both marks of a good metaphor, both the *shock* and the *recognition?* Do these metaphors both disorient and reorient? Do they evoke a response of hearing something new and something interesting? Are they both disclosive and illuminating, both a revelation and in some sense true? I wish at all costs to avoid the "tyranny of the absolutizing imagination," which would insist that our newly suggested metaphors are the only or the permanent ones for expressing God's saving love. No such claims will be made; instead, a case will be presented to show that the metaphors are appropriate, illuminating, and better than some alternatives.

The Monarchical Model

The *monarchical model* of God as King was developed systematically, both in Jewish thought (God as Lord and King of the Universe), in medieval Christian thought (with its emphasis on divine omnipotence), and in the Reformation (especially in Calvin's insistence on God's sovereignty). In the portrayal of God's relation to the world, the dominant western historical model has been that of the absolute monarch ruling over his kingdom.[5]

This imaginative picture is so prevalent in mainstream Christianity that it is often not recognized as a picture. Nor is it immediately perceived as oppressive. More often it is accepted as the natural understanding of the relationship of God and the world—and one we like. Think for a moment of the sense of triumph, joy, and power that surges through us when we join in singing the "Hallelujah Chorus" from Handel's *Messiah*. Probably we do not think about the implications of the images we sing, but we know they make us feel good about our God and about ourselves as his subjects: "King of Kings and Lord of Lords," "for the Lord God omnipotent reigneth." Our God is really God, the almighty Lord and King of the universe whom none can defeat, and by implication we also are undefeatable.

It is a powerful imaginative picture and a very dangerous one. As we have already noted, it has resulted in what Gordon Kaufman calls a pattern of "asymmetrical dualism" between God and the world, in which God and the world are only distantly related and all power, either as domination or benevolence, is on God's side.[6] It supports conceiving of God as a being existing somewhere apart from the world and ruling it externally either directly through divine intervention or indirectly through controlling the wills of his subjects. It creates feelings of awe in the hearts of loyal subjects and thus supports the "godness" of God, but these feelings are balanced by others of abject fear and humiliation: in this picture, God can be God only if we are nothing. The understanding of salvation that accompanies this view is sacrificial, substitutionary atonement, and in Anselm's classic rendition of it the sovereign imagery predominates. Since even a wink of the eye by a vassal against the Liege Lord of the universe would be irredeemable sin, we as abject subjects must rely totally on our sovereign God who "became man" in order to undergo a sacrificial death, substituting his great worth for our worthlessness. Again, we feel the power of this picture: because we are totally unable to help ourselves, we will be totally cared for. We not only are forgiven for our sins and reconciled to our King as once again his loyal subjects but we can also look forward to a time when we shall join him in his heavenly kingdom.

This picture, while simplistic and anachronistic, continues in spite of its limitations, because of its psychological power: it makes us feel good about God and about ourselves. It inspires strong emotions of awe, gratitude, and trust toward God and, in ourselves, engenders a satisfying swing from abject guilt to joyous relief. Its very power is part of its danger, and any picture that seeks to replace it must reckon with its attraction. Many have criticized the monarchical model, and it has been severely rejected by a wide range of contemporary theologians.[7] My criticism of it here focuses on its inability to serve as the imaginative framework for an understanding of the gospel as a destabilizing, inclusive, nonhierarchical vision of fulfillment for all of creation. In that respect, it has three major flaws: in the monarchical model, God is distant from the world, relates only to the human world, and controls that world through domination and benevolence.

The relationship of a king to his subjects is necessarily a distant one: royalty is "untouchable." It is the distance, the difference, the otherness of God that is underscored with this imagery. God as king is in his kingdom—which is not of this earth—and we remain in another place, far from his dwelling. In this picture God is worldless and the world is Godless: the world is empty of God's presence, for it is too lowly to be the royal abode. Time and space are not filled with God: the eons of human and geological time stretch as a yawning void back into the recesses, empty of the divine presence; the places loved and noted on our earth, as well as the unfathomable space of the universe, are not the house of God. Whatever one does for the world is not finally important in this model, for its ruler does not inhabit it as his primary residence, and his subjects are well advised not to become too involved in it either. The king's power extends over the entire universe, of course, but his being does not: he relates to it externally, he is not part of it but essentially different from it and apart from it.

Although these comments may at first seem to be a caricature rather than a fair description of the classical Western monarchical model, they are the direct implications of its imagery. If metaphors matter, then one must take them seriously at the level at which they function, that is, at the level of the imaginative picture of God and the world they project. If one uses triumphalist, royal metaphors for God, certain things follow, and one of the most important is a view of God as distant from and basically uninvolved with the world. God's distance from and lack of intrinsic involvement with the world are emphasized when God's real kingdom is an otherworldly one: Christ is raised from the dead to join the sovereign Father—as we shall be also—in the true kingdom. The world is not self-expressive of God: God's being, satisfaction, and future are not connected with our world. Not only, then, is the world Godless but God as king and lord is worldless, in all but an external sense. To be sure, kings want their subjects to be loyal and their realms peaceful, but that does not mean internal, intrinsic involvement. Kings do not have to, and usually do not, love their subjects or realms; at most, one hopes they will be benevolent.

But such benevolence extends only to human subjects; in the monarchical model there is no concern for the cosmos, for the non-human world. Here is our second objection to the model. It is simply blank in terms of what lies outside the human sphere. As a political model focused on governing human beings, it leaves out nine-tenths of reality. One could say at this point that, as with all models, it has limitations and needs to be balanced by other models. Such a comment does not address the seriousness of the monarchical model's limitations in regard to nonhuman reality, for as the dominant Western model it has not allowed competing or alternative models to arise. The tendency, rather, has been to draw other models into its orbit, as is evident with the model of God as father. This model could have gone in the direction of parent (and that is clearly its New Testament course), with its associations of nurture, care, guidance, concern, and self-sacrifice, but under the powerful influence of the monarchical model, the parent became the patriarch, and patriarchs act more like kings than like fathers: they rule their children and they demand obedience.

The hegemony of the monarchical model means that its blankness concerning what lies outside the human sphere is a major problem. If we seek a model that will express the inclusive, non-hierarchical vision of the gospel, this is not it. The model's anthropocentrism (the other side of its lack of concern for the natural world) can be seen, for instance, in classical Protestantism's emphasis on the the Word of God. The monarchical model and an aural tradition fit together naturally, for kings give orders and subjects obey, but the model has no place for creatures who cannot hear and obey. An interpretation of Christianity that focuses on hearing the Word, on listening to the Word as preached and on the Scriptures in which the Word is written, is a tradition limited to human beings, for they alone are linguistic. God is present in words and to those who can hear, and if Francis of Assisi preached to the birds, few have followed his example. An aural tradition is anthropocentric: we are the only ones who can "hear the Word of the Lord." A visual tradition, however, is more inclusive: if God can be present not only in what one hears but also in what one sees, then potentially anything and everything in the world can be a symbol of the divine. One does not preach *to* the birds, but a bird can be a metaphor to express God's intimate presence in the world: ". . . the Holy Ghost over the bent world broods with warm breast and with ah! bright wings."[8]

A visual tradition has a place for birds and for much else; if one allows in the other senses of smell, taste, and touch, then, as Augustine puts it in book 10 of the *Confessions,* one loves "light and melody and fragrance and food and embrace" when one loves one's God. In other words, one has let the whole world in: not just words are expressive of God's saving presence but everything can be.[9] The world can be seen as the "body" of God. It is not, then, just a book, the Scriptures, that is special as the medium of divine presence, but the world is also God's dwelling place. If an inclusive vision of the gospel must include the world, it is evident that the monarchical model, which not only cannot include the world but is totally anthropocentric and excludes alternative models, is sadly lacking.

This anthropocentric model is also dualistic and hierarchical. Not all dualisms are hierarchical; for instance, in the Chinese understanding of yin and yang, a balance is sought and neither is considered superior to the other, for too much of one or the other is undesirable. But a dualism of king and subjects is intrinsically hierarchical and encourages hierarchical, dualistic thinking of the sort that has fueled many kinds of oppression, including (in addition to that of the nonhuman by the human) those arising from the cleavages of male/female, white/colored, rich/poor, Christian/non-Christian, and mind/body. The monarchical model encourages a way of thinking that is pervasive and pernicious, in a time when exactly the opposite is needed as a basic pattern. The hierarchical, dualistic pattern is so widespread in Western thought that it is usually not perceived to be a pattern but is felt to be simply the way things are. It appears natural to many that males, whites, the rich, Christians, and the mind are superior, and to suggest that human beings, under the influence of powerful, dominant models such as the monarchical one, have constructed these dualistic hierarchies is to these people not believable. Or to put it with more subtlety, though tolerance is a contemporary civil virtue and not many would say openly that these dualisms are natural, deep down they believe they are.

We come, then, to the third criticism of the monarchical model: in this model God not only is distant from the world and relates only to the human world, but he also controls that world through a combination of domination and benevolence. This is the logical implication of hierarchical dualism: God's action is on the world, not in it, and it is a kind of action that inhibits human growth and responsibility. (Such action represents the kind of power that oppresses—and indeed enslaves—others; but enough has been said already in these pages and by others on that aspect of the model, which is its most obvious fault.) What is of equal importance is the less obvious point that the monarchical model implies the wrong kind of divine activity in relation to the world, a kind that encourages passivity on the part of human beings.

It is simplistic to blame the Judeo-Christian tradition for the ecological crisis, as some have done, on the grounds that Genesis instructs human beings to have "dominion" over nature; nonetheless, the imagery of sovereignty supports attitudes of control and use toward the nonhuman world.[10] Although the might of the natural world when unleashed is fearsome, as is evident in earthquakes, tornadoes, and volcanic eruptions, the power balance has shifted from nature to us, and an essential aspect of the new sensibility is to recognize and accept this. Nature can and does destroy many, but it is not in a position to destroy all, as we can. Extinction of species by nature is in a different dimension from extinction by design, which only we can bring about. This chilling thought adds a new importance to the images we use to characterize our relationship to others and to the nonhuman world. If we are capable of extinguishing ourselves and most if not all other life, metaphors that support attitudes of distance from, and domination of, other human beings and nonhuman life must be recognized as dangerous. No matter how ancient a metaphorical tradition may be and regardless of its credentials in Scripture, liturgy, and creedal statements, it still must be discarded if it threatens the continuation of life itself. What possible case can be made for metaphors of the God-world relationship which encourage attitudes on the part of human beings destructive of themselves as well as of the cosmos which supports all life? If the heart of the Christian gospel is the salvific power of God, triumphalist metaphors cannot express that reality *in our time,* whatever their appropriateness may have been in the past.

And this is so even if God's power is seen as benevolence rather than domination. For if God's rule is understood benevolently, it will be assumed that all is well—that the world will be cared for with no help from us. The king as dominating sovereign encourages attitudes of militarism and destruction; the king as benevolent patriarch encourages attitudes of passivity and escape from responsibility.[11] In the triumphalist, royal model the victory has already been won on the cross and in the resurrection of Jesus Christ, and nothing is required of us. We can rest comfortably in the assurance that our mighty Lord will deal with all present and future evil as he has always dealt with evil. Such a view of God's benevolence undercuts human effort of any sort.

The monarchical model is dangerous in our time: it encourages a sense of distance from the world; it attends only to the human dimension of the world; and it supports attitudes of either domination of the world or passivity toward it. As an alternative model, I suggest considering the world as God's body. Questions abound with this piece of "nonsense." It is a shocking idea; is it also an illuminating one? What does it mean from God's side and what from our side? Is it pantheistic? Is God or are we reduced to the world? With this metaphor how would one speak of God knowing and acting in the world as well as loving it? What about evil? About sin? What of *our* freedom, individuality, and behavior in such a world?

The World as God's Body

We are letting the metaphor of the world as God's body try its chance.[12] We are experimenting with a bit of nonsense to see if it can make a claim to truth. What if, we are asking, the "resurrection of the body" were not seen as the resurrection of particular bodies that ascend, beginning with Jesus of Nazareth, into another world, but as God's promise to be with us always in God's body, our world? What if God's promise of permanent presence to all space and time were imagined as a worldly reality, a palpable, bodily presence? What if, then, we did not have to go somewhere special (church) or somewhere else (another world) to be in the presence of God but could feel ourselves in that presence at all times and in all places? What if we imagined God's presence as in us and in all others, including the last and the least?

As we begin this experiment we must once again recall that a metaphor or model is not a description. We are trying to think in an as-if fashion about the God-world relationship, because we have no other way of thinking about it. No metaphor fits in all ways, and some are more nonsense than sense. The king-realm kind of thinking about the God-world relationship sounds like sense because we are used to it, but reflection shows that in our world it is nonsense. For a metaphor to be acceptable, it need not, cannot, apply in all ways; if it did, it would be a description. One has to realize how not to apply a metaphor (to say God is the Father does not mean that God has a beard!) and also where it fails or treads on shaky ground. The metaphor of the world as God's body has the opposite problem to the metaphor of the world as the king's realm: if the latter puts too great a distance between God and the world, the former verges on too great a proximity. Since both metaphors are inadequate, we have to ask which one is better in our time, and to qualify it with other metaphors and models. Is it better to accept an imaginative picture of God as the distant ruler controlling his realm through external and benevolent power or one of God so intimately related to the world that the world can be imagined as God's body? There are, of course, different understandings of "better." Is it better in terms of our and the world's preservation and fulfillment? Is it better in terms of coherence, comprehensibility, and illumination? Is it better in terms of expressing the Christian understanding of the relationship between God and the world? All these criteria are relevant, for a metaphor that is all or mostly nonsense has tried its chance and failed.

Therefore, a heuristic, metaphorical theology, though hospitable initially to nonsense is constrained as well to search for sense. Christians should, given their tradition, be inclined to find sense in "body" language, not only because of the resurrection of the body but also because of the bread and wine of the eucharist as the body and blood of Christ, and the church as the body with Christ as its head. Christians have a surprisingly "bodily" tradition; nonetheless, there is a difference between the traditional uses of "body" and seeing the world as God's body: when the world is viewed as God's body, that body includes more than just Christians and more than just human beings. It is possible to speculate that if Christianity had begun in a culture less dualistic and antiphysical than that of the first-century Mediterranean world, it might have been willing, given the more holistic anthropology and theology of its Hebraic roots, to extend its body metaphor to God.[13] At any rate, in view of the contemporary holistic understanding of personhood, in which embodiment is the sine qua non, the thought of an embodied personal deity is not more incredible than that of a disembodied one; in fact, it is less so. In a dualistic culture where mind and body, spirit and flesh, are separable, a disembodied, personal God is more credible, but not in ours. This is only to suggest that the idea of God's embodiment—the idea as such, quite apart from particulars—should not be seen as nonsense; it is less nonsense than the idea of a disembodied personal God.

A more central issue is whether the metaphor of the world as God's body is pantheistic or, to put it another way, reduces God to the world. The metaphor does come far closer to pantheism than the king-realm model, which verges on deism, but it does not totally identify God with the world any more than we totally identify ourselves with our bodies. Other animals may be said to be bodies that have spirits; we may be said to be spirits that possess bodies.[14] This is not to introduce a new dualism but only to recognize that although our bodies are expressions of us both unconsciously and consciously, we can reflect about them and distance ourselves from them. The very fact that we can speak about our bodies is evidence that we are not totally one with them. On this model, God is not reduced to the world if the world is God's body. Without the use of personal agential metaphors, however, including among others God as mother, lover, and friend, the metaphor of the world as

God's body would be pantheistic, for the body would be all there were. Nonetheless, the model is monist and perhaps most precisely designated as panentheistic; that is, it is a view of the God-world relationship in which all things have their origins in God and nothing exists outside God, though this does not mean that God is reduced to these things.[15] There is, as it were, a limit on our side, not on God's: the world does not exist outside or apart from God. Christian theism, which has always claimed that there is but one reality and it is God's—that there is no competing (evil) reality—is necessarily monist, though the monarchical imaginative picture that has accompanied it is implicitly if not blatantly dualistic. It sets God over against competing, presumably ontological, powers, and over against the world as an alien other to be controlled.

Nevertheless, though God is not reduced to the world, the metaphor of the world as God's body puts God "at risk." If we follow out the implications of the metaphor, we see that God becomes dependent through being bodily, in a way that a totally invisible, distant God would never be. Just as we care about our bodies, are made vulnerable by them, and must attend to their well-being, God will be liable to bodily contingencies. The world as God's body may be poorly cared for, ravaged, and as we are becoming well aware, essentially destroyed, in spite of God's own loving attention to it, because of one creature, ourselves, who can choose or not choose to join with God in conscious care of the world. Presumably, were this body blown up, another could be formed; hence, God need not be seen to be as dependent on us or on any particular body as we are on our own bodies. But in the metaphor of the universe as the self-expression of God—God's incarnation—the notions of vulnerability, shared responsibility, and risk are inevitable. This is a markedly different basic understanding of the God-world relationship than in the monarch-realm metaphor, for it emphasizes God's willingness to suffer for and with the world, even to the point of personal risk. The world as God's body, then, may be seen as a way to remythologize the inclusive, suffering love of the cross of Jesus of Nazareth. In both instances, God is at risk in human hands: just as once upon a time in a bygone mythology, human beings killed their God in the body of a man, so now we once again have that power, but, in a mythology more appropriate to our time, we would kill our God in the body of the world. Could we actually do this? To believe in the resurrection means we could not. God is not in our power to destroy, but the incarnate God is the God at risk: we have been given central responsibility to care for God's body, our world.

If God, though at risk and dependent on others, is not reduced to the world in the metaphor of the world as God's body, what more can we say about the meaning of this model from God's side? How does God know the world, act in it, and love it? How does one speak of evil in this metaphor? In the monarchical model, God knows the world externally, acts on it either by direct intervention or indirectly through human subjects, and loves it benevolently, in a charitable way. God's knowledge, action, and love are markedly different in the metaphor of the world as God's body. God knows the world immediately just as we know our bodies immediately. God could be said to be in touch with all parts of the world through interior understanding. Moreover, this knowledge is empathetic, intimate, sympathetic knowledge, closer to feeling than to rationality.[16] It is knowledge "by acquaintance"; it is not "information about." Just as we are internally related to our bodies, so God is internally related to all that is—the most radically relational Thou. God relates sympathetically to the world, just as we relate sympathetically to our bodies. This implies, of course, an immediacy and concern in God's knowledge of the world impossible in the king-realm model.

Moreover, it implies that the action of God in the world is similarly interior and caring. If the entire universe, all that is and has been, is God's body, then God acts in and through the incredibly complex physical and historical-cultural evolutionary process that began eons ago.[17] This does not mean that God is reduced to the evolutionary process, for God remains as the agent, the self, whose intentions are expressed in the universe. Nevertheless, the manner in which these intentions are expressed is internal and, by implication, providential—that is, reflective of a "caring" relationship. God does not, as in the royal model, intervene in the natural or historical process in deus-ex-machina fashion nor feel merely charitable toward the world. The suggestion, however, that God cares about the world as one cares about one's body, that is, with a high degree of sympathetic concern, does not imply that all is well or the future is assured, for with the body metaphor, God is at risk. It does suggest, however, that to trust in a God whose body is the world is to trust in a God who cares profoundly for the world.

Furthermore, the model of the world as God's body suggests that God loves bodies: in loving the world, God loves a body. Such a notion is a sharp challenge to the long antibody, antiphysical, antimatter tradition within Christianity. This tradition has repressed healthy sexuality, oppressed women as sexual tempters, and defined Christian redemption in spiritualistic ways, thus denying that basic social and economic needs of embodied beings are relevant to salvation. To say that God loves bodies is to redress the balance toward a more holistic understanding of fulfillment. It is to say that bodies are worth loving, sexually and otherwise, that passionate love as well as attention to the needs of bodily existence is a part of fulfillment. It is to say further that the basic necessities of bodily existence—adequate food and shelter, for example—are central aspects of God's love for all bodily creatures and therefore should be central concerns of us, God's co-workers. In a holistic sensibility there can be no spirit/body split: if neither we nor God is disembodied, the denigration of the body, the physical, and matter should end. Such a split makes no sense in our world: spirit and body or matter are on a continuum, for matter is not inanimate substance but throbs of energy, essentially in continuity with spirit. To love bodies, then, is to love not what is opposed to spirit but what is at one with it—which the model of the world as God's body fully expresses.

The immanence of God in the world implied in our metaphor raises the question of God's involvement with evil. Is God responsible for evil, both natural and humanly willed evil? The pictures of the king and his realm and of God and the world as God's body obviously suggest very different replies to these enormously difficult and complex questions. In the monarchical construct, God is implicitly in contest with evil powers, either as victorious king who crushes them or as sacrificial servant who (momentarily) assumes a worldly mien in order to free his subjects from evil's control. The implication of ontological dualism, of opposing good and evil powers, is the price paid for separating God from evil, and it is a high price indeed, for it suggests that the place of evil is the world (and ourselves) and that to escape evil's clutches, we need to free ourselves from "the world, the flesh, and the devil." In this construct, God is not responsible for evil, but neither does God identify with the suffering caused by evil.

That identification does occur in the metaphor of the world as God's body. The evil in the world, all kinds of evil, occurs in and to God as well as to us and the rest of creation. Evil is not a power over against God; in a sense, it is God's "responsibility," part of God's being, if you will. A monist position cannot avoid this conclusion.[18] In a physical, biological, historicocultural evolutionary process as complex as the universe, much that is evil from various perspectives will occur, and if one sees this process as God's self-expression, then God is involved in evil. But the other side of this is that God is also involved, profoundly, palpably, personally involved, in suffering, in the suffering caused by evil. The evil occurs in and to God's body: the pain that those parts of creation affected by evil feel God also feels and feels bodily. All pain to all creatures is felt immediately and bodily by God: one does not suffer alone. In this sense, God's suffering on the cross was not for a mere few hours, as in the old mythology, but it is present and permanent. As the body of the world, God is forever "nailed to the cross," for as this body suffers, so God suffers.

Is this to suggest that God is helpless in relation to evil or that God knows no joy? No, for the way of the cross, the way of inclusive, radical love, is a kind of power, though a very different kind from kingly might. It does imply, however, that unlike God the king, the God who suffers with the world cannot wipe out evil: evil is not only part of the process but its power depends also on us, God's partners in the way of inclusive, radical love. And what holds for suffering can be said of joy as well. Wherever in the universe there is new life, ecstasy, tranquillity, and fulfillment, God experiences these pleasures and rejoices with each creature in its joy.

When we turn to our side of this picture of the world as God's body, we have to ask whether we are reduced to being mere parts of the body? What is our freedom? How is sin understood here? How would we behave in this model? The model did not fit God's side in every way, and it does not fit ours in every way either. It seems especially problematic at the point of our individuality and freedom. At least in the king-realm model, human beings appear to have some freedom since they are controlled only externally, not internally. The problem emerges because of the nature of bodies: if we are parts of God's body—if the model is totally organic—are we not then totally immersed, along with all other creatures, in the evolutionary process, with no transcendence or freedom? It appears, however, at least to us, that we are a special part. We think of ourselves as the *imago dei*, as not only possessing bodies but being agents. We view ourselves as embodied spirits in the larger body of the world which influences us and which we influence. That is, we are the part modeled on the model: self:body::God:world. We are agents and God possesses a body: both sides of the model pertain to both God and ourselves. This implies that we are not mere submerged parts of the body of God but relate to God as to another Thou. The presence of God to us in and through God's body is the experience of encounter, not of submersion. For the saving love of God to be present to human beings it would have to be so in a way different from how it is present to other aspects of the body of the world—in a way in keeping with the peculiar kind of creatures we are, namely, creatures with a special kind of freedom, able to participate self-consciously (as well as be influenced unconsciously) in the evolutionary process. This gives us a special status and a special responsibility: we are the ones like God; we are selves that possess bodies, and that is our glory. It is also our responsibility, for we alone can choose to become partners with God in the care of the world; we alone can—like God—mother, love, and befriend the world, the body that God has made available to us as both the divine presence and our home.

Our special status and responsibility, however, are not limited to consciousness of our own personal bodies or even of the human world but extend to all embodied reality, for we are that part of the cosmos where the cosmos itself comes to consciousness. If we become extinct, then the cosmos will lose its human, although presumably not its divine, consciousness. As Jonathan Schell remarks, "In extinction a darkness falls over the world not because the lights have gone out but because the eyes that behold the light have been closed."[19] The tragedy of human annihilation by war, even if some plants and some other animals survived, would be that there were no one to be conscious of embodied reality: the cosmos would have lost its consciousness.

It is obvious, then, what sin is in this metaphor of the world as God's body: it is refusal to be part of the body, the special part we are as *imago dei*. In contrast to the king-realm model, where sin is against *God*, here it is against the world. To sin is not to refuse loyalty to the Liege Lord but to refuse to take responsibility for nurturing, loving, and befriending the body and all its parts. Sin is the refusal to realize one's radical interdependence with all that lives: it is the desire to set oneself apart from all others as not needing them or being needed by them. Sin is the refusal to be the eyes, the consciousness, of the cosmos.

What this experiment with the world as God's body comes to, finally, is an awareness, both chilling and breathtaking, that we as worldly, bodily beings are in God's presence. It is the basis for a revived sacramentalism, that is, a perception of the divine as visible, as present, palpably present in our world. But it is a kind of sacramentalism that is painfully conscious of the world's vulnerability, its preciousness, its uniqueness. The beauty of the world and its ability to sustain the vast multitude of species it supports is not there for the taking. The world is a body that must be carefully tended, that must be nurtured, protected, guided, loved, and befriended both as valuable in itself—for like us, it is an expression of God—and as necessary to the continuation of life. We meet the world as a Thou, as the body of God where God is present to us always in all times and in all places. In the metaphor of the world as the body of God, the resurrection becomes a worldly, present, inclusive reality, for this body is offered to all: "This is my body." As is true of all bodies, however, this body, in its beauty and preciousness, is vulnerable and at risk: it will delight the eye only if we care for it; it will nourish us only if we nurture it. Needless to say, then, were this metaphor to enter our consciousness as thoroughly as the royal, triumphalist one has entered, it would result in a different way of being in the world. There would be no way that we could any longer see God as worldless or the world as Godless. Nor could we expect God to take care of everything, either through domination or through benevolence.

We see through pictures. We do not see directly: the pictures of a king and his realm and of the world as God's body are ways of speaking, ways of imagining the God-world relationship. The one pictures a vast distance between God and the world; the other imagines them as intrinsically related. At the close of day, one asks which distortion (assuming that all pictures are false in some respects) is better, by asking what attitudes each encourages. This is not the first question to ask, but it may well be the last. The monarchical model encourages attitudes of militarism, dualism, and escapism; it condones control through violence and oppression; it has nothing to say about the nonhuman world. The model of the world as God's body encourages holistic attitudes of responsibility for and care of the vulnerable and oppressed; it is nonhierarchical and acts through persuasion and attraction; it has a great deal to say about the body and nature. Both are pictures: which distortion is more true to the world in which we live and to the good news of Christianity?

It may be, of course, that neither picture is appropriate to our time and to Christianity; if so, others should be proposed. Our profound need for a powerful, attractive imaginative picture of the way God is related to our world demands that we not only deconstruct but reconstruct our metaphors, letting the ones that seem promising try their chance. It is in this spirit that we continue our heuristic, metaphorical theology, turning now to the specific models of God as mother, lover, and friend of the world.

God as Mother, Lover, Friend

Our task is to suggest an imaginative picture of the relationship between God and the world that will express the saving presence of God in our present. That saving presence we have interpreted as a destabilizing, inclusive, nonhierarchical vision of fulfillment for all of creation. If what is sought is a likely account of the relationship between God and world, is there value in looking at the cosmos as God's bodily presence in all times and places? If we accept that picture, will the metaphors of mother, lover, and friend, be suitable ones for God's relationship to the world? Before developing that imaginative picture in detail (chaps. 4–6), we need to deal with some preliminary issues regarding personal metaphors. Throughout our discussion so far we have assumed divine personal agency. The analogy of self:body::God:world rests on this assumption, but we must now ask about its viability.

Two questions are central in any discussion of personal metaphors for understanding the God-world relation: Why use any personal metaphors? Why use these particular ones? Not all religious traditions use personal metaphors, or at least they do not use them to the degree the Judeo-Christian tradition does. Some mystical religions, as well as those intimately involved in nature's cycles, are far less personalistic in their imagery. If our task is to suggest imagery that will overcome the distance between God and the world while underscoring the immanence of God in the world, is it not counterproductive to continue using personal metaphors? This is a very serious question and is not a concern solely in our present ecological, nuclear crisis. To many people for a long time, the notion of a personal God has seemed incredible, for it appears to support the notion of a being existing somewhere whose only way to act on the world is to intervene in its affairs. It is not possible to trace here the modern history of this issue, but the remote God of the deists was certainly a first step away from an interventionist, personal God, and both Schleiermacher's turn to the self as the place where the presence of God is felt and Hegel's near-identification of God and the world are part of the history. These patterns were picked up by Bultmann's refusal to talk of God and divine activity except as implications of human states and by Tillich's wariness about personal images of God and his preference for "Being-itself" as the primary designation. One can see the direction that the issue of a personal God has taken during the past two centuries, by bringing to mind the embarrassment that such a "primitive" concept of God appears to present, as well as the genuine bewilderment it causes when we try to conceive the activity of such a God in a world that is understood as an evolutionary, causal nexus permitting no interference by outside agents. Is not a personal God both an anachronism from the childhood of humanity, best now discarded, and an impossibility in a time when agency, whether divine or human, is understood to take place in a highly complex ecological, evolutionary matrix of multiple agents, a matrix characterized by chance and necessity? Would it not be better, as Gordon Kaufman suggests, to conceive of God in terms of the multifarious physical, biological, and historicocultural conditions that have made human existence possible, rather than in quasi-personal terms? Kaufman finds that the political, personal images of the tradition undergird militaristic and passive attitudes, whereas the familial images are too individualistic to function effectively in our evolutionary, ecological world. At most, Kaufman says, one can speak of the "hidden creativity" or "unpredictable grace" that works in and through the incredibly complex physical, biological, and historicocultural matrix that has resulted in our present situation. I agree thoroughly with much of what Kaufman says and especially with his comment that "devotion to a God conceived in terms other than these [the physical, biological, historicocultural matrix] will not be devotion to God, that is, to that reality which has (to the best of our understanding) in fact created us."[20] We must understand God and the activity of God in the world in a fashion that is not just commensurate with an ecological, evolutionary sensibility but intrinsic to it. I disagree with Kaufman's position, however, in that I do not believe that the reduction of the personal God to hidden creativity or unpredictable grace is desirable or necessary.[21]

It is not desirable because, as I suggested earlier, any imaginative picture attempting to unseat the triumphalist, royal model must be at least as attractive as it is. It must be an understanding of the God-world relationship that will move people to live by it and work for it; it must come from a place deep within human experience. It is no accident that much of the tradition's most powerful imagery does come from this place. It is imagery reflecting the beginning and continuation of life, imagery of sex, breath, food, blood, and water, as in the second birth, the breath of the Holy Spirit, bread and wine, the blood of the cross, the resurrection of the body, and the water of baptism. This language continues to be powerful because images arising from the most basic level of physical existence—the level of our tenuous hold on existence and what is needed to keep it going—are images of life and death. I am not suggesting that there are some sacred, permanent metaphors that can replace the royalist, triumphalist model; but there may be a place to look for metaphors that goes even deeper than the political arena, from which most long-term models of the God-world relationship in the West have come. In the political arena the concern is with how we govern our lives; a deeper question is how we live at all and how well we live. Metaphors of mothers, lovers, friends, and bodies come from this level, as does the classic model of father understood as parent. If the imagery of mothers, lovers, friends, and bodies proved credible for picturing the God-world relation, it would certainly also be attractive, for it is unmatched in power: it holds within it the power not of mere kings but of life and death.

But although it may not be desirable to do away with personal imagery for God, it may still be necessary. How can personal metaphors be credible in our time? Do they not presuppose an external, interventionist understanding of the relationship between God and the world? Many apparently do not think so, for besides a movement during the last two centuries away from the model of personal agency for God there has been a countervailing movement toward it. Hence, another way to see the theological history of the past two centuries is as a movement toward taking the human self and the relationship between the self and the body, as a, if not the, prime model for imaging God and God's relationship to the world. It is not just mystics like Teilhard de Chardin or process theologians like Charles Hartshorne who press this case but a surprising range of theologians from a variety of perspectives.[22] Much of the reason for this shift lies in the current understanding of persons not as substantial individuals, separated from one another and from the world, who enter into relationships of their own choice, but as beings-in-relationship of the most radical and thoroughgoing nature. The model, as outlined in chapter 1, is not of a machine with separate parts relating externally but of an organ with all aspects intrinsically and internally related. The human person is the most complex organ known to us, and it exists as an embodied whole within an incredibly rich organic complex of mutually interrelated and interdependent parts, aspects, and dimensions. To be a person, therefore, is not to be a being related externally to other individual beings but to be part of—and to the best of our knowledge, the most sophisticated, complex, and unified part of—an organic whole that embraces all that is. If, then, we speak of God in personal metaphors, we will not be speaking of a

being that is related externally to the world, as, for instance, a king
to his realm, but we will be conceiving God on the model of the
most complex part of the whole that is the universe—that is, on the
model of ourselves. There are several points to make in support of
the personal model for the God-world relationship: it is the one we
know best; it is the richest; and the kind of activity of God in the
world it suggests is both credible in our time and needed by it.

It is perhaps simplistic to put weight on the fact that the personal
model is the one we know best, but cases against the model often
overlook that fact. It is the only metaphor we know from the inside:
there is nothing we can say about God with the help of any other
model that has the same credibility to us, because there is no other
aspect of the universe that we know in the same way, with the
privilege of the insider. The tradition says we are the *imago dei*, and
that inevitably means we imagine God in our image. Presumably, if
dolphins or apes have inklings of a higher reality, they imagine it
after the model they know best—themselves. That is said not in jest
but to bring home why personal metaphors, those modeled on
human beings as we understand them today, are suitable for us.
Another way to make this point is to consider the alternative to a
personal model. Nonpersonal metaphors would be either metaphors from nature (other animals or natural phenomena such as the
sun, water, sky, and mountains) or concepts from one or another
philosophical tradition (such as "Being-itself," "substance," and
"ground of Being"), which at some level are also, of course, metaphorical. We are limited in the ways we can model the God-world
relationship, and although we should certainly include a wide
range of metaphors from many sources, to exclude the one we know
best or to make it secondary to ones we know less well seems
foolish.

It would also be unwise for another reason: it is the richest model
available to us. This is not anthropocentric hubris but simply a
recognition that since we are the most complex, unified creature we
know, with what to us are mysterious and fathomless depths, we
are the best model. Given the nature of heuristic, metaphorical
theology, that is not to say that God *is* a person or that personal
language describes or defines God. It is to say, rather, that to speak
of God with the aid of or through the screen of such language is

better than some other ways of speaking. It is, for instance, more interesting, illuminating, and richer to speak of God as a friend than as a rock, though "A mighty fortress is our God" has a place in talk about God. Its place, however, is a limited one, and the rock metaphor does not begin to suggest the potential for elaboration that the metaphor of a friend does. To speak of God's saving presence in our present only with the help of images about rocks and wind, or with any other natural metaphors, is to overlook the richest source we have—ourselves.

Finally, the strongest argument for personal metaphors in our time is that the current understanding of personal agency allows personal metaphors to reflect a view of God's activity in the world as radically relational, immanental, interdependent, and noninterventionist. Current theological attention to the issue of divine activity in the world is considerable and varied, but there is widespread agreement that the understanding of the self, both in relation to its own body (as embodied self) and in relation to others (as profoundly embedded in and constituted by those others), is a helpful and illuminating model.[23] The evolutionary, organic complex is widely considered the context in which to interpret personal agency—with the agent as part of an intricate causal network that both influences it and is influenced by it—and this allows for an understanding of personal presence credible within the new sensibility. Moreover, it is the model for God's activity in the world that we need today, for to imagine God as the personal presence in the universe who epitomizes personhood, that is, *who has intrinsic relations with all else that exists*, is to possess a highly suggestive model for God's saving presence. If, on the model current today, a person is defined in terms of relationships, then, as Schubert Ogden says, God as "the Thou with the greatest conceivable degree of real relatedness to others—namely, relatedness to *all* others—is for that very reason the most truly absolute Thou any mind can conceive."[24] If personhood is defined in terms of intrinsic relations with others, then to think of God as personal in no sense implies a being separate from other beings who relates externally and distantly to them, in the way that the king-realm personal model suggests. On the contrary, it suggests, I believe, that God is present in and to the world as the kind of other, the kind of Thou, much closer to a mother, lover, or friend than to a king or lord. The intrinsic, interdependent relationships we know most about are also the most intimate, interpersonal ones: they are the ones that begin, support, and nurture life.

This defense of the personal model for understanding the God-world relationship has brought us finally, then, to the issue of the particular metaphors of mother, lover, and friend. If one accepts the personal model, one must ask which personal models are most appropriate for expressing the saving power and presence of God in our time. Although most personal metaphors in the Judeo-Christian tradition have come from the political arena, an understanding of the gospel as a destabilizing, inclusive, nonhierarchical vision of fulfillment for all of creation should look elsewhere. It should look to that level of human experience concerned with the beginnings, continuation, and support of life, the level not of how we govern our lives but of how we live at all and the quality of that life. In an understanding of the gospel for a holistic, nuclear age, when the continuation and the quality of life must be seen as central, we need to return to the most basic realities of existence and to the most basic relationships, for metaphors in which to express that understanding. The symbols of sex, food, water, breath, and blood (all that makes it possible for embodied life to begin and continue) and the relationships of mothers (and fathers), lovers, and friends (those most basic of all relationships, which more than any others contain potential for expressing the most profound fulfillment)—it is from such sources that metaphors for God's saving presence in our time should be drawn.

In particular I would make a case for experimenting in our time with mother, lover, and friend as three models that have been strangely neglected in the Judeo-Christian tradition. All three models represent basic human relationships; indeed, one could say that the three, along with the model of father, represent the most basic human relationships.[25] Hence, if one is going to employ a personal model for God, it makes sense to consider these three seriously. And they have been considered seriously in most religious traditions, for the simple reason that when people are attempting to express the inexpressible, they use what is nearest and dearest to them: they invoke the most important human relationships. One basic human relationship, that of father, has received massive attention in our tradition; the others have been, at best, neglected and, at worst, repressed. There are traces of them in Scripture and the tradition, but they have never become, or been allowed to become, major models.

Yet I hope that it has become evident that, given the kind of understanding of the gospel appropriate for a holistic, nuclear age, they may well be the most illuminating personal metaphors available. In different ways all three models suggest forms of fundamental intimacy, mutuality, and relatedness that could be a rich resource for expressing how in our time life can be supported and fulfilled rather than destroyed. They are all immanental models, in contrast to the radically transcendent models for God in the Western tradition. As we have seen, part of the difficulty with the dominant model of God is its transcendence, a transcendence undergirded by triumphalist, sovereign, patriarchal imagery that contributes to a sense of distance between God and the world. The relatedness of all life, and hence the responsibility of human beings for the fate of the earth, is supported by models of God as mother, lover, and friend of the world.

Moreover, these metaphors project a different view of power, of how to bring about change, than the royal model. It is not the power of control through either domination or benevolence but the power of response and responsibility—the power of love in its various forms (agape, eros, and philia) that operates by persuasion, care, attention, passion, and mutuality. The way of being in the world which these metaphors suggest is close to the way of the cross, the way of radical identification with all which the model of servant once expressed. It is a way of being with others totally different from the way of kings and lords.

A final question remains before we close out the case for personal models and especially for the ones chosen. Are they perhaps too intimate and too individualistic? We have already touched on the issue of intimacy: the more intimate, in the sense of the closer to the most basic realities of human existence, the better. An ascetic strain, however, has kept Christianity from acknowledging the physical and often sexual basis of many of its most powerful symbols, and its wariness in dealing with maternal and erotic language for God arises from this same puritanism. Part of the task of a heuristic theology is to consider what has not been considered, especially if the possibilities for illuminating certain aspects of the God-world relationship are great, as I believe they are in the metaphors of mother and lover. (The model of friend is less problematic in this regard, but as we will see, there have been other reasons for its neglect.)

The charge that these metaphors may be individualistic just at a time when radically relational, inclusive metaphors are needed is a serious one. It would be unanswerable if the metaphors had to be interpreted as suggesting a one-to-one relationship between God and individual human beings. Admittedly, in a context where God's saving power is understood as directed to specific individuals (who are also perceived as independent entities), speaking of God as mother, lover, and friend only accentuates the already particularistic understanding of salvation. But a radically inclusive view of the gospel means that the basic relationship between God and all others cannot be one-to-one; or rather, that it is one-to-one only as it is inclusive of all. The Gospel of John gives the clue: for God so loved the *world*. It is not individuals who are loved by God as mother, lover, and friend but the world. This means that we do not have to interpret these personal metaphors as suggesting a one-to-one relationship between God and individual human beings: we can use the metaphors that have the greatest power and meaning to us in a universal way, and in fact, only as we apply them universally can they also pertain individually. As mother to the world, God mothers each and all: the divine maternal love can be particular only because it is universal. If we understand God's saving presence as directed to the fulfillment of all of creation—with each of us part of that whole—we participate in God's love not as individuals but as members of an organic whole, God's body. Therefore, metaphors that could indeed be individualistic become radically socialized when applied to the world. Moreover, they have the potential for becoming politicized as well, for as the *imago dei*, we are called to mother, love, and befriend the world, both other human beings and the earth. Whether or not we are in our own personal lives mothers or fathers, or have a lover or even a friend, is not important: these most basic of loves lie deeply within us all. The model of God as mother, lover, and friend of the world presents us with an ethic of response and responsibility toward other human beings and other forms of life, in which our deep parental, erotic, and companionable instincts can be socialized and politicized.

In summary, the personal models for the God-world relationship have been defended as the ones we know best, as the richest, and as credible and needed in our time. The particular metaphors of mother, lover, and friend, which come from the deepest level of life and are concerned with its fulfillment, have been suggested as illuminating possibilities for expressing an inclusive, nonhierarchical understanding of the gospel. It has been claimed that the object of this gospel is not individuals but the world, and it has been proposed that the world—the cosmos or universe—be seen as God's body.

We have attempted to imagine the resurrection promise of divine presence—"Lo, I am with you always"—as a worldly reality, as the presence of God in the body of our world. In this, we have imaged God as both caring deeply for that world and calling us to care as well. This imaginative picture is radically different from that of a risen, ascended king in relationship with his realm but remarkably appropriate to an understanding of the story of Jesus of Nazareth as a surprising invitation to the last and the least, expressed in his parables, table fellowship, and cross. That destabilizing, inclusive, nonhierarchical vision of fulfillment can be perceived as continuing when we conceive of the world as God's body to which God is present as mother, lover, and friend of the last and the least in all of creation.

PART TWO | *Models of God for an Ecological, Nuclear Age*

Introduction

To say that God is present in the world as mother, lover, and friend of the last and least in all creation is to characterize the Christian gospel as radical, surprising love. We are attempting to see the possibilities for expressing that love with the help of images reflecting the most intimate and important human love relationships—those of parent to child, lover to beloved, and friend to friend. Our experiment will suggest that these metaphors be allowed to try their chance at representing for our time the creating, saving, and sustaining activities of God in relation to the world and that, together, the three metaphors of God as parent, lover, and friend form a "trinity" expressing God's impartial, reuniting, and reciprocal love to the world. In other words, we will advance the claim that the picture of God as a parent of the world represents God as a creator intimately and impartially concerned with life in all its manifestations and levels. God as parent is on the side of life as such. Life is not something alien to God but as God's body (which is not identical with God) is expressive of God's very self, even as children, although independent, are expressive of their parents. Furthermore, we will consider that the picture of God as lover of the world represents God as a savior whose passion—both as desire for and suffering with the beloved—is oriented toward healing and reuniting all parts of the body. God as lover values life, finds the world attractive and precious, as lovers find their beloved to be. Finally, we will reflect that the picture of God as friend represents God as a sustainer whose immanent presence is the faithful companion working reciprocally with us to bring about the healing of all parts of the body. God as friend needs us

91

as co-workers in the mutual project of extending fulfillment to all of creation.

All three loves—creative, salvific, and sustaining—are united in that each points to a desire for union; each, in a different way, draws attention to the interrelatedness and interdependence of all life. Creative love (or agape) is the love of God for being as such; it is the affirmation of all creatures by the parent who bodies forth all that is. Salvific love (or eros) is the passionate manifestation— the "incarnation"—of divine love for us, the beloved; it is going to the limit for the world so there can be no doubt but that the last and the least are accepted and reunited. Sustaining love (or philia) is the immanent, companionable love of God who continues always with us as we work together toward the fulfillment of all. Each kind of love also suggests an accompanying ethic or dimension of Christian discipleship: justice (agape), healing (eros), companionship (philia). A Christian lifestyle modeled on God as parent, lover, and friend would be one committed to the impartial continuation of life in its many forms, the healing and reunification of all dimensions of life, and the sharing of the basic needs of life as well as its joys.

In the next three chapters we will look at each of the models with the three issues already intimated in the foregoing comments in mind: What sort of divine love is suggested by each model? What kind of divine activity is implied by this love? What does each kind of love say about existence in our world? Though we will be dealing with God as parent, lover, and friend in seriatim fashion, the ways in which God loves the world and the ways that we, modeling ourselves on our models of God, are called to love the world are interrelated and overlapping. The goal of a metaphorical theology is not an exhaustive, systematic treatment of all the issues usually dealt with in traditional theology; nevertheless, many of these subjects will be considered here in a fashion that aims toward a reasonably comprehensive and unified conceptual understanding of the God-world relationship suggested by our models. Metaphorical theology departs from systematic theology in that its principal concern is the elucidation of an imaginative picture of the God-world relationship rather than the construction of an ordered system in which all traditional aspects of the God-world relationship are included; nonetheless, its form will bear some resemblance to a system. This is the case because just as the reigning monarchical model implies a theology, so do our models.

If our theology departs somewhat in form from traditional theologies, it will differ in content as well, for, as is already obvious, the models of God as mother, lover, and friend of the world as God's body imply views of the creative, salvific, and sustaining activities of God that are radically different from what we find in the monarchical model. For instance, the monarchical model implies that the crucial divine activity is the redemption of rebellious humanity, which is loved in spite of its unlovableness, whereas our models suggest that the crucial divine activity is the creation of a world, which is loved passionately to the limit of God's very being. These are basically different understandings of the God-world relationship, and although the monarchical model is the dominant one, especially in late medieval Catholicism as well as in classical Protestantism and much popular piety, the other pattern, even if seldom explicitly accompanied by models of God as mother, lover, and friend, is just as ancient to and characteristic of Christianity. The monarchical model could be said to find its biblical base in Paul, with his stress on the atoning victory of Christ, the Second Adam; the other model locates itself in John, with his emphasis on the illuminating love of Christ, the Word made flesh.

In making these connections I am by no means saying that all Pauline theologies are monarchical or that all Johannine theologies have characteristics of the theology emerging from models of God as mother, lover, and friend. Obviously, neither is the case; I am suggesting that to see God as mother, lover, and friend of the world as God's body is to identify with a long theological tradition, beginning with John (although, as we shall see, with earlier roots in the wisdom tradition) and gathering others along the way—such as, for instance, Irenaeus, Augustine, Schleiermacher, Hegel, Teilhard de Chardin, Rahner, Tillich, the process theologians, and some feminist theologians. The sensibility informing all these theologies can be characterized as monistic (presuming the basic oneness of all of reality, including the unity of God and the world) in contrast to the other sensibility which is dualistic in its awareness of the distance between God and humanity caused by sinful rebellion. The first tends to be cosmological and sees salvation as the reuniting of all reality in harmonious interrelationship, whereas the second tends to be anthropological and sees redemption as the atonement for human willfulness reconciling God and humanity. Though the characteristics of theologies identifying themselves with either of these sensibilities vary greatly, both sensibilities embody ancient traditions. Thus, even though the models of God as mother, lover, and friend of the world as God's body are relatively novel as means for expressing the Christian gospel, they fall within one of the two principal historical theological tracks: the monistic track.

The peculiar difficulty of monistic theologies is that they tend toward identification of God and the world, and this difficulty is clearly seen in the notion of the world as God's body. How can the world as the body of God be anything but a part of God? Is not God's fate tied to the destiny of the world if the latter is God's body? We have already ventured some answers to these questions, but the questions persist, for if God is modeled as the mother, lover, and friend of the world, which is imagined to be God's body, is not divine love merely self-love, love for what is one's own? When God mothers, loves, and befriends the world, is this not narcissistic— loving the divine body? The metaphor certainly tends in that direction, but with two qualifications. First, as a metaphor, the relationship of divine agency and the world as God's body, to human agency and the human body, is one of analogy, not correspondence—that is, it both fits and does not fit. If it is illuminating in certain respects, it is nonsense in others, and part of the skill in using metaphors appropriately is knowing the difference. It may be disclosive of the depths of divine love to imagine our world as God's body, but it is obviously ridiculous to think of the world (with its shoes and ships and sealing wax and cabbages and kings) as the same kind of body as ours or in the same relationship to its agent. For the sake of the shock of recognition that the organic model brings—the recognition that we are profoundly interrelated with all forms of life, including God's—we must risk its nonsense as well. Second, if our model does tend toward the claim that in loving the world, God loves what belongs to God, is this not a desirable and indeed necessary direction for a vision of the Christian faith as inclusive of all beings? Would it be more appropriate to speak of God as loving what is alien or belongs to another reality? Moreover, the single most important recognition for the continuation, not to mention fulfillment, of life in our threatened nuclear world is the awareness that "we are not our own," that we owe our existence to the life that came before us, and must pass life along to those who will come after. Awareness of the intricate, interdependent network of life, with God at its center as well as at every periphery, needs to become part of our daily, functioning sensibility: the model of God as the parent, lover, and friend of the world as God's body is a promising candidate to give imaginative reality to that sensibility.

4
God as Mother

"Father-Mother God, loving me, guard me while I sleep, guide my little feet up to thee." This prayer, which theologian Herbert Richardson reports reciting as a child, impressed upon his young mind that if God is both father and mother, then God is not like anything else he knew.[1] The point is worth emphasizing, for as we begin our experiment with the model of God as mother, we recall that metaphors of God, far from reducing God to what we understand, underscore by their multiplicity and lack of fit the unknowability of God. This crucial characteristic of metaphorical language for God is lost, however, when only one important personal relationship, that of father and child, is allowed to serve as a grid for speaking of the God-human relationship. In fact, by excluding other relationships as metaphors, the model of father becomes idolatrous, for it comes to be viewed as a description of God.[2] Hence, one reason for including maternal language in a tradition where paternal language has prevailed is to underscore what the negative theological tradition has always insisted: God is unlike as well as like our metaphors.[3]

But there are additional reasons for using female as well as male metaphors of God. The most obvious is that since human beings are male and female, if we seek to imagine God "in the image of God"—that is, ourselves—both male and female metaphors should be employed. Because the point is self-evident, one wonders what all the fuss is about when the suggestion is made that God be imaged in female terms or addressed as "she." But fuss there is, and it is best to address it head on. For whatever reasons, Western thought—certainly Western theology—has been deeply infected by both a fear of and a fascination with female sexuality.[4] The most basic reason, it appears, for uneasiness with female metaphors for God is that unlike the male metaphors, whose sexual character is cloaked, the female metaphors seem blatantly sexual and involve the sexuality most feared: female sexuality.

There are at least three points being made here that need to be addressed briefly. First, to speak of God as father has obvious sexual connotations (as is evident in the trinitarian language of the "generation" of the Son from the Father), but given the Hebraic tradition's interest in distinguishing itself from Goddess religions and fertility cults, as well as the early and deep ascetic strain in Christianity, the sexual implications of paternal imagery were masked. This leads into the second point: the blatant sexuality of female metaphors. It is by introducing female metaphors for God that the sexuality of both male and female metaphors becomes evident, though it appears, because we are familiar with the male metaphors, that only the female ones are sexual. In other words, the shock of unconventional language for God—female imagery—jolts us into awareness that there is no gender-neutral language if we take ourselves as the model for talk about God, because we are sexual beings. Hence, traditional language for God is not nonsexual; on the contrary, it is male. The third point, the fear and fascination associated with female sexuality, is related to the first two points: female sexuality would not, I suspect, be so feared or found so fascinating if sexuality, both female and male, had been accepted in a more open and healthy manner both as a human good and as an important way to model the activity of God in relation to the world.[5] It is treated in this fashion in many religions, and Western thought, including Christianity, with its warped view of female sexuality as well as its reluctance to imagine God in female terms, has much to learn from these sources.

The first thing to insist upon, then, is that in spite of Western and Christian uneasiness over female imagery for God, since the *imago dei* is twofold, female as well as male, both kinds of metaphors ought to be used.[6] The question then arises how God should be imaged as both female and male (as well as, of course, beyond both). I would make two points here: first, God should be imagined in female, not feminine, terms, and second, the female metaphors should be inclusive of but not limited to maternal ones. On the first point: the distinction between "female" and "feminine" is important, for the first refers to gender while the second refers to qualities conventionally associated with women.[7] The problem with introducing a feminine dimension of God is that it invariably ends with identifying as female those qualities that society has called feminine. Thus, the feminine side of God is taken to comprise the tender, nurturing, passive, healing aspects of divine activity, whereas those activities in which God creates, redeems, establishes peace, administers justice, and so on, are called masculine. Such a division, in extending to the godhead the stereotypes we create in human society, further crystallizes and sanctifies them.[8]

But to image God in female personal terms, as she as well as he, is a very different matter. It is not, at the outset, to identify God with any particular set of characteristics, unless one is slipping in feminine stereotypes under the cover of simple gender appellation. All that has been done is to use a personal pronoun for deity and this, we have insisted, is not only our tradition, the tradition of addressing God as Thou, but desirable and necessary in our time. Since all agents are either male or female, either pronoun and both pronouns can and should be used. If we use only the male pronoun, we fall into idolatry, forgetting that God is beyond male and female—a fact that the use of both pronouns brings home to us as the opening prayer to "Father-Mother God" illustrated. If we refuse to use any pronouns for God, we court the possibility of concealing androcentric assumptions behind abstractions.[9] If we are, then, to be concrete, personal, and nonidolatrous in our talk about God, we have no alternative but to speak of God in female as well as male terms, to use "she" as well as "he," and to realize that in so doing we are not attributing passive and nurturing qualities to God any more than we are attributing active and powerful qualities. Or to say it differently, we are attributing human qualities: we are imaging God on analogy with human beings, and so far that is all that we are doing: God is she and he and neither.

We come now, however, to the second point: female metaphors for God should be inclusive of but not limited to maternal ones. One of the important insights emerging from current research into Goddess religions is that in these traditions all divine activities are imaged by both male and female deities: both Ishtar and Horus, for instance, engage in creating, governing, nurturing, and redeeming.[10] In other words, neither masculine nor feminine characteristics are attributed to deities; rather, divine activities are attributed equivalently to male and female agents. Both male and female deities operate in both the private and the public arena; both engage in activities of power as well as care.[11] The Hebraic-Christian tradition does not, of course, worship multiple deities, but this fact in no way lessens the point being made—that if we accept the reasoning behind addressing God as "she" as well as "he," we should do so in a fashion that does not stereotype divine activities. This is not a new or radical notion in Christianity, despite the fact that the only female "component" in the tradition has been the quasi-divine figure of Mary, whose characteristics have certainly been stereotypically feminine.[12] But an earlier hypostasis of God—Sophia, or Wisdom, in Hebrew religion—was identified not only with the earth and sexuality but also with order and justice.[13] Moreover, medieval piety freely attributed a wide range of activities to God, some in female form, some in male, some in both.[14]

What, then, about the model of God as mother? Is that not stereotyping by suggesting as a major model for God *one* activity of females and the one most closely identified as stereotypically feminine, namely, giving birth to and raising children? My answer is twofold. First, although this particular essay will focus on God as mother in order to balance and provide a new context for interpreting God as father, other divine activities will also be imaged in female form, especially those concerned with creation and justice. Second, although mothering is a female activity, it is not feminine; that is, to give birth to and to feed the young is simply what females do—some may do it in a so-called feminine fashion, and others may not. What is more important for our purposes is that the symbolic material from the birthing and feeding process is very rich and for the most part has been neglected in establishment Christianity. It is also, as I shall try to show, powerful imagery for expressing the interrelatedness of all life, which is a central component in both a holistic sensibility and an understanding of Christian faith as an inclusive vision of fulfillment.

In this essay the model I have employed has sometimes been

"God as mother" and sometimes "God as parent"; the emphasis will be on the former, but the latter will have a role as well. Our tradition has thoroughly analyzed the paternal metaphor, albeit mainly in a patriarchal context. The goal of my work will be to investigate the potential of the maternal model but to do so in a fashion that will provide an alternative interpretive context for the paternal model—a parental one.

We turn now to an analysis of the model of God as mother, with three issues in mind: What sort of divine love is suggested by this model? What kind of divine activity is implied by this love? What does this kind of love say about existence in our world? The shorthand answers to these questions are agape, creating, and justice.

The Love of God as Mother: Agape

Hidden away in the third volume of Paul Tillich's *Systematic Theology* is the suggestion that the symbolic dimension of the "ground of being" "points to the mother-quality of giving birth, carrying, and embracing, and, at the same time, of calling back, resisting independence of the created, and swallowing it."[15] He goes on to say that the uneasy feeling that many Protestants have about the first statement about God—that God is the power of being in all being—arises from the fact that their consciousness is shaped by the demanding father image for whom righteousness and not the gift of life is primary. What the father-God gives is redemption from sins; what the mother-God gives is life itself. But there is another reason that one might feel uneasy about Tillich's suggestion, for it implies divine resistance to independence for created being, whereas Western thought has prized its image of independent individuals who are saved one by one, either by their own moral choices or by divine grace. But what if the power in us, that which gives us our very existence, is not primarily judging individuals but calling us back, wanting to be more fully united with us, or as Tillich graphically puts it, wanting to "swallow" us? Our first reaction is fear of the maternal maw and a cry that we are independent, owing nothing to anyone, ready to face the consequences of our own actions.

But Tillich's symbolic suggestion for imaging the ground of being, the depths of divinity, as mother-love, which both gives life to

all and desires reunification with all life, is helpful as we attempt to
answer the question of the kind of love implied in the model of God
as mother. We have characterized this love as agape, but that designation needs considerable qualification since the usual understanding of agape sees it as totally unmotivated, disinterested love.[16]
Obviously, if God as the power of being, God as mother, calls us
back and wants to be reunited with us, her love is not totally disinterested. But one must ask, why should we *want* it to be? The
discussions on the nature of divine love, principally in Protestant
circles and principally motivated by the desire to expunge any trace
of need or interest on the part of God toward creation, paint a
picture of God as isolated from creation and in no way dependent
on it. As C. S. Lewis says, God is "'at home' in the land of the
Trinity," presumably finding relations with the other "persons" sufficiently satisfying so that, needing nothing, God "loves into existence wholly superfluous creatures."[17] Discussions about agape as
definitive of divine love have, unfortunately, usually focused on
redemption, not creation, and as a result have stressed the disinterested character of God's love, which can overlook the sin in the
sinners and love them anyway.[18] In other words, even though we
are worthless, we are loved—but disinterestedly. Needless to say,
this is a sterile and unattractive view of divine love and a view that
most of us would not settle for even as a description of human love.
If, among ourselves, we want to be loved not in spite of who we are
but because in some sense we are valuable, desirable, and needed,
then is this not the case also with divine love? If God's creative love
is agapic love, then is it not a statement to created beings: "It is good
that you exist!"?[19] Agape has been characterized as the love that
gives (usually in contrast with eros as the love that takes), and as
such it belongs with the gift of life, creation. If it is considered in
that context instead of the context of redemption, it need not be
disinterested; in fact, it should not be.

As "interested," divine agape cannot be isolated from the other
forms of love, eros and philia. If, with Tillich, one understands love
as the "moving power of life," as that "which drives everything that
is towards everything else that is," then elements of need, desire,
and mutuality are evident in all forms of love.[20] An understanding
of love as unifying and reuniting is basic to an interpretation of

Christian faith as destabilizing, inclusive, nonhierarchical fulfillment for all. It is the love that underscores the interdependence of
life in all its forms, the desire to be with other beings in both their
needs and their joy. Nonetheless, the *depth* of divine love can be
characterized as agapic, for the distinctive feature of this love is its
impartiality, its willing of existence and fulfillment for all being.

God as the giver of life, as the power of being in all being, can be
imaged through the metaphor of mother—and of father. Parental
love is the most powerful and intimate experience we have of giving love whose return is not calculated (though a return is appreci-
ated): it is the gift of *life as such* to others. Parental love wills life
and when it comes, exclaims, "It is good that you exist!" Moreover,
in addition to being the gift of life, parental love nurtures what it
has brought into existence, wanting growth and fulfillment for all.
This agapic love is revolutionary, for it loves the weak and vulnerable as well as the strong and beautiful. No human love can, of
course, be perfectly just and impartial, but parental love is the best
metaphor we have for imaging the creative love of God.

An important caveat is necessary at this point: the parental
model in its siding with life as such is not "pro-life" in the sense of
being antiabortion. This is the case because of two features of our
model: it is concerned with all species, not just human beings (and
not with individuals in any species), and it is concerned with the
nurture and fulfillment of life, not just with birth. On the first
point: whereas we as biological or adoptive parents are interested
in only one species—our own—and with particular individuals
within that species, God as the mother of the universe is interested
in all forms of life. One indication of human pride is our colossal
ego in imagining that of the millions of forms of life in the universe,
we are the only ones that matter. Why should our birth, nurture,
and fulfillment be the only concern of the power that gives life to
all life? God as mother, on the side of life as such, does not therefore mean on the side of only one species or on the side of every
individual human birth (or every individual birth in any other species). This first point on the goodness of creation, "It is good that
you exist!" must be followed immediately by the second: the household or economy of the universe must be ordered and managed in a
way so as to bring about the nurture and fulfillment of life—and

again, this cannot mean every individual life that could be brought into existence. In a closed ecological system with limits on natural resources, difficult decisions must be made to insure the continuation, growth, and fulfillment of the many forms of life (not just one form and not all its individuals). Population control, both for our own species and other species, is one such decision. The balance between quantity and quality of life is one that a contemporary sensibility must keep to the forefront. To be on the side of life means participating in the decisions necessary to keep that balance. It cannot mean being "pro-life" in terms of one species or in terms of unlimited numbers, for such a perspective would in the long run mean being against life in its many and varied forms.

Let us now consider our model in more detail: the model of parental love for God's agapic, creative love. Why is this a powerful, attractive model for expressing the Christian faith in our time? If the heart of Christian faith for an ecological, nuclear age must be profound awareness of the preciousness and vulnerability of life as a gift we receive and pass on, with appreciation for its value and desire for its fulfillment, it is difficult to think of any metaphors more apt than the parental one. There are three features basic to the parental model which will give flesh to this statement: it brings us closest to the beginnings of life, to the nurture of life, and to the impartial fulfillment of life.

Much of the power in the parental model is its immediate connection with the mystery of new life. Becoming a biological parent is the closest experience most people have to an experience of creation, that is, of bringing into existence. No matter how knowledgeable one is biologically, no matter how aware that human beings by becoming parents are simply doing what all animals do in passing life along, becoming a biological parent is for most people an awesome experience, inspiring feelings of having glimpsed the heart of things. We are, after all, the only creatures who can think about the wonder of existence, the sheer fact that "things are," that the incredible richness and complexity of life in all its forms has existed for millions of years, and that as part of the vast, unfathomable network of life, we both receive it from others and pass it along. At the time of the birth of new life from our bodies, we feel a sense of being co-creators, participating at least passively in the great chain of being. No matter how trite and hackneyed the phrases have become—"the miracle of birth," "the wonder of existence," and so on—on becoming a parent one repeats them again and joins the millions of others who marvel at their role in passing life along.

There are other ways of being parental besides being a biological parent, and I want to stress this point at the outset, because much of the case for the models of mother (father), lover, and friend rests on their extensions beyond their physical and immediate base. One can, of course, be an adoptive parent as well as a biological one, but even more important for our purposes is that all human beings have parental inclinations. All human beings have the potential for passing life along, for helping to bring the next generation (of whatever kind of beings) into existence, nurturing and guiding it, and working toward its fulfillment. These tendencies are so basic, widespread, and various that it is difficult to catalogue all the ways they are expressed. Some of the ways that come most readily to mind, such as in teaching, medicine, gardening, and social work, are only the tip of the iceberg, for in almost any cultural, political, economic, or social activity, there are aspects of the work that could be called parental.

Having made this point, however, let us return to the base of the model, in the physical act of giving birth. It is from this base that the model derives its power, for here it joins the reservoir of the great symbols of life and of life's continuity: blood, water, breath, sex, and food. In the acts of conception, gestation, and birth all are involved, and it is therefore no surprise that these symbols became the center of most religions, including Christianity, for they have the power to express the renewal and transformation of life—the "second birth"—because they are the basis of our "first birth." And yet, at least in Christianity, our first birth has been strangely neglected; another way of saying this is that creation, the birth of the world and all its beings, has not been permitted the imagery that this tradition uses so freely for the transformation and fulfillment of creation. Why is this the case?

One reason is surely that Christianity, alienated as it always has been from female sexuality, has been willing to image the second, "spiritual," renewal of existence in the birth metaphor, but not the first, "physical," coming into existence.[21] In fact, as we shall see, in the Hebraic-Christian tradition, creation has been imaginatively pictured as an intellectual, aesthetic "act" of God, accomplished through God's word and wrought by God's "hands" much as a painting is created by an artist or a form by a sculptor. But the model of God as mother suggests a very different kind of creation, one in keeping with the world as God's body but not one that the central tradition has been willing to consider. And it is clearly the parent *as mother* that is the stronger candidate for an understanding of creation as bodied forth from the divine being, for it is the imagery of gestation, giving birth, and lactation that creates an imaginative picture of creation as profoundly dependent on and cared for by divine life.[22] There simply is no other imagery available to us that has this power for expressing the interdependence and interrelatedness of all life with its ground. All of us, female and male, have the womb as our first home, all of us are born from the bodies of our mothers, all of us are fed by our mothers. What better imagery could there be for expressing the most basic reality of existence: that we live and move and have our being in God?

If the symbol of birth were allowed openly and centrally into the tradition, would this involve a radical theological change? Would it mean a different understanding of God's relation to the world? We will be dealing with that issue soon in more detail, but the simple answer is yes, the view associated with birth symbolism would be different from the distant, anthropocentric view in the monarchical model: it would be an intimate view, inclusive of the cosmos, but not one that identifies God and the world. By analogy, mothers, at least good ones, encourage the independence of their offspring, and even though children are products of their parents' bodies, they are often radically different from them.[23]

The power of the parental model for God's creative, agapic love only begins with the birth imagery. Of equal importance is the ability of the model to express the nurturing of life and, to a lesser extent, its impartial fulfillment. It is at these levels that the more complex theological and ethical issues arise, for the divine agapic love that nurtures all creatures is a model of justice at the most basic level of the fair distribution of the necessities of life, and divine agapic love impartially fulfilling all of creation is a model of *inclusive* justice. In our understanding of Christianity as a destabilizing, inclusive, nonhierarchical vision of fulfillment for all, the parental model of God is especially pertinent as a way of talking about God's "just" love, the love that attends to the most basic needs of all creatures. It is important to look more closely at the way the model expresses the nurture and inclusion of all of life.

Parents feed the young. This is, across the entire range of life, the most basic responsibility of parents, often of fathers as well as of mothers. Among most animals it is instinctual and is often accomplished only at the cost of the health or life of the parent. It is not principally from altruistic motives that parents feed the young but from a base close to the one that brought new life into existence, the source that participates in passing life along. With human parents, the same love that says, "It is good that you exist!" desires that existence to continue, and for many parents in much of the world that is a daily and often horrendous struggle. There is, perhaps, no picture more powerful to express "giving" love than that of parents wanting, but not having the food, to feed their starving children.[24]

The Christian tradition has paid a lot of attention to food and eating imagery. In fact, one could say that such imagery is probably at the center of the tradition's symbolic power: not only does the New Testament portrait of Jesus of Nazareth paint him as constantly feeding people, and eating with outcasts, but the church has as its central ritual a eucharistic meal reminiscent of the passion and death of Jesus and suggestive of the eschatological banquet yet to come. Christianity may be reticent in regard to birth imagery, especially as associated with natural, female processes, but it has shown no comparable reluctance to use the experience of eating as a symbol of spiritual nourishment. In fact, as many have pointed out, the Christian eucharist has obvious overtones of cannibalism! But the power of the food imagery is precisely in not fearing the physical connection, for the use of food as a symbol of the renewal of life must be grounded in food's basic role as the maintainer of life. Unfortunately, however, although the power of food imagery has been preserved in Christianity, the practical truth that food is basic to all life has often been neglected. A tradition that uses food as a symbol of spiritual renewal has often forgotten what parents know so well: that the young must be fed.

A theology that sees God as the parent who feeds the young and, by extension, the weak and vulnerable understands God as caring about the most basic needs of life in its struggle to continue. One can extend nurture to include much more than attention to physical needs, but one ought not move too quickly, for the concern about life and its continuation that is a basic ingredient in the sensibility needed in our time has too often been neglected by Christianity in its interest in "spiritual" well-being. An evolutionary, ecological sensibility makes no clear distinction between matter and spirit or between body and mind, for life is a continuum and cannot flourish at the so-called higher levels unless supported at all levels. God as parent loves agapically in giving, with no thought of return, the sustenance needed for life to continue. This is creative love, for it provides the conditions minimally necessary for life to go on.

Finally, God as parent wants *all* to flourish. Divine agapic love is inclusive and hence a model of impartial justice. This is a difficult point to make without falling back into the old view of agape as disinterested; moreover, parental love can model the impartiality of divine love only in a highly qualified way. Yet it is central to the essence of agapic love to stress that it is impartial, or as I would prefer to say, inclusive.[25] This is a better way to express what is at stake than to call the love disinterested, which suggests that God's love is detached, unconcerned, or perfunctory. In fact, the opposite is intended, for agapic love functions in spite of obstacles and in this way can be love of *all*, whatever the barriers may be. God as mother is parent to *all* species and wishes all to flourish. We can reflect this inclusiveness in the model of parent only in partial and distorted fashion, for as parents we tend by instinct to focus on our own species and on particular individuals within that species. To be sure, when we extend the model beyond its physical base to include our parental inclinations toward human children not our own, as well as toward life forms not our own, a measure of impartiality, of inclusiveness, emerges, but only as a faint intimation of divine agape. It is imperative to recognize when a model falters. This one falters here.

With most recent understandings of agape, however, our model would have faltered long ago, for if divine love is seen as totally different from all forms of love that we know, as entirely "giving" whereas human love is only "taking," no human love will serve as a metaphor for God's love. But we have maintained that dimensions of divine agapic love, especially those involved in the creating and sustaining of life, can be modeled with great power by parental love. What this model or any model cannot do is express the mystery that *all* are included, even the last and the least.

The Activity of God as Mother: Creating

The kind of theological statement issuing from the model of God as mother is, of course, the doctrine of creation. The doctrine of creation, so basic to the Hebraic-Christian tradition, has in the past three hundred years undergone various revisions as scientific knowledge has questioned the received view of many centuries. The received view consisted of a nest of shared beliefs, but the two most important for our concern are that God created *ex nihilo,* from "nothing," and that God created hierarchically, with the physical subordinated to the spiritual.[26] Both of these notions support dualism: the absolute distinction of God from the world, and the inferiority of matter to spirit, body to mind.[27] Quite apart from the scientific difficulties of the traditional view of creation, the imaginative picture it paints is of a God fashioning the world, either intellectually by word (a creation of the mind) or aesthetically by craft (a creation of the hands), but in either case out of what is totally different from God, and in a manner that places humanity above nature, spirit above body. The principal elements of the artistic model of creation are evident in the Genesis stories: the earth that was "without form and void"; the "words" of God that bring into existence light and earth, sky and water, plants and animals; the special creation of man, sculpted by God from the earth; the superiority of human beings to nature, which they are to "subdue"; and the superiority of man over woman, who is formed from his side. The two versions of the story differ, but the picture that endured and fed into the tradition's consensus was of a creation totally dependent upon God and at the same time totally different, descending through angels (all spirit), to man (mainly spirit), to woman (mainly body), and on down the line. Although this picture has been discredited scientifically and has certainly faded considerably in the popular mind as well, its principal force hangs on, bespeaking distance and difference between God and

the world, and the superiority of spirit to body, humanity to nature. It hangs on in part because, in spite of impressive philosophical and theological attempts at revision, ranging from deism and
idealism to process thought, no new imaginative picture has replaced the old one.[28]

But just such an alternative imaginative picture does emerge from
the model of God as mother. The kind of creation that fits with this
model is creation not as an intellectual or aesthetic act but as a physical event: the universe is bodied forth from God, it is expressive of
God's very being. It is not something alien to or other than God but is
from the "womb" of God, formed through "gestation."[29] There are
some implications of this picture that we need to follow out, but first
we must remind ourselves once again that this is a picture—but then
so is the artistic model. We are not claiming that God creates by
giving birth to the world as her body; what we are suggesting is that
the birth metaphor is both closer to Christian faith and better for our
world than the alternative picture.

The first implication of this model is that the universe and God
are neither totally distant nor totally different. Is this not going
against the heart of Christian faith, which proclaims the utter
majesty and sovereignty of God, the transcendence of God over all
reality, the absolute difference between the infinite and the finite?
I submit that the rendering of Christianity implied in this question
derives from the monarchical model, aided as it was by Aristotelian
and Platonic notions of the distance of God from the world. It does
not come from the Hebraic roots of Christianity, where even the
high, holy One was in intimate, covenantal relationship with his
chosen people, nor from Christian beginnings, for however one
interprets the incarnation, it implies that God has "come near." To
say that the universe and God are neither distant nor different
implies that they are close and similar, in a way, for instance, that
a mother and her child have a sense of affinity and kinship. What
is critical in our model of creation from God as mother is not
whether this makes God and the world identical, for obviously it
does not; what is critical is that the model underscores, as the
artistic model does not, God's closeness to us in the world in which
we live rather than God as a being miraculously intervening in our
lives or public affairs. Creation is God's self-expression, formed in

God's own reality, bodied forth in the eons of evolutionary time, and supplied with the means to nurture and sustain billions of plants and creatures.

The affinity between God and the world in this model can be brought out by considering the difference between the ways an artist and a parent react to their creations. An artist, upon completing a work, makes a judgment whether it is good or bad; the judgment is an aesthetic one based on critical standards. The artist may, of course, decide at a future time that what was good is no longer. But a child, the product of our bodies, is not judged in this way. Certainly children may also be considered good or bad, yet the criteria applied are not aesthetic ones, that is, neutral standards, unrelated to the parent. Rather, it is the quality of the relationship between parent and child that is most important; we judge, then, in categories of love, not art. Thus also, by analogy, would God as mother judge the world not as an artist but as a parent.

Is this creation, then, God's child or God's body? The model of creation as the birth of the universe from God wavers at this point, and its nonsense side emerges. For when we give birth it is not to our bodies but to children of our bodies. We are not creators, we are only those who pass life along, and though at the time of giving birth we may feel like co-creators, we are mainly the passive conduits of the life growing in and passing through our bodies. But God is creator, the source of life, of all forms of life: that is the critical theological statement, and the theological way to imagine that statement for our time must be commensurate with the holistic, evolutionary sensibility. The picture of the universe as the visible creation coming from God's reality and expressive of God—the picture of God giving birth to her "body," that is, to life, even as we give birth to children—provides a model of kinship, concern, and affinity markedly different from the distance and difference of the artistic model. The dualism of God and the world is undercut.

The other implication of our model is that it overturns as well the dualism of body and mind, flesh and spirit, nature and humanity. God's body, that which supports all life, is not matter or spirit but the matrix out of which everything that is evolves. In this picture, God is not spirit over against a universe of matter, with human beings dangling in between, chained to their bodies but eager to escape to the world of spirit. The universe, from God's being, is properly body (as well as spirit), because in some sense God is physical (as well as beyond the physical). This shocking idea—that God is physical—is one of the most important implications of the model of creation by God the mother. It is an explicit rejection of Christianity's long, oppressive, and dangerous alliance with spirit against body, an alliance out of step with a holistic, evolutionary sensibility as well as with Christianity's Hebraic background.

To say that God is physical is not, however, to reverse the hierarchy and to proclaim a new gospel celebrating nature and the body. Christianity is not a nature religion or a fertility cult. But that should not be taken to mean, as it has often been, that Christianity is antinature and antibody. In fact, if God is to be found not only as spirit but also as body, both are to be affirmed. But more important still, there will be no hierarchy between them, for each is necessary to the other.

Surely this is the case with living creatures. Whatever evidences of spirit we see in other creatures (such as their experiences of pleasure and pain) and certainly in ourselves, as highly self-reflective beings with immense potential beyond our bodies, none of this spirit exists apart from its physical base, as death so painfully illustrates. But what of God? Does God not exist apart from her body, apart from creation? The doctrine of the trinity, especially what is called the immanent trinity, is often called on to answer this question affirmatively. In this understanding of the trinity, God does not need the world, because God is relational without it: the three eternal persons of the trinity relate to one another so that, rather than being an isolated monad, God is, in God's own otherworldly self, social.[30] God is not dependent on the world, and the implication is that we too, as basically spiritual beings, are only minimally dependent on the world. To model ourselves after this God is to want to escape from the confines of the body or, alternatively, to see salvation as freedom from the pain and disappointment of worldly existence. But if the universe is God's "other," if God's body is the entire organic complex of which we are a part—that is, if something similar to but not identical with God is God's other—then, God is physical as well as spiritual. God will therefore need the world, want the world, not simply as a dependent inferior (flesh subordinated to spirit) but as offspring, beloved, and companion.

We will expand on these relations in pages to come, but here the crucial point is that two critical implications of the artistic model of creation—the distance as well as the difference between God and the world, and the subordination of the physical to the spiritual—are blocked in the model of God as mother of creation.

We turn now to a consideration of the characteristics of God as mother. How should we address her and what are her functions? She is, as we have suggested, creator, but she is also judge. To join creator and judge in a metaphor may at first glance seem unusual, but the metaphor of God as mother which we have been considering is built not upon stereotypes of maternal tenderness, softness, pity, and sentimentality, but upon the female experience of gestation, birth, and lactation. This experience in most animals, including human beings, engenders not attributes of weakness and passivity but qualities contributing to the active defense of the young so that they may not only exist but be nourished and grow. Whatever thwarts such fulfillment is fought, often fiercely, as mother bears and tigers amply illustrate. Our model, we hasten to say, is not built on the extremes of the maternal instinct, but the value of leaning in that direction rather than in the direction of maternal stereotypes is that we see the toughness in the model. Those who produce life have a stake in it and will judge, often with anger, what prevents its fulfillment.

In addressing the mother-God as both creator and judge—as both the giver of life and the judge who is angry when for any reason the fulfillment of the life given is thwarted—we find a clue to the nature of sin. God as mother is creator and judge in a way quite different from the way in which God as artist is envisioned to be creator and judge, for in the picture of God as artist, God is angry because his good, pleasing creation is spoiled by what upsets its balance and harmony, or because what he molded rebels against the intended design, whereas in the picture of God as mother, God is angry because what comes from her being and belongs to her lacks the food and other necessities to grow and flourish. The mother-God as creator is necessarily judge, at the very basic level of condemning as the primary (though not the only) sin the inequitable distribution of basic necessities for the continuation of life in its many forms. In this view, then, sin is not "against God," the pride or rebellion of an inferior against a superior, but "against the body," the refusal to be part of an ecological whole whose continued existence and success depend upon a recognition of the interdependence and interrelatedness of all species. The mother-God as creator, then, is also involved in "economics," the management of the household of the universe, to insure the just distribution of goods.

As was mentioned earlier, most religions image both male and female deities as involved in generative functions and also image both as involved in ordering and justice activities—for the two go together naturally. And to the extent that God as father in the Hebraic-Christian tradition is understood in parental rather than patriarchal terms, the same is the case there. God as father (patriarch) judges disobedience against his command, whereas God as father (parent—the Abba of Jesus of Nazareth) cares for the lilies of the field and causes the rain to fall on the just and the unjust. The patriarchal judge objects to human rebellion, whereas the parental judge orders the heavens and earth so as to bring about maximal fulfillment for all, and condemns those who obstruct this goal.

The relationship between generative and justice activities is not often imagined in a female form of the deity in the Hebraic-Christian tradition. There are, however, a few instances where the female form plays a theological role, and it is instructive to look briefly at some of these, for they underscore more heavily than male models the unity of nature and history. If God is profoundly involved in the natural world, in giving life, then this God must be involved in the ordering of history as well, so as to bring about the fulfillment of life. The converse holds equally: the God involved in history, which is the God the Hebraic-Christian tradition has usually portrayed, must also be nature's God, the one who embraces all that is.

An important example of the unity of nature and history, of generative and justice activities, is found in Wisdom, or Sophia, in the Hebrew tradition. Sophia is not God in a female form but a secondary persona of God, especially as the immanent presence of God in all things. Although she is involved in creation, her activities are not limited to the natural order but they embrace much more, including the revelation of the mind of God and the reconciliation of humanity to God. Moreover, as Elisabeth Schüssler Fiorenza points out, Sophia is especially concerned with the poor, the suffering, and the outcast and is pictured as seeking out people in order to invite them to eat with her and become "friends of God."[31] She appears not only as the compassionate nurturer of those who are hungry and suffer injustice but also as "the leader on the way, the preacher in Israel, the taskmaster and creator God."[32] She is, in other words, a full deity (even if a subordinate one) who functions at the levels of both body and mind, nature and history. She functions in a way very similar to that eventually of the Logos, the second person of the trinity, and the tension between the two resulted in her demise. But what is interesting is that many of the characteristics attributed to both Jesus of Nazareth and the Logos are qualities earlier attributed to Sophia—from eating and drinking with outcasts to serving as God's agent in creation, redemption, and preservation.[33] In the picture of Sophia we do not see the split between flesh and spirit, female and male, nature and history, which was later to become so dominant in the tradition.

Nor do we see that dualism in Julian of Norwich's theology of the motherhood of God, in the fourteenth century. Unlike early Cistercian monks who, employing a kind of sentimental maternal imagery for God, praised the nurturing "breasts" of God, Julian discovered in the depths of God (and not simply in God's nurturing actions) a reason for attributing motherhood to God: "We owe our being to him, and this is the essence of motherhood."[34] Birth imagery is central to Julian for speaking not only of our creation but also of our renewal: as mother, God loves us in creation (first birth), in grace (second birth), and in work (the nurturing food of the sacraments).[35] What is interesting about this theology is that practically alone among extensive medieval attribution of maternal imagery to God, it focuses on an understanding of God as "substantially" and not just "accidentally" female. Moreover, as female, God here not only creates but brings her creation to fulfillment through nurture and through redemption. Our "Mother Jesus" bears us in his pain and death; "he alone bears us for joy and for endless life, blessed may he be."[36] Despite its brevity and

incomplete development, Julian's theology is one of the most definite statements of God the mother who as creator is also redeemer
and sustainer: "To the property of motherhood belong nature, love,
wisdom, and knowledge, and this is God."[37]

Finally a contemporary example of female naming of God which
includes both generative and justice functions, both nature and
history, is Rosemary Radford Ruether's God/ess as Matrix, "as the
foundation (at one and the same time) of our being and our new
being," which "embraces both the roots of the material substratum
of our existence (matter) and also the endlessly new creative potential (spirit)."[38] Although she objects, on the one hand, to maternal
(and parental) language as prolonging "spiritual infantilism" and,
on the other hand, to the negation of matter by some kinds of
liberation theologies that set out to liberate history from nature,
she finds in the God/ess a contemporary way to express the truth
of the ancient Primal Matrix: the divine is "beneath and around us
as encompassing source of life and renewal of life: spirit and matter
are not split hierarchically."[39] This truth survives as well, she says,
in the "metaphor of the divine as the ground of being."[40]

This returns us to where we began, with Tillich's cryptic statement that the ground of being can be symbolized in maternal
imagery. Both Ruether and Tillich note the difficulty with this
imagery: it can tend toward infantilism; it can suffocate and
"swallow." These are important restrictions, and reasons that
other, balancing metaphors for God's relationship to the world
must be used. But they are not reasons to discard the maternal
model, for it is among the most powerful and attractive models we
have. By it, in a way we can match with no other metaphor, we can
model God the creator as the one in whom we live and move and
have our being and as the one who judges those who thwart the
well-being and fulfillment of her body, our world.

The Ethic of God as Mother: Justice

We all know, some by heart, the two great commandments: we
are commanded to love God with all our heart, soul, and mind, and
our neighbor as ourselves (Mark 12:28–31; Matt. 22:34–40; Luke
10:25–28). Many Christians, especially Protestants, have felt uneasy about these commandments, for not only are sinners unable to

love God genuinely, that is, with "giving" (agapic) love, but they ought not to love the neighbor with love based on *self*-love.[41] But in the context of the doctrine of the created world as the body of our mother-God in which we all live and have our being, the commands take on a very different complexion. In this context it is impossible to consider loving God apart from loving the others (human and otherwise) that constitute the body of the world, and love toward the others, the agapic love of creation, is a very basic love: the affirmation of existence. In an ecological, nuclear world, the "as ourselves" of the commandment is first of all the affirmation of existence for the others as we also, and most fundamentally, affirm it for ourselves. Loving others "as yourself" means—whatever else it may also mean—willing for others the existence, the right to birth, nurture, and fulfillment, that one wills for oneself. Not to wish this for oneself is to wish for death, but in the context of our doctrine of creation, the commandment to love others is to wish for them what one, unless suicidal, wishes for oneself: life.

As simple as that sounds, the fulfillment of the command is complex and "impossible"—but then the fulfillment of the commandments, on any interpretation, has always been considered impossible. What is important, however, is the direction they give for human living. The direction suggested by the present interpretation is toward bedrock justice: the establishment of the conditions of a just order in which the necessities of existence are shared. God as mother-judge condemns those who selfishly refuse to share. When judgment is connected to the mother-creator, it is different from when it is connected to the king-redeemer. In the picture of the king-redeemer, individuals are condemned who rebel against the power and the glory of the monarch, assigning to themselves the status that only the king deserves. The king judges the guilty and metes out punishment, or as the Christian story happily concludes, takes the punishment upon himself and thus absolves those condemned. In the picture of the mother-creator, however, the goal is neither the condemnation nor the rescue of the guilty but the just ordering of the cosmic household in a fashion beneficial to all. God as mother-creator is primarily involved not in the negative business of judging wayward individuals but in the positive business of creating with our help a just ecological economy for the well-being of all her creatures.[42] God as the mother-judge is the one who establishes justice, not the one who hands out sentences.[43] She is concerned with establishing justice now, not with condemning in the future.

But how, more specifically, can such an ethic of justice be pertinent in our day? Before answering this question, we must recall that our experiment is not meant to suggest a life style for individual Christians so much as it is meant to suggest a framework, a heuristic picture, for interpreting Christian faith in a holistic, nuclear age. It is not expected that human beings can bring about a just order for all life, for such a vision is utopian and apocalyptic—a way of expressing what the tradition has meant by the "kingdom of God." Nonetheless, the picture that one holds of utopia makes a difference in the way one conducts daily business. If one thinks of it as individual election to an eternal otherworld, one will act differently than if one thinks of it as a just order for all in this world: both are utopian in the sense that fulfillment is always partial, but each serves as a goal and a goad, as an attraction and a critique.

According to some liberation theologies, the establishment of a just social, political, and economic order is the gospel of the Christian faith. And this, we agree, is the heart of the ethic of justice implicit in God as mother-creator. But even within most liberation theologies the right to existence and the basics necessary to live and live decently have been narrowly allocated. They have been allotted to human beings, with little regard for the rights of other levels of being and little concern with these other levels apart from their support of the human population. At a still deeper level little attention has been given to the right to existence of unborn generations of our own as well as other species, a right that we as the creatures who have the power to cut off birth, to extinguish ourselves and all others, can withhold. In most liberation theologies, the justice issue has not been joined with the ecological and nuclear issues but has been dealt with largely as a human, historical, economic problem. Therefore, Marxism has seemed adequate for analyzing the situation and, with ancillary insights from the Christian tradition, for dealing with it. But if one considers the justice issue in an ecological, nuclear context, there is no way to separate history from nature in this way, and though one can rightfully speak of liberation from oppressive structures, one must also speak of caring for the world that provides all the necessities that we would distribute justly.

As we have indicated earlier, an ethic of justice in a holistic, nuclear world implies an ethic of care, for with the shift of power from nature to human beings there is no way we can deal justly with other orders of beings, either in recognition of their intrinsic worth or as the necessary support for our existence, unless we become caretakers.[44] It is here that the model of parent, mother and father, becomes especially relevant as a way to envision human behavior that is concerned to bring about justice through care. We should become mothers and fathers to our world, extending those natural instincts we all have, whether or not we have children of our bodies (or adopted children), to what Jonathan Schell calls "universal parenthood."[45] Schell uses the term in regard to the nuclear threat of extinction, in which birth would become extinct. In this context, universal parenthood is the will to allow others to come into existence, the desire for the renewal of life which birth always brings. It appeals to that level deep within all of us that links death and birth: we can stand the thought of the one because of the link with the other. Even though each of us must die, others will be born: this, up to now, one could always count on. But, says Schell, there is now the possibility of a "second death." The first death is our own individual death, which, difficult as it is to face, we can and do face, because we know that birth will bring others who will succeed us: life will be passed on. The second death, however, is the death of life itself: extinction. It is the death of birth, for none will be born, but it is also the death of death, for there will be none to die. The second death we can scarcely imagine, but once imagined, it is too revolting and appalling to dwell on, especially when we know that we are responsible. It is at this level, and nothing short of it, that we must ask, In such a situation, how should we model our behavior?

If we were to see ourselves as universal parents, as profoundly desiring not our own lives to go on forever but the lives of others to come into being, we would have a model highly appropriate to our time. Schell limits the model to the human species and to birth (or the simple willing of others into existence); I, on the other hand, would extend it both to other species and to nurturing activities beyond birth and feeding. Before amplifying these two points, however, I would stress that the power of the model rests on the base Schell has given it: the will deep within all of us which could be called the parental instinct, the will not to save ourselves but to bring others into existence. Most broadly, whether or not one is a biological or adoptive parent, the parental instinct says to others, "It is good that you exist!" even if this involves a diminishment and, in some cases, the demise of the self. Or to put it a little differently, we realize, if we contemplate the possible death of our species (or worse still, the extinction of all life), that it is not our own individual end that is most appalling to us but the death of birth. We all want to be life givers, to pass life on, and when we do we can face our own deaths more easily. Therefore, to suggest universal parenthood as a model to help bring about justice through care calls upon our deepest instincts, where life and death mingle and where the preservation of life for others takes precedence over concern for the self.

Universal parenthood, however, cannot be limited to our species or to birth. To limit it to our species displays the anthropocentric focus that fails to appreciate the interdependence and interrelatedness of all levels of life. Since human beings are the only "conscious" parents—that is the only ones who can, both for their own species and as surrogate parents for other species, will to help birth take place—we have the special responsibility to help administer the process: to join God the creator-mother in so arranging the cosmic household that the birth and growth of other species will take place in an ecologically balanced way, both for our own well-being and for the well-being of other species.[46] We must become the gardeners and caretakers of our Eden, our beautiful, bountiful garden, not taming and ruling it, let alone despoiling and desecrating it, as we so often do, but being to it as a universal parent, willing the existence of all species and, as a good householder, ordering the just distribution of the necessities of existence. We are, of course, speaking here of an attitude, of a role model that, if assumed, can begin to change both how one sees the world and how one acts in and toward it. If one thought of oneself as parent to the world, that is, if one moved oneself inside that model and walked around in it, acting the role of parent, what changes might come about in, say, how one spent one's time, one's money, one's vote? The universalizing of our most basic loves, extending them beyond the confines of our immediate families and primary communities and even beyond our own species, is, I believe, the necessary direction in our search for models for behavior in an ecological, nuclear age.

The other direction in which we must universalize parenthood is in extending it beyond birth and an attention to basic nurture, to an attention to the entire well-being of our successors. As creator, God the mother is concerned not only with birth and nourishment but also with fulfillment. We have noted that female deities in other religious traditions and female attributes or personas of God in ours were not limited to bearing and caring for new life but were also pictured as involved in the fulfillment of life through the ordering of justice, the impartation of wisdom, the invitation to the oppressed, the transformation of life, and so forth. Parenthood is not limited to birth and nurture but includes all creative activities supporting the next generation—and by implication, the weak and vulnerable as well.[47] This, of course, once again undercuts the split between nature and history, for in the human species at least, nurture and fulfillment involve all ranges of the body, mind, and spirit. All people, therefore, who engage in work, paid or unpaid, that helps to sustain the present and coming generations are universal parents. The agapic, just love that we have designated as parental, the love that gives without calculating the return, that wills the existence and fulfillment of other beings—this love is manifest in ways beyond counting. It is found in the teacher who gives extra time to the slow or gifted student, in the social worker whose clients are drug-addicted pregnant women, in the librarian who lovingly restores old books, in the specialist in world population control whose days are spent on planes and in board meetings, in the zoologist who patiently studies the behavior of the great apes in the wild, in the owner of the local supermarket who employs ex–juvenile delinquents, in the politician who supports more funds for public education, in the botanist who catalogues new strains of plants, in rock stars who give their talents to famine relief. All of these are examples of universal parenthood: the examples are independent both of gender and of biological parenthood and are not limited to our own species. Nor are they unusual. In fact, much paid work in any society and almost all volunteer work have potential parental dimensions. It is these dimensions that need to be uncovered and encouraged in order to work within the ethic of God as mother-creator, the ethic of justice.

Needless to say, individual examples alone will not accomplish revolution. Is it possible to think of governments modeling themselves as universal parents? The model in most capitalist democracies is a mechanical one, balancing the rights and responsibilities of various constituencies while focusing on the freedom of the individual. In such a model the vulnerable and the weak, including children and the natural world, tend to do poorly, since they do not have a voice strong enough—if they have any voice at all—to sway the balance of power or to protect themselves against rapacious individualism. Some forms of socialism do approach the parental model more closely, both in understanding the political order in organic rather than mechanistic terms and in providing better support for the necessities of life to the young, the sick, and the vulnerable.

The intention of these remarks on the ethic of God the mother-creator as justice is not, however, to provide a blueprint for the reconstitution of society but to sketch the change in attitude, the conversion of consciousness, that could come about were we to begin to live inside the model and allow it to become a lens through which we looked out on the world. We would no longer see a world we named and ruled or, like the artist God, made: mothers and fathers to the world do not rule or fashion it. Our positive role in creation is as preservers, those who pass life along and who care for all forms of life so they may prosper. Our role as preservers is a very high calling, our peculiar calling as human beings, the calling implied in the model of God as mother.

In closing this chapter on God as mother we return to our opening prayer "Father-Mother God, loving me, guard me while I sleep. . . ." God as mother does not mean that God is mother (or father). We imagine God as both mother and father, but we realize how inadequate these and any other metaphors are to express the creative love of God, the love that gives, without calculating the return, the gift of the universe. Nevertheless, we speak of this love in language that is familiar and dear to us, the language of mothers and fathers who give us life, from whose bodies we come and upon whose care we depend. We in turn pass on that life, and in this model of birth, nurture, and fulfillment, we dimly perceive a pattern of giving and receiving in which to speak of God as creator. It is partial at best, inadequate and false at places, and in need of other balancing models. Yet this bit of nonsense is, I believe, also an illuminating expression of an inclusive Christian vision of fulfillment appropriate to a holistic, nuclear age.

5
*G*od as Lover

If there is one word the Christian tradition has been willing to apply unqualifiedly to God it is "love." God is love, and the tradition has carefully refused the converse, that love is God. Hence, God exemplifies love, God is the model of love. We learn what love is by looking to God, not to ourselves. But how is this done? It is done, we are told, by looking at the story of Jesus of Nazareth, his teachings, death, and resurrection, as the revelation of God's love to us. This deceptively simple instruction, however, scarcely answers the question; on the contrary, it presses it, for that story is open to multiple interpretations on many matters, including the nature of God's love. Some who insist on looking to revelation rather than to ourselves to learn what genuine love means do so in order to avoid any contamination of divine love with need or interest. Christian love, they say, like God's agapic love, should be totally giving, with no thought of finding value in the loved object and no need of response from the one loved. We have already suggested some problems with this understanding of love and will address others shortly, but prior to dealing with substantive issues regarding the model of God as lover, we need first to deal with—from a Christian perspective—the *incredibility* of it.

The Christian tradition not only insists that God is love and refuses to say love is God but it also recoils from using the noun "lover." Christians do not speak of God as lover, or at any rate, only a fringe group of medieval mystics do. And here, of course, we encounter the issue of eroticism. Just as female sexuality had to be squarely faced with the proposal of God as mother, so eroticism must be openly considered with the model of God as lover. That is

125

not the only hindrance in this model; in fact, in my view, this hindrance is not a central one, for as we shall see, the model cannot be reduced to eroticism. Nevertheless, it deters many people from considering the model seriously, for the slightest suggestion of passion in God's love is thought to contaminate it. Not only should God's love contain no need or interest, it should also contain no desire. It should, in other words, be totally gratuitous, disinterested, and passionless. Setting aside for the moment whether this description of divine love is adequate, let us try to dispel some of the incredibility surrounding the notion of God as lover. We have assumed in our experiments with models of God that important personal relationships are prime candidates for expressing the gospel of Christianity as an inclusive, nonhierarchical vision of fulfillment. Is there any reason, on the face of it, that the relationship of lover to beloved should be kept from trying its chance? In fact, should we not ask the opposite question: Why, given its importance to and power in human life, has this model *not* been included centrally in Christianity? As the most intimate of all human relationships, as the one that to the majority of people is the most central and precious, the one giving the most joy (as well as the most pain), does it not contain enormous potential? If the relationship between lovers is arguably the deepest human relationship, then it should be a central metaphor for modeling some aspects of the God-world relationship. Could a relationship be of such crucial importance in our existence and be irrelevant in our relationship with God? Does that not suggest dualistic thinking again, that the divine and the human, the spiritual and the physical, have no intrinsic relationship? If we are not willing at least to consider this model with an open mind, are we not cutting off a central dimension of human experience as outside the concern of the Christian gospel? Are we not saying that the most intimate and important kind of human love is inappropriate for expressing some aspects of the God-world relationship? The love of parents to children and perhaps friend to friend is allowed but not lover to beloved. But why not? What is wrong with desire, with passion? Or more positively, what is good, appropriate, and right about it as a model of God's relationship with the world? In these opening comments we are not attempting a full or systematic answer to the question but are only trying to dispel some of the incredibility surrounding the metaphor.

Let us consider a few ways in which desire or passion, though not exhaustive of the love between lovers, is an important dimension both of that relationship and of the relationship between God and the world. We begin with the simple reminder that the Song of Songs is part of our scriptural tradition. Many have ignored the book or found it an embarrassment, but it has served to check those who would like to say that Christianity has no place for passion except in marriage and for the sake of procreation.[1] Although the Song of Songs praises human love and nowhere mentions the deity, some, especially medieval mystics, have not hesitated to use it as an analogy for the relationship between the soul and God. Thus, Bernard of Clairvaux takes the line by the woman to her lover "O that he would kiss me with the kisses of his mouth!" (1:2) as an analogy for the incarnation: Jesus is God's "kiss"! "Happy kiss! in which God is united to Man . . .," writes Bernard.[2] Whatever one may think of the theology here, the imagery powerfully expresses divine passion for the world as well as extraordinary intimacy between God and the world. The tradition has often turned to the lover model in order to express closeness, concern, and longing between God and human beings; thus, we have the image of God as the faithful husband in Hosea, the Johannine passages in which Christ prays "that they may be one even as we are one, I in them and thou in me" (17:22b–23a), and of course, the metaphors of the soul as bride to God, in medieval mysticism, or the church as the bride of Christ.[3] Some of these images are sexist in subordinating the female to the male, especially the bridal ones, and some are individualistic, especially the mystical ones, but they at least serve as a reminder that the Judeo-Christian tradition, if wary of the lover model and preferring to keep it well within the safe boundaries of marriage, has nonetheless not been able to eliminate it entirely.

One may then be inclined to ask why this metaphor refuses to stay submerged. It refuses quite simply because it is so central to human life: we never feel better than when we are in love, when we love and are loved. The crux of being in love is not lust, sex, or desire (though these are expressions of a human love relationship);

the crux is *value*. It is finding someone else valuable and being found valuable. And this perceiving of valuableness is, in the final analysis, unfounded. After all the reasons have been given on both sides for why each loves the other, the reasons do not add up to the love. Lovers love each other for no reason or beyond all reasons; they find each other valuable just because the other person is who he or she is. Being found valuable in this way is the most complete affirmation possible. It says, I love you just because you are you, I delight in your presence, you are precious beyond all saying to me. In the eyes of the beloved, one sees a different image of oneself: one sees a valuable person. Perhaps for the first time in one's life one realizes that one might be lovable: to see with the lover's vision is to see oneself as lovable.[4] And in a love relationship, one responds in kind: one values the valuer.

Is it any surprise then that the Christian tradition in its attempt to sum up the goal of human existence has done so in lover's language? From Augustine through Thomas and to the Westminster Confession, the "end of man" was to "know" and "enjoy" God forever. Beyond fear of judgment and punishment for sins, and beyond relief and gratitude for forgiveness, lies loving God for God's own sake—because God is God, attractive, valuable, lovely beyond all knowing, all imagining. In the beatific vision, we are promised, through analogy with the relationship between lovers, the fulfillment of our deepest longings. We will be united, permanently and totally, with the One whom we find most valuable, whom we love beyond all else, and who finds us, the beloved, valuable as well beyond all reckoning. We, being totally affirmed for who we are, embrace the source of our being and our value: we are "in love" with the Lover. Our hearts, no longer restless, have found their rest in love itself.

We feel uneasy with this language, however, and with good reason: it is individualistic, dualistic, and otherworldly, possessing characteristics of the tradition that we have attempted to counter at every turn. If, however, the lover model is seen in the context of the world as God's body, if the lover is God and the beloved the world rather than individuals, then the individualistic, dualistic, and otherworldly aspects dissolve. For now God as lover is seen to love not spirits individually in a world apart from the one we know, but all creatures, body and spirit, here and now. And we in turn do not love God one by one in vertical relationships of beloved to lover, but as we love the world, God's body—as we find it attractive and precious, valuable for its own sake—we are in this loving of the world loving God. With our model of the world as God's body, we avoid the dualism, individualism, and otherworldliness of the tradition's use of the lover model. What we do not want to lose, however, is the passion in the model, the desire to be united with the beloved. But now the beloved cannot be God alone: it must also be the world that is the expression of God and that God loves.

Can we feel passion for the world? Is that not too strong a feeling to be a base for Christian behavior? Even if one were willing to grant that the lover model may have possibilities—that it is not just individualistic, dualistic, otherworldly eroticism—still, one would want to ask whether it is not too strong, too intimate, as a way to speak of how God loves us and we should love our neighbors. It may be instructive at this point to note that "passion" has two distinct principal meanings, neither of which is limited to sexual desire, although one meaning includes it. Passion means suffering, and it also means deep feeling of any sort: hope, fear, love, joy, grief, and desire.[5] It is perhaps no coincidence that the passion of Jesus of Nazareth has carried both of these motifs: his suffering has not been seen as passive, indifferent endurance but as agony brought on by great love toward those who need love most: the last and the least. The bond between the two meanings of passion emerges in the story of Jesus of Nazareth, whose deep feeling for those who believed themselves to be without value brought on his suffering with and for them. Disciples who model themselves on God the lover will inevitably find the same connection to obtain.

Having built a preliminary case for at least considering the model of God as lover, we turn now to a more substantive treatment of the model, with three questions in mind: What sort of divine love is suggested by this model? What kind of divine activity is implied by this love? What does this kind of love say about existence in our world? One-word answers to these questions are eros, saving, and healing.

The Love of God as Lover: Eros

There is *passion* in the universe: the young stars, the whirling galaxies—the living, pulsing earth thrives in the passionate embrace of life itself. Our love for one another is the language of our passionate God. . . . It is *desire* that spins us round, *desire* that sends the blood through our veins, *desire* that draws us into one another's arms and onward in the lifelong search for God's face. And in the love of one another we see that face—in the touch of each other's hands we feel God's presence.[6]

We speak of God as love but are afraid to call God lover. But a God who relates to all that is, not distantly and bloodlessly but intimately and passionately, is appropriately called lover.[7] God as lover is the one who loves the world not with the fingertips but totally and passionately, taking pleasure in its variety and richness, finding it attractive and valuable, delighting in its fulfillment. God as lover is the moving power of love in the universe, the desire for unity with all the beloved, the passionate embrace that spins the "living pulsing earth" around, sends the "blood through our veins," and "draws us into one another's arms."

This is a poetic way of saying what many others have said of eros, from Plato (love is the "everlasting possession of the good") to Tillich (love is the desire for union with the valuable).[8] This is the love that finds goodness and beauty in the world and desires to be united with it. By itself, unqualified by other kinds of love, it can become aesthetic and elitist, but its importance, as we have seen, is that it expresses better than any other kind of love the *valuableness* of the beloved. In a time such as ours, when the intrinsic value of our world must be stressed, eros as the love of the valuable is a necessary aspect of both divine and human love. This is a critical dimension of our model and will figure prominently in our understanding of the work of God as lover, for we shall understand salvation to be the making whole or uniting with what is attractive and valuable, rather than the rescuing of what is sinful and worthless.

The assumption that eros is the desire for union with, or possession of, the valuable suggests, however, that it lacks what it would have. It assumes a situation of separation, a situation of alienation in contrast to a situation of original unity. And it is this lack or

need—what Tillich calls the "urge toward the reunion of the separated"—that is the point of identity in all forms of love, from epithymia (desire, including sexual desire), to agape, eros, and philia.[9]
In fact, one sees it most clearly in sexual desire: the act that both
brings new life into being and gives the most intense pleasure to all
living creatures is a powerful symbol of the desire for unity with
others that is shared by all forms of life.[10] Agape, the love that gives
with no thought of return; eros, the love that finds the beloved
valuable; and philia, the love that shares and works for the vision of
the good—none of these can be reduced to sexual desire, but all of
them in different ways attest to the oneness of love, so evident in
sexual union, as "that which drives everything that is towards everything else that is."[11] Sex is the most basic physical symbol for
unity, and therefore, in a theology concerned to express the Christian vision as an inclusive one of fulfillment for all creation, it must
be allowed its hallowed place as the one act that up and down the
ladder of creation signifies the desire to be united with others. As
with birth, eating, and other basic physical acts, we use sex in a
vast multitude of ways to communicate all manner of complex human emotions, but they all depend for their meaning on the power
of the original base. Love cannot be reduced to sex, but it cannot
escape it either, or if it tries, it becomes bloodless, cold, and sterile,
no longer the embrace that spins our pulsing earth, sending blood
through our veins and drawing us into each other's arms.

This description of eros—that it is a passionate attraction to the
valuable and a desire to be united with it—may initially mark it as
a strange candidate, from a traditional Christian perspective, for
expressing God's saving love. It implies that the world is valuable,
that God needs it, and that salvation is the reunification of the
beloved world with its lover, God. As we investigate each of these
implications in more depth, we must remind ourselves again that
we are experimenting with one model in order to let it try its
chance in expressing certain aspects of the God-world relationship in our time. We are not making pronouncements but experimenting, not dealing with all possible models but only one, not
suggesting our model comprises a complete doctrine of God
but only certain aspects, not claiming the model is for all time but
only for our time. The heuristic, limited, and timely character of

metaphorical theology must always be kept at the forefront: imaginative boldness is not the same as dogmatic pronouncement, and the criteria for judging each differ. If we can make a case for our model, it will at best be plausible, illuminating, and timely; it will not be the one and only truth.

Our strange candidate for expressing God's saving love implies that the world is valuable. The Christian tradition has always claimed the original valuableness of the world—God pronounced in Genesis that the creation was good—but from human sin the initial harmony and right order have gone awry and the world, along with human beings, has fallen. What our model claims, however, is that our present world is attractive and valuable. What then about sin? Does not sin ruin creation? We shall treat sin in more detail soon but the short answer, from the perspective of our model, is no.

To be sure, in a love relationship, betrayal and estrangement can turn feelings of attraction into feelings of anger; great love engenders strong emotions at both extremes. At such times, however, the will to love, commitment to the other, continues because, even though estranged, the beloved is still valuable. One of the characteristics of genuine love is that it endures, it is faithful through all manner of barriers and difficulties, finding the beloved valuable even when others may not see value or may not see it any longer. In a long-term relationship that includes illness, defeat in both personal and public ways, the processes of aging and decline, and of course death, the testing of continued valuableness between lovers becomes acute. The great lovers, not just the Abélards and Héloïses but also the unsung and unknown faithful lovers, are the ones who *no matter what* continue to find the beloved valuable beyond all reasons that can be given. It is important to distinguish this kind of valuation from love that continues "in spite of." The latter kind of love continues despite the fact that the other is worthless, sinful, or whatever, whereas the former kind of love persists because the other is, given whatever negative qualities, still worthy and desirable. To be sure, human beings cannot in some circumstances attain this ideal: changes in a partner through mental deterioration or drug addiction, for instance, are painful reminders of our limits to loving "because" rather than "in spite of." But as a model for God's love to us (and hence ours to others) in our time, which is better? Is it better as has been usual in the tradition to love others in spite of their worthlessness (recall the old adage "Hate the sin but love the sinner") or because of their valuableness? Do we want to be loved in spite of who we are or because of who we are? That is, if we are talking about the "greatest love there is"—God's love—is it not far greater to be loved as God's beloved than as a rebellious sinner?

Granted that it may be better to be loved in this way in that we may prefer it, is it better in other respects as well? This kind of love is, I believe, a crucial aspect in the change of consciousness needed in an ecological, nuclear era. One of the greatest barriers to developing the sensibility needed in our time is the traditional Christian, and especially Protestant, view of sin as corrupting, depraving, and making worthless both human beings and the rest of creation. It results in a low view of l. fe, in general and in particular. It is difficult to permeate this mind-set with a radically different view of life, both human and otherwise, a view that finds life in all its complexity and diversity—in its breadth and depth—wondrous, attractive, and valuable beyond all imagining. There is little in the traditional view of God's loving "in spite of" that will aid in creating the sensibility needed today. Life is not worthless, nor is it made worthy only through divine forgiveness; as such, it is valuable and precious, and we need to feel that value in the marrow of our bones if we are to have the will to work with the divine lover toward including all the beloved in the circle of valuing love. We need to value life and deeply desire all forms of life to survive and prosper if we are to have any hope of attaining an ecologically balanced, nuclear-free world.

The second implication of our model of God as lover is that God needs the world. Lovers need each other, and in fact, the classic treatment of eros in Plato's *Symposium* describes it as the love that would complete us and make us whole. Plato says that love (eros) is the child of Plenty and Poverty and hence has a dual nature that drives it from finite and transitory embodiments of the good and beautiful up the ladder until it reaches the Forms of absolute goodness and beauty. So lovers start with their beautiful bodies and proceed to the beauty of the mind. This view of eros as using valuable objects and persons as steppingstones to intellectual self-fulfillment is certainly part of the reason eros has received such negative treatment in Christian circles. However, the model of God as lover of the world who needs the world does not have the utilitarian, dualistic, and self-centered characteristics of Plato's view.

Nonetheless, there is still the issue of divine need. Certainly a radically transcendent, triumphalist view of God, of God as either the unmoved mover or the absolute monarch, cannot conceive of God as needing anything, let alone an intimate relationship with her creatures. But our model of God as mother-creator and as lover to the beloved world puts need in a very different light. As many have pointed out, neither the covenantal God of the Hebrew Scriptures who pleaded with Israel to be his faithful partner nor the compassionate God of Jesus of Nazareth who healed the sick and cast out demons is an unmoved mover or an absolute monarch entirely outside the circle of need. Need, of course, implies change and growth, and though some societies, like that of ancient Greece, find change and growth inferior to immutability and motionlessness, our society does not.[12] Change, growth, and development are all positive attributes for contemporary human beings; they are also characteristics of an evolutionary view of the universe. Hence, on the principle that we image God according to what we find most desirable in ourselves and what we find constitutive of our world, there is reason to include change as a divine attribute.

Moreover, unless we understand God as needing us, we will lack the will to take responsibility for the world. We alone among all the beloved of God know that we are loved; we are the only ones who can consciously respond, returning the love. One of the great assets of the lover model for God is that, unlike the monarchical model, and in a more central way than the maternal model, it underscores the need that God has of us. Kings do not need subjects (except to obey orders), and even mothers, though hoping for a response from children, give love without it. But lovers want and need a response.[13] They are enriched and fulfilled by response. How, then, should we speak of our responsive love that fills a need in God the lover? We will not do so in the tradition of erotic mysticism, where the relationship between a soul as bride to God as bridegroom has encouraged an individualistic, dualistic, otherworldly understanding of Christian love imagery. On the contrary, the response of the beloved, the need we fill in God, is directed toward God's body, the world. What should be evident is that we are, so to speak, the mind as well as the hands and feet of the body; we are the conscious part that can respond to the cosmic lover as workers, as healers, to help bring about the reunification of all parts of the body that God desires.

The response that God as lover needs is from us not as individuals but as parts of the beloved world; God as lover is interested not in rescuing certain individuals from the world but in saving, making whole, the entire beloved cosmos that has become estranged and fragmented, sickened by unhealthy practices, and threatened by death and extinction. God as lover finds all species of flora and fauna valuable and attractive, she finds the entire, intricate evolutionary complex infinitely precious and wondrous; God as lover finds himself needing the help of those very ones among the beloved—of us human beings—who have been largely responsible for much of the estrangement that has occurred. We are needed lest the lover lose her beloved; we are needed so that the lover may be reunited with his beloved. The model of God as lover, then, implies that God needs us to help save the world! This is, as we shall see, a different view of salvation from the traditional one, where God does the entire work of salvation and we can do nothing but accept God's gift with gratitude.[14]

Finally, the model of God as lover implies that salvation is the reunification of the beloved world with its lover, God.[15] We will deal with salvation in detail presently, but here we note only that in the lover model salvation as reunification suggests grounds for a kind of sacramentalism.[16] The model of God the creator as mother suggests an ontological (or cosmological) sacramentalism: the world is born from the being of God and hence will be like God. The model of God the savior as lover suggests a personal (or anthropological) sacramentalism: the world is in a responsive relationship to God as his beloved and hence will, in different ways, manifest that relationship. The first kind of sacramentalism, the sacramentalism of creation, is the more basic, for it implies that all phenomena in reality have potential for reflecting the deity.[17] The second kind of sacramentalism is more selective, for it suggests that human beings as the *imago dei*, those with the greatest potential for responding as beloved to lover, can be revelatory of the God-world relationship in a special way.[18] Thus, in our models of God as mother of creation and as lover of the world, we can speak of God's incarnation in two ways: first, creation as a whole (God's body) is a sacrament or sign of the presence of God, and second, human beings, particularly those human beings especially open and responsive to God, are sacraments or signs of God the lover. God becomes incarnated, "in the flesh," both in the body of the world as a whole and in the bodies and spirits of certain creatures who have special capacity to respond to God as lover and hence to manifest that love.

One can, in our model of God as lover, understand the incarnation of God in Jesus of Nazareth in this way.[19] Jesus' response as beloved to God as lover was so open and thorough that his life and death were revelatory of God's great love for the world. His illumination of that love as inclusive of the last and the least, as embracing and valuing the outcast, is paradigmatic of God the lover but is not unique. This means that Jesus is not ontologically different from other paradigmatic figures either in our tradition or in other religious traditions who manifest in word and deed the love of God for the world. He is special to us as our foundational figure: he is our historical choice as the premier paradigm of God's love. But all creation and all human beings have potential as the beloved of God to reflect or respond to their lover. That many, most, human beings do not is in our model the definition of sin, the refusal to be the special part of creation, of God's body, that we are called to be— namely, those who among the beloved can respond to God as lover by working to reunite and heal the fragmented world. Those who do respond are called the disciples, and they, like the paradigmatic life and death they follow, are signs or incarnations of divine love: John Woolman, Sojourner Truth, Dietrich Bonhoeffer, Dorothy Day, Martin Luther King, Jr., to name a few of the better-known disciples. Their lives are sacraments of God's great love for the world, sacraments of the value of the world to God. To insist as we have done, however, on the value of the world, on its attractiveness and preciousness, raises the issue of what went wrong. If the world is the beloved creation of God as mother and lover, why are we in our present predicament, headed for ecological and perhaps nuclear disaster? What about sin and evil?

The Activity of God as Lover: Saving

One of the most impressive features of the Judeo-Christian tradition is its understanding of sin and evil. Often more convincing than its proposed solutions to these issues is its analysis of them. One way to characterize the classic Christian analysis of sin and evil is as anthropological, radical, and tragic: human beings, while not responsible for all the evil in the cosmos, are responsible for much of it, yet even their sin, as far-reaching as it is, cannot account for the profoundly tragic character of existence.[20] In other words, the classical view underscores the deeply ambivalent situation that most sensitive people acknowledge: that the magnitude of human evil both private and public is enormous, but that it occurs in a situation so flawed that one feels as much victim as perpetrator.[21] It is Christianity's acknowledgment of the mystery surrounding the issues of sin and evil—that they are in the final analysis beyond our comprehension and our ability to redress—that continues to be persuasive.

An understanding of sin and evil within the context of our model of God as lover of the world will not only retain but deepen this classical perspective. For the world God loves and finds valuable, and would have us love and find valuable, is an incredibly complex ecological whole that even if we want to love it rightly, we often do not know how to.[22] The sheer immensity of the household of God, the unfathomable number of phenomena that need to be kept in some sort of balance, means that the ancient notion of a flawed universe in which evil powers and principalities operate takes on new significance. We realize that, even when we are motivated by the best of intentions, our efforts to be sensitive to the needs of some parts of God's body, some species of flora and fauna, will inevitably mean the deterioration and demise of others. We exist in a no-win situation, in a way that an ecological sensibility brings home to us more profoundly than an individualistic one does: one can imagine that certain (elect) individuals will be saved—and can hope that one is part of that company—but when the vision of salvation is an inclusive one of fulfillment for all, it is evident that many individuals and some species will be sacrificed for others. There is, then, a tragic aspect to our model: if we see ourselves and

every other creature as parts of the body of God and if we see that
body as the universe in all its complexity which has evolved over
eons of unrecorded and recorded time, then we will realize that,
whatever salvation means, it must take into account the organic
solidarity of our actual situation. We cannot be loved apart from
that state of affairs, and given its immensity, complexity, and intricacy, not all phenomena can reach the same degree of fulfillment,
since many will have to suffer or to be sacrificed for others.[23] Far
from being a sentimental view, the model of God as lover, as understood in an ecological context, is painfully tough-minded. One is
reminded of Jonathan Edwards's notion of the "consent to being,"
an acknowledgment that one's own puny existence is not the center
of things, for each of us is part of a scheme so awesome, mysterious, and enormous that, at a profound level, we can only "consent"
to the state of things.[24]

If the ecological context produces a deepening of the situation
in which human sin occurs, the nuclear threat does so even more.
To live permanently with nuclear knowledge, with the knowledge
forever of how to destroy ourselves and other life, is to go beyond
the temptation the serpent in the garden of Eden offered human
beings. He told them they could be "like God, knowing good and
evil" (Gen. 3:5b).[25] Nuclear knowledge, the special serpent of our
time, tempts us to be like God not merely by knowing good and
evil but by exercising ultimate power over good and evil. We have
a tempter no other generation has had: we face the temptation to
end life, to be the un-creators of life in inverted imitation of our
creator.[26] Like the serpent in the garden, nuclear power is simply
part of nature, simply there as a part of the complex. In itself it
is neither good nor evil, and yet as a temptation to human self-
aggrandizement, it strikes *us* as evil. We wish it were not there: the
knowledge that this temptation will always be in our garden,
threatening to ruin it if we even once give in to its lure, makes us
aware as perhaps nothing else can that our situation is a tragic one
in which we are victims as well as perpetrators. We find our situation to be unfair. The cards are stacked against us, and we feel
certain to fail. It is difficult to imagine a symbol more powerful
than nuclear knowledge for the human dilemma as understood
classically in the Christian tradition. According to this tradition,

human beings are responsible for sin, for refusing to accept their place, for wanting to be like God, yet the temptation to exceed one's place is a constant, attractive lure which so invades existence that it appears inevitable that we succumb. The threat of a nuclear holocaust symbolizes the ultimate sin of which human beings are capable. That we are truly capable of such sin is manifest in the other holocaust, the Jewish one. We stand between these two holocausts, which witness to the depths of human evil and illuminate the nature of sin as such: it is the desire to be like God, with control over good and evil, life and death.

Granted that the situation we inhabit is flawed and tragic, granted that we feel victimized, is there not also, in most of us in our more honest moments, a sense of responsibility? Responsibility for what and to whom? Here we take exception to the classical view of sin, for the answer to these questions in the Augustinian-Thomistic synthesis is that we are responsible for turning away from God in pride and unbelief. The picture of the universe in which this turning-away and centering on the self occur is a hierarchical, dualistic one, in which one should order one's allegiance, the direction of one's will, toward God and away from the world since things temporal and physical are inferior to things eternal and spiritual.[27] Sin is understood as operating against God, the highest being and source of all being, and as involving other beings only to the extent that one loves them rightly or wrongly—rightly if they are loved as means to one's own salvation, and wrongly if they are loved for their own sake. One uses but does not enjoy the things of this world; to enjoy the world is to turn away from God and find satisfaction in the world.

From the perspective of our model of God as lover of the world, it is obvious why this description of sin is lacking. Nonetheless, within a nonhierarchal, holistic ontological context, it can be interpreted with fresh power. That is, in the context of our model, sin is the turning-away not from a transcendent power but from interdependence with all other beings, including the matrix of being from whom all life comes. It is not pride or unbelief but the refusal of relationship—the refusal to be the beloved of our lover God and the refusal to be lover of all God loves.[28] It is the retention of hierarchies, dualisms, and outcasts so as to retain the superiority of

the self. It is a horizontal refusal to be part of the body of God
rather than a vertical refusal to be inferior to God. Nonetheless,
there is much that unites the classical view and the present revision,
most especially in the notion that sin is a turning of the self that
disrupts the right balance of things. In the classical view, the balance was conceived hierarchically and dualistically, whereas in our
model it is understood ecologically and holistically. But in both
cases it is the "inordinate desire" of the self (what the tradition has
called concupiscence) that disrupts the balance. In other words, it is
love gone awry: the deepest desire in all life for union with everything else that is—the love symbolized by sexual union—is now
perverted into self-love. What in the nature of our being was meant
to be our direction toward unity with others is given an about-face
in the love of self. Concupiscence, intense desire, becomes the desire of the self for the self rather than the desire to be united with
other beings. Desire gets out of hand: the passion that is attracted
to others as valuable and lovable turns its direction inward, narcis-
sistically loving the self, refusing the relationality that in our model
of God as the lover of the world is the nature of things.

By refusing the balance of radical interdependence, we, the only
conscious ones among the beloved—the ones responsible in special ways—disrupt the ontological order and threaten life itself.
The extent of our freedom to do this and of our power to disrupt
the order of things is only too evident in our oppression of others
owing to gender, race, or class, and in the genocide of other
peoples, the deterioration of the ecosphere, and the threat of nuclear disaster. It would be difficult to find a better illustration of
Augustine's view of sin as engendering chaos in all dimensions
and aspects of life than we find in our present situation. We continue to stress the flawed, tragic context in which sin occurs;
nonetheless, much of what we call evil does stem from human
selfishness, from the desire of the self for the self, from the refusal
to direct one's passion, one's innate drive toward unity, outward
toward others. What results is estrangement and alienation, the
wounding of the body of God, the fragmenting of relationships,
the refusal of interdependence. Hierarchies, dualisms, and outcasts become the norm: the inclusive vision of fulfillment for all is
perverted beyond all recognition.

But is God, then, not in some sense responsible for the horrendous evil that has already occurred in evolutionary and in human
history, and for that which lies ahead, including the possible extinction of life? In a monist ontology, one has to give a qualified yes
to the question: since there is no evil power comparable to God,
God is in some sense responsible for the worst that happens in the
cosmos. But qualifications are crucial. First, the universe is, as an
evolutionary phenomenon, so immense and complex, with so many
constituent phenomena interrelating in so many ways, that evil is a
relative concept. What is evil to some species, what diminishes or
destroys them, is good to other species, for it brings them satisfaction and fulfillment. This is a modern version of what has been
called the Augustinian theodicy, in which the aesthetic panorama
of the whole justifies the sacrifice of some of the parts.[29] God is the
artist of the universe and alone can see the beauty of the whole. The
Augustinian theodicy is implicit in God's answer to Job: "Where
were you when I laid the foundation of the earth?" (Job 38:4a). This
rhetorical answer introduces a list of the wonders of the divine
artistry, of which Job is but a puny part. To defend in this way
God's part in the world's evil may be intellectually and aesthetically satisfying, but it is a cold, unfeeling defense, which makes
one feel that God is not involved and does not care about the
suffering of her creation. Nonetheless, when translated into an evolutionary context this explanation of evil underscores the unfathomable complexity of the cosmic whole in which good for some will
inevitably mean evil for others. It also cautions us against special
pleading for oneself or one's kind—as for instance, in thanking
God that one has escaped a disaster that befell others.[30]

The second qualification of God's responsibility for evil recognizes human freedom. We are responsible for a great deal of the
evil, but says the Irenaean theodicy, the experience of evil is educational. God in this theodicy is not the artist but the educator who
is slowly forming us through many trials to enter into fuller fellowship with him. We are the children being trained for a greater
future through the evils that befall us. The price is high, that is,
the inevitable misuse of our freedom, but the alternative is to be
puppets on a string, pets in a cage, creatures with no freedom.
God's caring involvement with us is more obvious here than in the

Augustinian theodicy, for God can be seen to identify with the pains of growth. This model of theodicy also has clear evolutionary overtones, allowing for change and transformation. Its tendency, however, is toward an easy optimism and sense of progress which neither contemporary evolutionary theory nor contemporary events—witness our two holocausts—support.

Therefore, although acknowledging the value of both the artist and the educator versions of theodicy—that, indeed, the complexity of the whole and the reality of human freedom qualify God's responsibility for evil—the lover model of theodicy offers something more. God as lover suffers with those who suffer. God was not in the Nazi death camps, but they are in God. God as lover is totally opposed to such monstrous treatment of the beloved and has no part in it (apart from having created the world in which it occurred and the creatures with free will who perpetrated it). When such events occur, God participates in the pain of the beloved as only a lover can. God as lover takes the suffering into her own being; God feels the pain in his own body in an immediate and total way.[31] God as lover cannot be aloof like the artist nor identify at a distance like the educator but will be totally, passionately involved in the agony of the evil that befalls the beloved. God's involvement with the world in its struggles with evil will embody passion as both deep feeling and suffering. Does such identification, such caring, justify the evil? No, and any theodicy that attempts a justification succeeds only to the extent that it sacrifices the persuasive ambivalence and the grounding in experienced reality of the classical Christian view of sin and evil. But the model of God as lover offers something perhaps more important than a defense of God: it offers the presence of God to the suffering beloved. We do not suffer alone. Does suffering, then, characterize the presence of God as lover of the world? Is salvation achieved merely through God's suffering with us? Such sharing is the passive side of passion and is the last, not the first, stance toward sin and evil. The first stance is one of resistance, active efforts to heal, make whole, mend the body that has been torn by hierarchies, dualisms, and outcasts. The understanding of salvation in the model of God as lover differs in significant ways from the reigning classical model of Jesus Christ, who by his substitutionary, sacrificial death makes amends for our sins, the benefits of which amends we receive through the preached word of forgiveness and the sacraments.[32] Our understanding of salvation will differ in terms of *who* brings it about, *what* its nature is, and *how* it is received.

In the classical view Jesus acts alone. What occurs, the atoning act, takes place for all time and for all people in one individual who represents and includes all other individuals. Just as all sinned in Adam, all are saved in Christ—so the reasoning goes. But this kind of thinking makes little sense in our day. The kind of solidarity that is ingredient in an ecological, evolutionary perspective is not the kind found in substantialist Greek thinking. There the idea is that we share a human 'substance' and hence can participate ontologically in an atonement wrought by one divine individual two thousand years ago. The kind of solidarity ingredient in the model of God as lover set in a holistic context is different: it is the solidarity of the body of God which in different ways and in different times can manifest God's love. In other words, who does the work of salvation is spread out, and it is work that must be done again and again. Salvation is not a once-for-all objective service that someone else does for us. Rather, it is the ongoing healing of the divided body of our world which we, with God, work at together. This, as I have already suggested, does not preclude special, paradigmatic manifestations of God's love: Jesus of Nazareth is certainly such a manifestation for Christians. But the kind of solidarity implicit in the model of God as lover in an ecological, evolutionary context does not allow the work of one individual to be effective for all space and time. We must all be involved in the work of salvation, and it must be ongoing.

In the model of God as lover, what that work is differs also from what it is on the classical view. The several versions of the classical view share a common presupposition: that atonement is made for sins. The stress is on sins, individually committed against God, for which some sort of amendment must be made before reconciliation can occur between God and human beings. We have already said that the classical view is individualistic and anthropocentric; we now add that it sees salvation as basically a negative event, with the focus on what has gone wrong. Salvation in the model of God as lover is not individualistic, anthropocentric, or negative; rather, it is holistic, inclusive, and positive, for the heart of salvation in this view is the making manifest of God's great love for the world. God as lover values the world and all its creatures so passionately and totally that God enters into the beloved, becoming one with them. From time to time we *see* God in these beloved ones, working and suffering to overcome the divisions and heal the wounds of selfish sinfulness and tragic evil.[33] The work of salvation is first of all the illumination that all of us are loved by God with the greatest love we can imagine—the love that loves us not in spite of who we are but because of who we are. The work of salvation is, in this model, the address not to a sinner but to the beloved; it assumes that the beloved is not evil but is loving wrongly, loving the self rather than God in the body of the world. It assumes that the first work toward making the body whole again is the revelation we could not imagine on our own: we are loved, loved deeply and passionately, by the power whose love pulses through the universe. What this knowledge does is what the announcement of the lover to the beloved at its best always does: it calls forth a response in kind. The beloved, feeling valuable, wants to return the love, wants to be at one with the lover.

The beloved in our model, we recall, is not this or that individual human being but the world: different phenomena in the world will have different ways of responding to the love of God. Our way is twofold: we are aware, through the illumination of God's great love for us, of a redirection of our love away from self and toward others in the beloved world, and we feel energized to work to overcome alienation, to heal wounds, to include the outcasts. One sees this twofold pattern of awareness of the depths of divine love, and active participation in love's inclusive, healing work, in the destabilizing inclusive, nonhierarchical life and death of Jesus of Nazareth. And one sees it as well in the lives and the deaths of others.

We may be inclined to ask, Is this enough? Is not the classical, objective understanding of redemption from sin and evil more satisfying? Does not the classical view with its assertion that God took the sins of the world upon himself once and for all, did battle with the powers of evil and won, make a stronger claim? Yes, that view may be more satisfying and make a stronger claim, but it is simply irrelevant to an understanding of sin and evil in an ecological, nuclear age. It is also part of an outmoded mythology. The sins we must deal with are not the sort that can be atoned for and forgotten; they are daily, present refusals, by all of us some of the time and some of us all of the time, to acknowledge the radical relationality and interdependence of all God's beloved with one another. Likewise, the evil we must deal with, epitomized in our systemic structures of oppression due to race, class, and gender, as well as the deterioration of the ecosphere and the monstrous escalation of nuclear weaponry, will not disappear through God's having "conquered" it in battle. We live with sin and evil that derive principally (though not totally) from ourselves and that are directed against others of our own kind of being as well as of other kinds. What is needed then is renovation on two fronts: on the springs of our own action, and on the devastation that our misdirected action has brought about. In other words, we need to become disciples of Jesus of Nazareth, become lovers of the world and healers of its wounds.

We come finally to how salvation is received or made effective. In the classical view, focused on an atoning event for human beings which occurred two thousand years ago, salvation is available through the preached word and the sacraments. In the preached word, individuals hear that their sins have been forgiven through Christ's death and resurrection, and in the sacraments, the forgiving word takes visible shape in the symbolic acts of baptism and the eucharist. For an understanding of the salvation that must be the present work of all the beloved working with the lover to overcome the painful estrangements in the body, the classical view of how salvation is made effective is not, however, persuasive.

In our model of God as lover, salvation is not something received so much as it is something performed: it is not something that happens to us so much as something we participate in. The lover loves the beloved, and wants and expects a response. In this model of salvation, it is not sufficient to be loved; it is necessary also to love. This implies a very close relationship between soteriology and ethics: that we are made whole only as we participate in the process of making whole. We participate, then, in our own salvation. This would, perhaps, be a heresy from the perspective of classical atonement theories, where it would mean that individuals helped to save themselves, but in the context of the model of God as lover

of the world, it means that we are loved and saved only as we love
and work to save the world. Salvation, as always, is a "matter of life
and death," but now it is the life and death of the whole body of the
world that is at stake, rather than the eternal life of some individuals after death. What is needed on this view of salvation is not the
forgiveness of sins so that the elect may achieve their reward, but a
metanoia —a conversion or change of sensibility, a new orientation
at the deepest level of our being—from one concerned with our
own salvation apart from the world to one directed toward the
well-being, the health, of the whole body of the world. Salvation,
then, is not a "second work" of God; it belongs intrinsically to the
"first work," creation. Salvation is a deepening of creation: it says to
all, even to the last and the least, not only, "It is good that you exist!"
but also, "You are valuable beyond all knowing, all imagining." The
saviors of the world are lovers of the world.

The Ethic of God as Lover: Healing

The link between salvation and healing is an obvious one: if
salvation is the making whole again of the ruptured body of the
world, then healing is the way to bring it about.[34] What belongs
together but has been broken and estranged in innumerable ways
must be pieced and sewn together again. At best, it is makeshift
work; there is no quick fix, no miraculous cure, and often the healers will become wounded in their work. Not all parts of the body
will survive, and the burdens of those who engage in this work will
often seem greater than they can bear. It is at such times that the
revelation of God in the paradigmatic figure of Jesus of Nazareth
empowers them to continue—the revelation that the source of all
being in the universe is on the side of the lovers of the world and
healers of the body of the world. As we do not suffer alone in
defeat, neither do we work alone: the source of healing power
comes from God, the lover of the world.

There are several characteristics of healing that make it an obvious image for the work of God as lover as well as the work of the
followers of this God.[35] First, and of great importance, the model of
healing undercuts the body/spirit split in traditional views of redemption. Classical treatments of redemption, in spite of affirming
the resurrection of the body, tend to separate the whole person into

two parts—primarily spirit, incidentally body—and of course the body of the world (nonhuman, physical matter) receives no attention. The healing model, however, is based in the physical, and only by extension, as in holistic medicine and psychotherapy, are the mental and spiritual dimensions included.[36] As with other models we have considered, the power of the healing model is its grounding in life and death: healers are those who are able to give and take away life.[37]

It is a model, then, that emphasizes the importance of bodies, and this is critical in our time in at least two respects. First, it brings out that reunification of our disordered world is primarily, whatever more it might be, attention to the basics that human (and other kinds of) bodies need in order to survive. In other words, God as lover and healer is at one with God as mother and judge in insisting on the health of bodies as the condition for other kinds of well-being.[38] A second, related point is that the healing model in its concern for bodies undercuts the heavy anthropocentrism of traditional Christian theories of redemption. If we are spirits who have bodies and other creatures are bodies who have spirits, an understanding of salvation as healing tips the balance in favor of what we share with all the rest of creation, rather than what is primarily ours. It is worth noting, finally, that although the body/spirit split is usual in most classical views of atonement, it is remarkably absent from the healing ministry of Jesus of Nazareth. Unlike some of his contemporaries, he never appeared to claim that sickness was divine punishment for sin; rather, he saw a proportionality between physical and spiritual health.[39] He appeared to see human beings as a unity of body and soul such that sin and evil could produce an imbalance in both. He had great sympathy for those in physical pain, and the healings, like the teachings, were signs of the kingdom.

A second important feature of the healing model is its appropriateness for imaging salvation in an ecological, evolutionary context. If one of the characteristics of health is a balanced integration of all parts of the organism, the health (or salvation) of the body of the world involves redressing the imbalances that have occurred in part through inordinate human desire to devour the whole rather than to be part of it. Inordinate human desire is sin, and the acceptance of limits, the willingness to share basic necessities, and the desire to bring order out of disorder are all aspects of the salvation our world needs. The health of the entire organism depends on an intricate balance not unlike the balance necessary in a much smaller but marvelously intricate organ, our own bodies.

An ecological understanding of the world, in viewing the world on an organic rather than a machine model, implies that what is wrong cannot be fixed by a technician; rather, the causes of the disorder, and its solution, are internal and involve a redress of imbalances. The role of the healer in this view will necessarily be somewhat indirect; it will not be of the miracle worker intervening to cure one diseased part but of a helper working to restore right relationships, proper balance among the parts. Finally, healing in an ecological, evolutionary context implies that there is no cure, only better or worse health, greater or lesser imbalances. Salvation or health in the complex world we inhabit is a relative concept and must be so if it is to be at all inclusive and if salvation and health are to attend to basic needs of the many beings who inhabit the universe. For some to be in "perfect health," given our limited resources, means for others to die. Moreover, the disorder, the imbalances—the evil, if you will—is so great that a cure is not realistic.[40] To love the world and to wish to alleviate the pain in its torn body is not to expect miraculous results; this view of salvation is a modest one, conscious of the great power of sin and its tragic consequences. At times it is only possible to refuse to join those who spread the disease.[41]

A third feature of the healing model which recommends it as a way to understand salvation is its dual emphasis on resistance and identification: resistance to disease, disorder, and chaos, in the fighting to overcome the ruptures in the wounded body, and identification with the sufferers in their pain.[42] The first, active phase has close connections with the model of liberator: God as lover of the world desires the beloved to be whole and free. As healer of the divisions in the body and liberator of those oppressed by others, God as lover of the world works actively to bring well-being to the beloved. It is no mere coincidence that the active phase of Jesus' ministry is well expressed in the metaphors of healing to the sick and liberation to the oppressed (Luke 4:18–19), for to be whole and free is what lovers want for their beloved, and one must work actively and relentlessly to help bring such conditions about. Healers and liberators must be tireless in their battle against the forces that bring disorder to the body, that enslave the spirit. The military imagery here, repugnant as it may be to some, is necessary in order to express the anger that God as lover feels toward those who wound the body and oppress the spirit of the beloved. God as mother-creator feels the same anger and judges those harshly who deny life and nourishment to her children. Those who join the healing and liberating work of God are invited, then, into a fighting unit that does not easily accept defeat. But two qualifications must be added immediately, lest misunderstanding occur. First, to fight does not necessarily mean to commit violence—as for instance, the relentless fight for India's independence led by Mohandas Gandhi illustrates. Second, to accept some inevitable personal injury (to "turn the other cheek") in the battle for wholeness and freedom does not entail passive acceptance of defeat—again, a point well illustrated by Gandhi.

The second, passive phase of the healing model—identification with the sufferers in their pain—is an inevitable dimension of the model if salvation is seen as involving God as lover.[43] The reason that God as lover wants the beloved world healed and made whole is his great love for it. A lover feels the pain of the beloved deep within himself and would undergo any sacrifice to relieve the pain.[44] One way to understand the passion of Jesus of Nazareth is as the suffering that inevitably came to him in his fight against the divisions separating people from God and one another—the hierarchies, dualisms, and existence of outcasts. The passion or death is the passive side of his active ministry as healer of the sick, prophet of inclusive love, liberator of the oppressed. The passive side witnesses to solidarity of each with all: in the model of God as lover there are no healers that do not feel wounded, no liberators that do not experience oppression.[45] This second, passive side must be seen as second: solidarity with the sufferings of the beloved is a permanent feature of the kind of love for the world implicit in the model of God as lover; nevertheless, if it is conceived as the primary feature of salvation, acceptance of the status quo and a romanticizing of suffering occur. In our model, suffering is not salvific but it is inevitable: it is a risk incurred by all who confront evil by siding with those who suffer and are oppressed.

Who, then, are the healers and the liberators—the "saviors" of the world? The tradition says there is only one, Jesus Christ, who does all the work. This position made sense in a time that understood the one thing needful to be atonement for sins, ransom from the devil, or reconciliation with an angry God, but if the one thing needful is reunification of the shattered, divided world, there must be many saviors. Jesus of Nazareth, as paradigmatic of God as lover, reveals God's passionate, valuing love for the world. In his teachings, healings, and death he seeks to make the beloved whole and free through overcoming hierarchies and dualisms, healing bodies and spirits, suffering in solidarity with the outcast and the oppressed. But as revelatory and powerful as that life was and continues to be, it cannot stand alone as accomplishing salvation if salvation is seen as the piecing together of the fragmented body of the world in one's own time and place. That work must be done and done again, by many minds, hearts, hands, and feet.

One sees from time to time other paradigmatic figures who reveal in their own lives and often deaths the same passionate, valuing, inclusive love for the world that we see in the figure of Jesus. Often they are disciples of Jesus, but they need not be. If such inclusive love is in any sense revelatory of reality, why should it be limited to one historical community? In the Christian tradition this passionate, inclusive love has centered on overcoming divisions among human beings; in Eastern and native American traditions the cosmos and other forms of life are often included.[46] In an ecological, evolutionary era our inclusive, valuing love needs to extend beyond our own species; nonetheless, those within our tradition who manifest this love to our own kind are paradigmatic healers of the divisions that separate people. There are several qualities that many of these people share, but two of the most outstanding are the *inclusive* and the *radical* character of their love for others.[47]

One thinks, for instance, of John Woolman, the eighteenth-century Quaker abolitionist, who not only spent his life fighting slavery as an itinerant crusader walking hundreds of miles (to protest the enslavement of the post boys who cared for the carriage horses) and wearing undyed clothing (to protest the slave-manned dye ships from the West Indies) but who also reasoned endlessly with the slaverholders whom he included in his ministry.[48] Or the case of Dietrich Bonhoeffer comes to mind: a brilliant young theologian in Nazi Germany, who as part of an assassination plot on Hitler's life was imprisoned and hanged but during his imprisonment not only held services for his guards but also came to a new understanding of Christianity as secular, contemporary suffering with *all* who suffer—a view far from his early, sectarian "Christian" theology.[49] One is also reminded of Sojourner Truth, an illiterate slave and mother of twelve children, all but one sold away from her, who was emancipated in 1827 to begin an itinerant ministry after a religious experience in which she responded, "Oh God, I did not know you were so big!": a ministry of abolitionism and women's rights, the overcoming of the divisions of slave and slaveholder, women and men.[50] One remembers also Dorothy Day, American journalist, member of the Communist Party, who as a convert to Roman Catholicism left her lover and the father of her child to spend a life founding hospitality houses in New York and other cities across the country for the most destitute outcasts, houses where she herself lived and worked to create an alternative society free of war and exploitation.[51] Another example is Mohandas Gandhi, Hindu and sometime Christian, peacemaker and healer of the enmity between Indian and South African, Indian and British, finally giving his life in his fight to unify Hindu and Muslim.[52]

There are many others like these, of course, and many whose lives of inclusive, radical love have passed largely unnoticed and usually unrecorded; nonetheless, all help to fill out the paradigm of saving love as willing to go to the limit to heal the wounds dividing people. These lives reveal once again the inclusive, nonhierarchical love of God, and they do so with the passion and intensity of those who find others, all others, valuable and worthy. None of these people, however, is a "saint": they are not miracle workers, and they did not reach their vision of inclusive love and their willingness to practice the healing ministry of this vision easily or quickly. In the stories of their lives which they themselves tell, all the warts show: they are at one level very ordinary human beings battling their own desire for money and comfort, afraid for their families, lonely in prison and frightened of death, discouraged by the slight gains they make against the forces of discrimination, fear, and prejudice that divide people. Nonetheless, they are, in our model of God as lover, illustrative of the many saviors of the world: their stories flesh out the paradigmatic story of Jesus of Nazareth.

Is the world going to be saved by these special but also very weak, ordinary human beings? Obviously not. Their lives, as reflections of the life and death of Jesus of Nazareth, are revelatory of God's love: to have faith in the God whom the lives of Jesus and these others reveal is to believe that the universe is neither malevolent nor indifferent but is on the side of life and its fulfillment. In our day this love must be imagined and conceived in a way that takes into account the ecological, evolutionary network in which we actually live, the incredibly complex natural, historical, and cultural web of existence, which includes ourselves and other beings. Moreover, we have become conscious of the deterioration of this web of life as well as of our power to extinguish it. In this situation, what can salvation mean except working along with the power who is on the side of life to heal the divisions that tear the world apart? We do not work alone, but the work cannot be done without us.

But is this not asking too much? In the traditional view of redemption, something is done for us; here we are asked to join the work. Moreover, we are asked to love others, all others, and to find them valuable. Is this not impossible? Two things must be said here. First, it is important not to water down the passionate love of God for the valuable world, which is the paradigm, whether fulfilled or not, of human love for the world. We recall that, however interpreted, the great commandments of love to God and neighbor have always been considered impossible. The traditional view that Christian love, following God's love, should be agapic—totally giving love with no thought of return—is no easier to live up to than the view that our love should value the world, finding it attractive and precious. Second, however, just as we extended the notion of parenthood beyond actual, physical parenting, so also we extend the lover model beyond the passionate, valuing love that is its base.

There is the obvious extension to include all whose work liberates and heals; that is to say, the work of salvation in this model is not done solely or even principally by the special, paradigmatic people. The healers and liberators of the world are many and diverse: all those whose work, whether paid or unpaid, brings together those who belong together and frees the oppressed are participating in salvation. The peacemakers on a city block or at an international negotiating table; the reformers of economic injustice, racial conflict, or sexual discrimination, whether at the personal, familial, or public level; the healers of torn bodies and broken spirits, whether of those at hand or treated by institutions we support; the ecological planners, whether of a backyard garden, a model town, or the world community—all these and many more participate in the work of salvation. Such work need not be seen as special or religious; rather, it is ordinary secular work oriented toward healing the world's divisions and freeing the world's oppressed. The ways such work can be done are limitless; the need for such work is equally limitless.

But there is another less obvious but equally important extension of the lover model. This extension involves a kind of empathy or sympathy, an identification, with all that lives, which, though not as intense as love, derives from the same base of desire for unity with everything else that is. It could be called fellow feeling (understanding "fellow" in neither a male- nor species-specific way), which unites all life at a deep level of affirmation based on the shared adventure in which we all participate, and on our imaginative ability to enter empathetically into the pain and pleasure of other beings, including nonhumans.[53] This is not agapic love, love that gives quite apart from the merits of the object, but it derives from a sense of relationship with other beings. It assumes that relationship, unity with others, is more basic than individuality, separation from others, and that although human beings differ enormously from one another and our species differs in untold ways from other species, there is a shared substratum that provides a basis for imaginative and sympathetic identification with others. Thus, to take two extreme examples, we can sympathize with the mortal terror of a bird or share "Jesus' despair in Gethsemane . . . regardless of our historical, racial and even human limitations."[54] This fellow feeling is the basis of a morality that, if not as radical as love for the valuable, is kin to it, for it desires healing for the wounded and liberty for the captive, on the basis of a common bond in suffering and joy. It is to this fellow feeling that appeals to feed starving peoples, support welfare programs for the young and the old, and end segregation of people by race can be made, for even if we have never experienced starvation, deprivation, or discrimination, we can imagine what it feels like and experience pain for such suffering. Likewise, it is possible to appeal to fellow feeling to avert actions that would be harmful to others even if these have not yet taken place, as in the case of further ecological deterioration and, most especially, a nuclear holocaust. We can imagine the disaster these events would bring to all with whom we share life, and we can will and work toward averting them.

As with universal parenthood, fellow feeling takes many forms and, were it to become part of our daily, operating sensibility, would have a powerful and at times revolutionary effect. It is not only those whose lives are totally and radically dedicated to inclusive love that do the healing work of love but also those whose sensibilities have been converted from an individualistic, divisive, dualistic way of thinking to a relational, unitive, holistic way. As one sees things differently, one begins to act differently, whatever one's position, influence, or occupation might be.

The attempt here to suggest the changed sensibility linked to the model of God as lover is not a *plan* for the systemic reformation of the institutions in our society that oppress human beings and divide them from one another and human life from other kinds of life. These institutions are many, wicked, and powerful, and working to reform if not to revolutionize them is a task demanding great ingenuity, intelligence, technical expertise, and dedication. But the will, the desire, to do that work comes from a sensibility that believes such work is worthwhile, necessary, and possible. Heuristic, metaphorical theology is not directly in the business of reforming or revolutionizing society. Its work is at the deep level where the most basic feelings about God and the world are formed: feelings of fear, alienation, estrangement, exclusion, divisiveness, separation, *or* of attraction, caring, valuing, inclusion, belonging, relatedness. Western Christianity has been part of and has contributed to the former sensibility regarding God and the world. But what if the inclusive sensibility became dominant? Such a sensibility is one that finds the world, its rich and varied life, valuable, and one that is enabled to work for its well-being, its salvation, in the knowledge and by the power of God, the lover of the world. A large part of such salvation would be systematizing the inclusive vision in economic, political, and social institutions. Thus, in this sense, metaphorical theology *is* in the business of reforming and revolutionizing society.

6
God as Friend

Unlike mothers and lovers, friends are unnecessary—or so some say. As C. S. Lewis puts it, "Friendship is unnecessary, like philosophy, like art, like the universe itself. . . ."[1] A recent study of life cycles of American males noted, "In our interviews, friendship was largely noticeable by its absence. As a tentative generalization we would say that close friendship with a man or a woman is rarely experienced by American men."[2] On the other side, we find Aristotle insisting that "without friends no one would choose to live even though he possessed all other goods."[3] And an account of a recent study by the psychologist Robert Sternberg, of Yale, states "that women, on average, report loving their best friends as much as they do their lovers. And they report liking, as opposed to loving, their best friends a bit more than they do their lovers."[4] No one denies that the love of mothers and lovers is central to human life, but what of friendship? There appears to be conflicting evidence. In part, this is due to the sliding definition of a friend: from someone who is not an enemy to, as Montaigne thought, someone in a relationship superior to marriage, the "alliance being that of one soul in two bodies."[5] By contrast, the definition of a mother or a lover is comparatively settled. But what, who, is a friend? Common usage does not help much, for one says both, "It's nothing serious: they are just friends," and, "She had many acquaintances but few friends."[6] We seem to sense there is something special about friendship but not to know exactly what it is.

In addition to disagreements over the importance of friendship and the definition of a friend, there is also disagreement over how basic friendly intentions are in human beings. As the substratum

157

out of which friendship emerges, Aristotle points to "good will" (*philotēs*), a benevolent attitude toward others, which Augustine and Thomas Aquinas also believed was a natural tendency in human beings. It is evident, Aristotle claims, in hospitality toward strangers and in the willingness to cooperate in civic ventures.[7] Are we basically sociable or basically aggressive beings? This controversy continues, for instance, in the work of Lionel Tiger versus that of Konrad Lorenz.[8] Aristotle and the tradition based on his work believe we are relational creatures, and, for very different reasons, so does an ecological, evolutionary perspective. But the other view, that we are aggressive and that friendships are formed only to combat a common enemy, has many supporters in a culture that promotes individual entrepreneurship.[9]

Finally, there is the issue of the credibility of the friendship model for imagining the relationship between God and the world. In an Aristotelian view of friendship, where the partners must be equal, there is no possibility of friendship between human beings and God: "If one party," says Aristotle, "stands at a vast remove, as God does, there can be no question of friendship."[10] But the possibilities may be different in a Christian view. The well-known scriptural passages on Jesus as friend are markedly egalitarian—for example, Matt. 11:19, where Jesus is called the "friend of tax collectors and sinners," and John 15:12–15, where Jesus tells his disciples that they are no longer servants but friends.[11]

Thus friendship, far from being a common, ordinary, and simple relationship that we all understand, is complex and even mysterious in ways that the relationships with mothers and between lovers are not. Or perhaps a more accurate thing to say is that we accept those relationships as complex and inexplicable, whereas friendship is an unplumbed mystery we believe we understand until we begin thinking about it seriously. How important is friendship? Who is a friend? Are we basically friendly beings? And can we be friends with God? These are but a few of the questions we will be dealing with as we look at the model of God as friend. Our introduction to this model has been different from that to God as mother or lover. In both those instances, a case had to be made, given our tradition, for even considering the model. Each appeared, for different reasons, incredible or inappropriate. A different issue faces

us with the model of God as friend: a case must be made that the
model is sufficiently important, sufficiently basic, to human existence to qualify as a potential candidate for imaging the God-world
relationship. Friendship to many appears lightweight, dispensable,
inessential, a sort of icing on the cake. As C. S. Lewis says, we can
live and breed without friendship: "Friendship is . . . the least
natural of loves; the least instinctive, organic, biological, gregari-
ous, and necessary."[12] Part of the power, as we noted, in the mother
and lover models was their grounding in biological processes of life
and its continuation. By contrast, friendship appears strangely unnecessary, yet, as we will try to show, it is this very lack that, as a
balance to the other models, is its strength, for it is of all human
relationships the most free. Practically all who have written about
friendship—Aristotle, Kant, Hegel, Bonhoeffer—agree that what
distinguishes friendship from other relationships is that it alone
exists outside the bounds of duty, function, or office. Bonhoeffer,
for instance, says that marriage, labor, the state, and the church
exist by divine decree, but friendship exists in freedom and as such
is the "rarest and most priceless treasure."[13] One does not choose
one's mother, and even falling in love seems to have a kind of
destiny about it, but friends choose to be together. There are other
qualities important in friendship, as we shall see, but at the center
of its power and mystery is that, of all our relationships, it is the
most free.

We will be investigating this and other assumptions as we turn to
a treatment of the model of God as friend, with our three questions
in mind: What sort of divine love is suggested by this model? What
kind of divine activity is implied by this love? What does this kind
of love say about existence in our world? Brief answers to these
questions are philia, sustaining, and companionship.[14]

The Love of God as Friend: Philia

We begin our analysis of this model as we have the others: with
its most concrete and troublesome characteristics. Although the
model of friend does not have a physical base, a base that provided
the mother and lover models their power as well as their problematic features, its foundation is as deep and potentially as problematic.
Friendship at its most elemental is the bonding of two people by

free choice in a reciprocal relationship. There are relationships we call friendship which are utilitarian or one-sided, relationships that either service needs or are unreciprocated, but true friendship is characteristically neither of these. Most basically, one chooses to be with a friend simply because one likes the person, and one allows one's friends "to be," just the way they are. As Kant puts it, friendship is composed of affection and respect.[15] Friendship, first of all, is a joyful, free attraction between two people: a friend is someone you like and someone who likes you. Children usually know a friend instinctively: a friend is someone fun to play with— and someone you can trust. Attraction, joy, freedom, trust: a friendship is a relationship that at one level is simply mutual delight in the presence of each to the other. In this sense, philia is close to eros, but without the sexual element. It is why phrases such as "kindred souls" or "soul mates" are often used to characterize this powerful, nonsexual bonding. Is it any surprise, then, that the metaphor of God as friend is frequent among the mystics, those who enjoy being in the presence of God and who undertake meditative exercises to achieve such closeness?[16] Nor is it any surprise that visions of paradise often reflect the qualities of deep friendship: the dance of the saved circling God in mutual attraction and joy.[17] The powerful, nonsexual bonding of friendship seems to be a "perfect" relationship, free of the complications of our other primary loves—free of guilt, fear, jealousy, resentment. It is for this reason that we sometimes assign it to children and to angels (or to paradise): it seems too innocent, too spiritual, too pure, for us.[18]

But in spite of these accolades for friendship, it has had a bad press in Christian circles. Philia is often compared unfavorably with agape: the former is preferential and exclusive, the latter is nonselective and inclusive. One should not, the argument goes, think of God's love as philia, for God has no favorites, chooses no friends.[19] The seemingly perfect relationship—the free bonding of two in a reciprocal relationship—has often been perceived as an elitist, individualistic, peripheral relationship, outside the bounds of society and hence lacking the seriousness and commitment of an adult relationship. Friendship is for children or, if for adults, for their leisure time. Part of the reason for this view lies in Aristotle's classic definition of friendship, which is highly individualistic and elitist; moreover, friendship is finally not love of another but of oneself. One needs a friend, says Aristotle, in order to exercise one's virtue; one needs someone to be good *to* in order to be good![20] His principal kind of friendship is the friendship of virtue, in which two good men enter into a singular relationship in order to become more noble. If, however, the main attributes of friendship are viewed in terms of the self—wishing what is good and noble for the self—then the other is finally superfluous except as a means to exercising one's virtue. Of course, one wishes for the friend the same good that one wishes for oneself, but one's best friend is not the other but oneself. One should, Aristotle says, love oneself best.[21] Thus, one might lay down one's life for a friend, but continues Aristotle, the reason would be that as one's own best friend, one always assigns oneself the greatest share of virtue. One can practice this kind of love with only a few like-minded individuals; hence, friendship from an Aristotelian perspective is an elitist, individualistic program of self-improvement.

It is easy to see why this understanding of philia has been unattractive to Christians across the ages. But to accept only this definition is shortsighted. One of the difficulties with friendship, however, is, as we have noted, that although it is very clear who a mother is and relatively clear who a lover is, being a friend means many different things to different people in different times and places. Apart from Aristotle, only a handful of writers, mainly philosophers and mainly men, have written about it;[22] it appears to be more important in organic, familial societies than in democratic ones;[23] it has suffered from hierarchical, dualistic relationships between men and women, receiving a second place to marriage, and often, when a single-sex relationship, it has been connected with homosexuality;[24] it appears in contemporary American life to be a relationship more important to women than to men.[25] Left with this plethora of diverse opinion, it is necessary to construct a case for friendship in a fashion not necessary for motherhood and the love of lovers. Assuming that friendship is a primary (though perhaps, for many, dormant) human relationship, what understanding of friendship is most relevant as a model of God in an ecological, nuclear context? We need not, I believe, be bound by Aristotle's view but should look to our own culture, and to significant ways human beings in our time relate to one another, for clues in understanding friendship.

We have already begun to construct a case for friendship with the understanding of it as a bonding of two by free choice in a reciprocal relationship. That definition does not exclude Aristotle's view, but it does not necessarily support it either, and in fact when we enter more deeply into the nature of friendship, especially in our contemporary context, we find a quite different view, one more ambivalent and enigmatic. From what we have sketched of friendship so far, three paradoxes are suggested: in a free relationship, a bonding occurs; in a relationship between two, an inclusive element is implied; in a relationship supposedly for children and angels, adult characteristics are required.

The basis of friendship is freedom, and that is part of its power: all other relationships are ringed with duty or utility or desire. But once chosen, a bond is created that is one of the strongest bonds: the bond of trust. It is the bond of commitment, each to the other, never to be disloyal. The sin against the friend is betrayal.[26] Thus Dante reserved the innermost circle of hell for the notorious betrayers: Judas, Brutus, Cassius. The betrayer is the one who "acts the friend" but opens the door from within to the enemy. What appears, then, as the freest of all relationships, with no obligations except to delight, to play, carries a hidden but powerful responsibility of commitment to the other, a commitment to stay true, to stay trustworthy. The sin against the friend is nothing less than treason. It is obvious, however, that if the highest good is to be loyal to another individual, one can betray—and people have betrayed—many others in being true to one. The case of loyalty in crime rings illustrates the point. Nonetheless, the power of the model of friend is manifest in the contempt most societies have heaped upon the betrayer. What one expects from a friend is, above all else, trust: reliability, constancy, loyalty. A friend is sincere, genuine, true, one who does not talk behind one's back, one who does not open the door, even a crack, to the enemy.[27]

There is, however, another and equally important kind of commitment in friendship, a kind that undercuts the individualism of the loyalty bond. It is, I believe, a major characteristic of friendship and one that distinguishes philia from eros. C. S. Lewis states it succinctly: "Lovers are normally face to face, absorbed in each other; friends, side by side, absorbed in some common interest."[28] If the common interest is something very particular and practical such as watching football or attending the opera, "acquaintances" would be a better term than "friends." The common interest that creates friends out of acquaintances is usually more inward: as Emerson expressed it, *Do you see the same truth?*—or at least, Do you *care about* the same truth?"[29] A common vision brings friends together, something more than a common activity, although what they can care about together is, of course, practically limitless. This element of common interest in friendship, however, opens it onto the world. Such friendship is no longer just delight in another but is now delight together in something, some vision or project, that unites the friends. Thus, the Quakers, known as the Society of Friends, illustrate this motif in friendship of engagement in a work that is sustained by a common vision. Likewise, the covenant between Yahweh and Israel can be understood as a common vision or project to which each was committed and which joined the partners, the friends, together. Or again, friendship between God and human beings in our time can be seen as focused on a common project: the salvation, the well-being of the earth. Friendship here, unlike friendship between God and certain mystics, is not between two facing each other but between two facing the common vision that is the basis of the friendship. The importance of a common vision in divine-human friendship cannot be overstated, for it frees friendship from the self-absorbed individualism of its classical roots. It does not, however, undercut the basic characteristics of friendship, as we shall see, for one still chooses freely and out of a sense of joy to join with God the friend in a mutual project of great interest to both: the well-being of the world. In sum, in a free relationship, which friendship preeminently is, bonding occurs: the bonding of trust and of commitment.

Our second paradox states that in a relationship between two, an inclusive element is implied, because commitment to a common vision is not limited to two. Many can stand side by side, or as is often the case when two become many, join hands in a circle, linked together by virtue of a common vision they share. Friendship of this sort is not exclusive; its sole interest is not in the other people as such, or to phrase it more positively, the like-mindedness it demands is a similar vision, not similar minds. The friends who join together united by commitment to a common cause, then, can be not only numerous but also different. In fact, in this sort of friendship, numbers and differences are an asset, for if what unites the friends is commitment to a common project, it will often be the case—as it is with the reunification and liberation of the world as the body of God—that many companions are needed as well as many diverse abilities.

The individualistic, exclusive character of friendship is also undercut when one questions the "two" of the classical definition. If one asks, "Between two *what?*" the traditional answer is between two equal (and usually good, noble, etc.) human beings, especially male human beings.[30] But given our basic description of friendship as a bonding by free choice of two people in a reciprocal relationship, equality and gender do not enter. The elitist, exclusive character of friendship which derived from its classical treatment in Aristotle, is not intrinsic to it. One can, at least theoretically, be friends with anyone across the barriers of gender, race, class, nationality, age, creed. As with all things human, there are some practical limits, but the notion of attraction to and bonding with other kinds of human beings is not absurd or illogical. Like-mindedness is not the only kind of attraction; difference has its delights as well. Friendship is, then, potentially the most inclusive of our loves, for though in its purest form it is highly particular (involving a unit of two), its other can be anyone. Moreover, if all life, including both subhuman and divine life, is basically relational, then in some extended sense, we can be friends across ontological barriers as well. We can be friends with other forms of life in our world—and we can be friends with God. In sum, from its base in the bonding of two by free choice, friendship, rather than being necessarily an exclusive, individualistic, and elitist relationship, is potentially inclusive in a number of ways. In fact, because it is the freest of all our primary relationships, it has the capacity to be the most inclusive: we can choose to be friends with any other.[31]

Finally, our third paradox states that in a relationship supposedly for children and angels, adult characteristics are required. The other two paradoxes have given us a clue to resolving the present one, for if trust, commitment, common vision, inclusiveness, and diversity are part of friendship—in addition to delight and attraction—then it is evident that, whatever the angelic potential might be for such a relationship, for us human beings it is not mere "child's play." In fact, a strong case can be made that of the three primary relationships we have considered, it is the most adult. This is the case primarily because of the mutuality, the reciprocity, intrinsic to friendship: it implies that one friend is not overly dependent on or taken care of by the other but that each has a responsibility to the other. This is the truth in the classic insistence that friends be equals. Our description does not demand equality, but it does include reciprocity and mutual responsibility. Children are obviously dependent on parents, and even the beloved is dependent on being valued by the lover, but friends are mutually interdependent in a way characteristic of adults.[32] Part of what we mean by becoming adult is being ready to take on responsibilities, being able to share in the work of the world rather than being sustained by others. Becoming adult need not mean, although it often has in our society meant, becoming independent in the sense of becoming a solitary individual. On the contrary, in an ecological, evolutionary context, becoming adult must mean the movement from dependent status to interdependence: the recognition that mature perception and activity in our world demand interrelating not only with other human beings but also with other forms of being, both nonhuman and divine. It is, above all, our willingness to grow up and take responsibility for the world that the model of friend underscores. If God is the friend of the world, the one committed to it, who can be trusted never to betray it, who not only likes the world but has a vision for its well-being, then we as the special part of the body—the *imago dei*—are invited as friends of the Friend of the world to join in that vision and work for its fulfillment. God as lover of the world gave us the vision that God finds the world valuable and desires its wounds healed and its creatures free; God as friend asks us, as adults, to become associates in that work. The right name for those involved in this ongoing, sustaining, trustworthy, committed work for the world is neither parents nor lovers but friends.

Our three paradoxes have resulted in an understanding of

friendship that could be called a solidarity, in contrast to a separatist, view. One must not undercut the power of friendship by diluting its basic character as a bonding of two people in a reciprocal relationship, but the deeper one penetrates into the nature and potential of that relationship, the richer and more complex become its possibilities as a model for the relationship of God to the world and of human beings to the world. Of the models we have considered, it stresses most strongly that we are relational beings, friendly beings as it were. This emphasis is due in part to the sliding character of the definition of a friend: it includes not only pure friendship and the fellow feeling discussed in the last chapter but also the friendship between acquaintances, companions, partners, colleagues, co-workers, and associates of many sorts. We exist in a wide variety of positive connections with others, a fact that the model of friendship expresses and elaborates. While a sense of radical interrelatedness is essential to the sensibility needed in our time and is supported by an ecological, evolutionary perspective, it is scarcely a novel insight. The opposite view—that we are isolated, independent individuals who choose to be or not to be in relationships with others—is, in spite of its currency in democratic capitalism, the more novel idea. Both Greek and Hebraic-Christian cultures in different ways support the solidarity view of human existence. Certainly Stoic pantheism supported a relational view of human existence, uniting human beings with one another as well as with the deity, but Aristotle did also, for in addition to his narrow view of friendship, he had a broad one: any and every mutual feeling between human beings is interpreted by him as a variety of friendship, and this includes the affection between parents and children, the hospitality to the stranger, and the political bond that holds together citizens of a state.[33] The relational character of existence in Hebraic culture is, of course, epitomized in the covenant that binds all Israelites not only to Yahweh but also to each other; and the Christian insistence on relationality, expressed scripturally in a number of different ways, received dogmatic status in the doctrine of the trinity. That doctrine can be variously interpreted, but one central insight it attempts to illuminate is that God is not an isolated monad for whom relationship is secondary or derivative. All too often, however, emphasis on relationships among the persons of the immanent trinity negates the very point the doctrine should make—that God, as intrinsically relational, is, as are we, the *imago dei,* interrelational with other forms of life.[34] What the model of friendship emphasizes in all the many kinds of relationship to which it can be extended is that we are friendly beings, in the sense that, from the cells of our bodies to the greatest visions we hold in common, relationship and interrelationship are at the heart of our existence. The solidarity view of friendship is built upon this assumption and as such has a firm foundation in the ecological understanding of reality current in our culture.

Solidarity friendship says, "We are not our own," but it also says, "We are not *on* our own." As a model of God's relationship with the world, it says that we do not belong to ourselves, but it also says we are not left to ourselves. In stressing mutuality, commitment, trust, common vision, and interdependence, it denies possession but defies despair. It is a model of hope: God is with us, immanent in the world as our friend and co-worker and immanent in the community of friends called the church, which is a gathering of those committed to the vision of a healed, liberated world.

The Activity of God as Friend: Sustaining

C. S. Lewis, after claiming that of all human loves, friendship is the least natural, organic, and necessary, and that it has no survival value, adds, "Rather, it is one of those things that give value to survival."[35] And, indeed, we have found this to be the case in our analysis of friendship, for the heart of the model is joy at being together with others. It is no accident that sharing a meal is the most common activity of friends, for the pleasure of good food and conversation with people one enjoys and trusts is symbolic of fulfillment at a very deep level. On such occasions one feels, in body and spirit, comfortable, accepted, satisfied. Most religious traditions—and ours is no exception—focus on the importance of sharing food, for food, like sex, unites all creatures at the levels of both need and pleasure. But the sharing of food, like friendship itself, is potentially a more inclusive phenomenon than sex, for food can be shared with any other and with all others. As we have noted, Jesus' table fellowship with the outcasts of society, his eating with them as a friend (Matt. 11:19), epitomized the scandal of

inclusiveness for his time, for he invited the others that were rejected to the fellowship of a meal.[36] Moreover, this table fellowship
became both a symbol of the messianic banquet, where all would
feast together in joy, and a precursor of the sacrament of the eucharist. Thus, Jesus' invitation to the outsiders to join him as friends
at the table became an enacted parable of God's friendship with
humanity: the God of Jesus is the One who invites us to table to eat
together as friends.

This is a homely image, perhaps, for eschatological fulfillment,
but it is profound in its simplicity. It not only shocks us (*we*, all of
us, are invited to be friends with *God?*) but also causes us to acknowledge that it is what we want most deeply. To be friends with
God is the most astounding possibility, for whereas a mother desires your existence and a lover finds you valuable, a friend likes
you. Friendship may be superfluous and lacking in survival value,
but it does indeed make survival valuable. Friendship is a relationship of joy. "Companion" means, literally, "together at bread"; companions share food and share the joy of being together while they
eat. One can eat alone, and eating with others has no survival
value, but scarcely anyone likes it. In fact, in almost all societies,
eating alone is a symbol of loneliness and rejection, a symbol of the
outsider and the stranger. Thus, hospitality to the outcast and the
stranger is the other side of table fellowship. And here, once again,
we see the ambivalence of our model of friendship, for its central
celebration, a shared meal, rather than being the exclusive ritual it
first appears to be, is intrinsically (and certainly in Christian beginnings and history) inclusive.[37] It reaches out to the outcast and
the stranger, inviting them in. God as mother says, "It is good that
you exist!"; God as lover says, "You are valuable beyond all imagining"; God as friend says, "Let us, all of us, break bread together in
fellowship and joy."

The work or activity of God as friend is not, then, different from
the work of God as mother or lover—even as the work of creation
and salvation are also one. Salvation is the reunification—the
healing and liberation—of the torn, alienated, enslaved body of
the world through the revelation of the depths of divine love for
the world which gives us the power both to work actively for
reunification and to suffer with the victims of estrangement. The

work of God is always of a piece; in our models of God as mother, lover, and friend we see different aspects of God's one love, the destabilizing, nonhierarchical, inclusive love of all. God's creative love (agape) emphasizes the right of different forms of life to existence and nourishment; God's salvific love (eros) stresses the value of these forms of life and God's desire that they be whole and free; God's sustaining love (philia) underscores the joy of all forms of life as companions united with one another and with the source of their life.

Let us now look more carefully at some features of the sustaining work of God in an ecological, nuclear world. The issues with which we will deal are summarized in two questions: Who is the sustaining God? And what sort of community is formed by the work of God the sustainer? In attempting to answer the first question, we recall that what solidarity friendship says, most fundamentally, is that we are not our own and we are not on our own. As a model for God's relationship with the world, it is a model of hope, defying despair. It says that God is with us, Emmanuel, our companion, who steadfastly accompanies us in both joy and suffering. We are not left alone to struggle against the forces of sin and evil, the forces in ourselves and our world that pit being against being, build walls of discrimination, deny nourishment to many, oppress some in order to privilege others. And this is also what the church and the tradition have said both in the appearance stories of Jesus, as noted earlier,[38] and in the arrival of the Holy Spirit at Pentecost (Acts 2).

The church has chosen the model of Spirit to designate who the sustaining God is, but I would like to suggest that the model of friend or companion is preferable for expressing the sustaining work of God in an ecological, nuclear age. Before suggesting the difficulties with the Spirit model, let us mention some of its assets. It is, as many have seen, non-gender-related. In a time when inclusive language is needed for both God and human beings, it offers obvious advantages. It is also an immanental metaphor in a tradition given to transcendent imagery: most uses stress that the Spirit is God's activity in and with human beings.[39] Moreover, as a way of understanding human virtue, whether the "in-spirited" life of Jesus of Nazareth or the "inspired" lives of his followers, it provides a way of understanding the relationship between God and individual human beings.

But each of these assets of Spirit as the major model of God's sustaining activity hides a liability. First, Spirit, though gender-free, is also amorphous, vague, and colorless. When it is used, as it often is, in the trinitarian formula along with Father and Son—two very rich images with many resonances—the liabilities of Spirit are evident. When one is attempting to experiment with alternative models of God appropriate for our time, it will not do to retreat to bland ones merely because they do not offend. To be sure, the Spirit is better than the Ghost it has replaced in many liturgies, but to many it still connotes something ethereal, shapeless, vacant. As a model in which to imagine the enduring, committed, immanent presence of God to and with the world, it lacks both interest and force.

Second, in the Christian tradition, Spirit, as an image of God's immanent presence, has been limited largely to divine activity in relationship to human beings.[40] Though the term "spirit" is associated in both its Hebraic and Greek background with breath and wind and hence could have taken a more cosmological turn, it did not; rather, it has contributed to the anthropocentric tendencies in Christianity. The corporeal understanding of *pneuma* among the Stoics, for instance, which implied that God and the world were made of the same substance, inclined Christian writers away from an understanding of Spirit as the breath or life in all things; that would, they thought, be identifying God and the world too closely.[41] But such identification is precisely what an inclusive vision of the gospel in an ecological, nuclear age requires, and the history of "Spirit" language in our tradition disqualifies it for that role. However much supporters may insist that Spirit is not in contrast to body, the limitation of the term to human beings, as well as the deep dualism in Western culture, which naturally thinks in spirit/body and mind/body categories, undercuts the viability of the term.[42]

Finally, although "Spirit" language is helpful as a way to speak about particular divinely inspired human beings, including Jesus of Nazareth, it tends toward an individualistic, existentialist understanding of Christianity.[43] As one contemporary analysis puts it,

"Salvation is essentially a relationship with God," and the result of that relationship is the bestowal of the virtues of faith, love, wisdom, hope, and other moral gifts.[44] In this and in similar analyses, one finds little mention of community, the cosmos, or the oppressive structures within which we exist.

For a number of reasons, then, Spirit is not a strong candidate for imaging God's sustaining activity. But is friend? We recall the description of friendship with which we have been operating in these pages: friendship is a free, reciprocal, trustful bonding of persons committed to a common vision. This description is an expansion of our original definition on the basis of the paradoxes we discovered as we investigated friendship more deeply. We found that far from being mainly an exclusive, preferential relationship between two, purely for their own amusement or benefit, it opened up, through the paradoxes, into an inclusive, binding relationship of commitment to a common good, requiring adult characteristics. As such, it is a highly suitable model for the sustaining activity of God in our time. For, as we have stressed over and over, the understanding of salvation which is needed in our time must be inclusive of all human beings as well as other forms of life; salvation must be a joint project involving human responsibility for the world, and it must be long-term commitment to the fulfillment of life at physical, social, economic, and political levels. God as sustainer—as the very word suggests—is the One who endures, who bears the weight of the world, working for its fulfillment, rejoicing and suffering with it, permanently. God has chosen to be in such a relationship with the world, to be bonded to it freely and in full commitment to its well-being. The image of God as sustainer does not tell us anything new about the nature of divine activity in and for the world; rather, the image underscores how God's vision of fulfillment for all could come about, and also gives us an intimation of what the fulfillment would be.

How that vision can be actualized involves us, as friends of the Friend of the world. What we learn from the "event" of Pentecost is that the friendship of God is permanent, totally trustworthy, entirely committed to our well-being. What is more, it is a choice freely undertaken, because, as we have to assume in this model, God likes us. God has, as Kant puts it, affection and respect for the world and, in a special way, for human beings as the ones able to join in the common venture consciously and fully. Of our three models, this one, asking for the most response from us, is the most adult, the most egalitarian, and the most demanding. It invites us freely to choose the God who has freely chosen us, but choosing such friendship means to be committed, in a trustworthy and per-severing manner, to God's vision of fulfillment for all. Who is the sustaining God, then, is answered by saying, "God as friend," but this answer is deceptive—suggesting a comfortable, cozy friend-ship of individuals with God—unless one adds that God's sustain-ing work involves an invitation to us to become friends of the Friend of the world.

When we ask for an intimation of what fulfillment of the com-mon vision shared by these friends is, we turn to the question of the sort of community formed by the work of God the sustainer. The sort of community is epitomized in the shared meal. That simple event, which is the oldest ritual of friendship, is also a ritual so basic to Christianity that a case could be made that it is *a*, if not *the*, central motif in Jesus' ministry and in the early church. Whether one thinks of Jesus' table fellowship, the feeding of the thousands, the parables of the prodigal son or the great supper, the last supper and the agape feasts of the early church, the recognition of the stranger on the road to Emmaus in the breaking of bread, Paul's insistence on inclusiveness at meals, or the heavenly banquet in the kingdom, the importance of shared meals can scarcely be over-stated. The shared meal among friends suggests some clues to the kind of community we seek: it is a joyful community; it is an inclu-sive fellowship; it is concerned with basic needs. These are not new insights; in fact, the love of God the creator, which desires exis-tence and just treatment for all forms of life, and the love of God the savior, which values the whole of the attractive world, come very much to the same thing. But the shared meal of friends em-bodies the vision of inclusive fulfillment concretely: in this one image we see joyful plenitude at all levels and for all beings. The shared meal that satisfies the body and delights the spirit, the meal to which all are invited, including both human and nonhuman outcasts, is the metaphor for the community established by God as friend. The sustaining work will be centered in a community formed by this image and the hope of its realization.

There is, however, a paradox implied in this shared meal: at a meal for friends, the stranger is welcome. Once again we see the ambivalence of the friendship model—hospitality extended to the stranger—and it is a phenomenon deep in Greek as well as Christian culture.[45] Both traditions recognized the interchangeability of the roles of host and stranger, though for somewhat different reasons. In Greek culture, where human beings could not count on the favor of the gods, the good will of human beings to one another, epitomized in the rite of hospitality, furnished solace and defense against divine caprice.[46] Providing basic necessities for the stranger before the identity of host or stranger was disclosed symbolized the bonding among human beings apart from the barriers of class, race, family, religion, and politics.[47] In a universe indifferent to human good or, worse still, with malevolent intentions toward it, the personal and political bonds of philia, both in the rite of hospitality and in the bond of good will uniting citizens, became essential. Today's host could be, and often was, tomorrow's stranger: the expected reversal of roles bound them together.

In the story of the stranger on the road to Emmaus (Luke 24:28–35), there is also a reversal of the roles of host and guest. In the breaking of the bread, which the stranger, acting as host, takes into his own hands, he becomes the host and the former hosts become the guests. But this reversal is different from that in the Greek situation: host and stranger are bound together not because of divine oppression but by divine presence. One of the characteristics of early Christian hospitality is the unexpected presence of God in ordinary exchanges between human beings—and especially in exchanges with the stranger, the outcast, the outsider,[48] as can be clearly seen, for instance, in the Matthean parable where care for the stranger and the needy is caring for God (25:31–46). The opposite of friend implied in the host-stranger relationship is not enemy but the outsider, the other, the unknown. It suggests not only that roles can be reversed, but of equal if not greater importance, that outsiders can be invited in.[49] Moreover, just as in Greek culture the rite of hospitality has its public extension in the good will among

the citizens of the polis, so in Christian culture the bonding of host
and stranger in divine presence is the catalyst for broader and more
inclusive partnerships of God with human beings, in which we become "companion builders of God's home on earth."[50] Such partnerships can, of course, be of many kinds: one of them has been called
the church (*ecclesia*). It is important to remember that if we take as
our model of the church the hospitality extended to the stranger, it
can in no way be a community of like-minded friends but must have
at its very heart the inclusion of the others, the different.

In addition to the bonding of host and stranger by divine presence and the inclusive character of the resulting partnerships, yet
another characteristic of the community formed by God as friend is
suggested by the rite of hospitality to the stranger: the community
is concerned with basic needs. This is obvious in the simple and
classic form of hospitality, for the guest's needs are the ones necessary to life itself: food, shelter, warmth, clothing, companionship.
Hospitality to the stranger illustrates an old Celtic proverb: "The
one who bids me eat wishes me to live."[51] It suggests that communities identified with God as friend are not just marginally or occa-
sionally concerned with economics but centrally and continually.
The partners in the *koinonia* are *oikonomoi*, economists, involved in
the just administration and distribution of goods and services.
Moreover, if the *koinonia* is understood to include not just like-
minded human beings but all human beings, and not just human
beings but all life, the serious ecological dimensions of such communities become evident.

We have identified some characteristics of the community
formed by God as friend, as implied in the shared meal and especially in hospitality to the stranger: it is a joyful community; its
bond is with and in divine presence; its fellowship is extended to
others, to the outsider; it is a sharing of the necessities of life. We
will continue to develop these themes as we turn to what the love of
God as friend implies about existence in the world.

The Ethic of God
as Friend: Companionship

One of the traditional images for the Christian church is as the
"body of Christ."[52] But throughout these pages we have spoken of the

world, the cosmos, as God's body, finding that this metaphor brought out the inclusive character of God's presence both to all human beings and to all forms of life. Thus, when we turn to the specific community and the mode of existence intrinsic to it that are identified with Jesus of Nazareth, the limitations of the image of the church as the body of Christ must be acknowledged. The community of Jesus' followers is not the body of God, it is not the universal community implicitly embracing all, but it is rather one way that this body, our world, is cared for and loved. This particular way is characterized by a vision of destabilizing, nonhierarchical, inclusive fulfillment, epitomized in the shared meal in which hospitality is extended to all outsiders. This is a specific vision of salvation, the characteristic notes of which suggest that an appropriate way to speak of those united by this vision is as a "community of friends" or, more precisely, a "fellowship of the friends of Jesus."[53] Such a community is obviously modeled not on the elitist, separatist view of friendship, as suggested by the church as the "communion of saints," but on the solidarity view, as epitomized in Jesus' table fellowship. To be friends of Jesus, in this sense, means to stand with him and with all others united by and committed to the common vision embodied in the shared meal extended to the outsider. It means choosing, freely and out of a sense of joy, to be friends of the world one likes and wishes to see fulfilled. It means being willing, as an adult, to join in mutual responsibility with God and others for the well-being of this world. It means being to it as a mother and father, a lover, and a friend. It means welcoming different others and many others into the community, for such a friendship is not limited to the like-minded few: it invites and needs all who share the vision.[54]

What creates this friendship is the common vision: in this model of fellowship, God and human beings are both friends of the world. In an ecological, nuclear era, salvation must mean this; hence, the friendship is not between two—God and individual human beings—but between all those who are united by love for the world.[55] As with the models of God as mother and lover, so with the model of friend, what appear to be individualistic images for the relationship between God and the world become universalized when the world, and not specific human beings, is seen as the focus of divine love.

Let us now look more specifically at two ways in which this fellowship of the friends of Jesus, this companionship of those who share meals with all, is especially pertinent as a mode of existence in an ecological, nuclear time. The first is in respect of what we shall call fear of others; the second, care for others. As to the first: One way to characterize the mentality promoting the escalation of nuclear weapons is as extreme xenophobia, a fear of the stranger, the other, the outsider.[56] That such fear is deep within all of us, human and nonhuman, is well illustrated by animal territorial patterns and by our national boundaries. If friendly feelings are intrinsic to human beings, unfriendly ones certainly are as well. Many in fact believe that unfriendly feelings are more intrinsic, since a case can be made that evolutionary survival depends not on cooperation but on superiority of various kinds.[57] Whatever may be the case with this hotly debated issue, it is difficult to think of a more precise symbol for xenophobia than a nuclear holocaust. In such an occurrence, all others would be extinguished, including, ironically, the like-minded who feared the others. It is suicidal xenophobia: such fear of the stranger that one wills the end of all existence, including one's own. The seriousness of xenophobia in our time can scarcely be overstated: the fact that we live in a global village and must accept that fact if we are to survive does not, unfortunately, mean that we will accept it or even that we know how to accept it in significant ways. It is not the task of a heuristic theology to deal with the complex technical, economic, political, and social dimensions of reducing xenophobia, but it is its task to offer contrary models. The inclusive character of the Christian vision, epitomized in the shared meal with the outcast and stranger—the image of the church as the community of friends—is a powerful countermodel to xenophobia. It focuses on exclusion as the heart of the problem, insisting that what we fear most and apparently are willing to kill and die for, namely, the outsider, is not necessarily the enemy but is rather only the stranger. What Greek culture recognized in the reversal of host and guest (that we all are potential strangers) and what Christian culture claims in befriending the stranger (that God is also present in such occurrences) suggest that the willingness to risk such encounters is central to overcoming xenophobia.[58] Openness to the different, the unexpected, the strange, an openness that identifies with the outsider as embodying a condition common to all and that is receptive to possible value in such encounters, can be seen as the negative side of our model to counter xenophobia. It merely suggests that strangers need not be enemies, that in a sense we are all strangers, and that when we risk encounters with strangers, surprising things can happen. In its negative work, the model raises the question whether exclusion is necessary or beneficial.

The positive side of the model of the community of friends concerns care for others. In an ecological, nuclear age, the decline of xenophobia is not sufficient; in addition, a new kind of community needs to be built, and the work of heuristic theology in this task is at the level of helping to form the sensibility necessary for the task. The sensibility is an inclusive one, and the term "companionship," which embraces many levels of friendly fellowship, including advocacy and partnership, is a good one for the range of care for others needed in the new kind of community. The shared meal of friends with outsiders of the Christian community is one form of an inclusive sensibility, but an inclusive sensibility is by no means solely the possession of Christians. Many cultures, especially those modeled on an organic image, have a version of it. An interesting case is found in the notion of civic friendship in Greek political life.[59] According to Aristotle, there is political bonding that is mutual well-wishing and well-doing by and for all citizens. There is reciprocal benefit in such civic bonding, to be sure, but it emerges out of warmth and attachment and not just from a sense of cold justice. In fact, in Aristotle's view, if friendship is present among citizens, the claims of justice become greater, for citizens who live in mutual well-wishing are not satisfied with a notion of justice as mere fairness and legality but insist on much more for a truly just society.[60] Thus, friendship has been called the "soul of socialism," giving the inside to justice, and justice has been seen as the outside of friendship, insuring that neither special interests nor preferential treatment dominates.[61] In a truly socialized society the assumption is that citizens should conduct themselves toward one another not just in terms of rectitude but also in terms of friendship. One can see in civic friendship expansion of the host-guest bond: "The city which forgets how to care for the stranger has forgotten how to care for itself."[62]

Our model of the church as a community of friends united by a common vision of fulfillment for all can also be seen as the product of an inclusive sensibility. Beginning with the image of a shared meal open to outsiders, it expands to include the entire cosmos in its circle of care. What is evident in both the Greek and Christian instances is a deprivatization of friendship: what is usually seen as a personal relationship between two (or a few) is politicized and becomes a model for public policy. Although some would prefer to keep friendship as a private and indeed romantic relationship, unconcerned and uninvolved with public matters, the qualities that we have found to be present in solidarity friendship are far too important to be relegated to the fringes of life.[63] Of all human loves, philia is the most free, the most reciprocal, the most adult, the most joyful, the most inclusive. Its range, from best friend to partner, as well as the depths we uncovered through an analysis of its paradoxes, reveals it to be eminently suited to participate in the formation of a new sensibility for the conduct of our public life and not just for our private pleasure. Thus, when we speak of the kind of care for the world that our model suggests, we extend the model (as we did with the mother model, in elaborating the idea of universal parenthood, and with the lover model, in elaborating the idea of fellow feeling) and suggest that to befriend the world is to be its companion—its advocate and partner.[64] In the solidarity view of friendship which we have promoted, private versus public is not a relevant division, for hospitality to the stranger, though ostensibly a private event, is in both its Greek and Christian forms implicitly and intrinsically public. For, once the door has been opened to the other, the different, the stranger one does not know, it has been opened to the world. All can become companions together, sharing the bread of life with one another in an atmosphere of both justice and concern. Both justice and friendship, both advocacy and partnership, then, are aspects of companionship. To participate in the ongoing, sustaining work of God as friend of the world means, as the word "sustain" suggests, to support the world, to be its companion, both as advocate for its needs and as partner in its joys and sufferings. What we are suggesting, therefore, is that the notion of companion of the world, modeled on God as the sustaining friend of the world, comprises being with the world in two ways: as an advocate fighting for just treatment for the world's many forms of life, and as a partner identifying with all the others. Both aspects of this public model of a "companionable sensibility" are extensions of hospitality to the stranger: they represent the just provision of necessities, epitomized in the shared meal, in an atmosphere of fellowship and concern.

Is such a sensibility possible as our public stance toward others? Or is it simple naive sentimentality to suggest something other than the xenophobic sensibility that fuels nuclear escalation and that not only denies to others what is justly theirs but does so "in cold blood"? A companionable sensibility is certainly needed in our time: one that accentuates neither dependence nor independence but interdependence. A companionable sensibility stresses, as no other model can, the reciprocity of all life, the mutual give-and-take, that is central to an ecological, evolutionary perspective. Is this sensibility an utter absurdity? It does not seem that it should be. One need not be a Christian or an adherent of any religion to be converted to a companionable sensibility. As we have seen, the awareness of divine oppression (or absence) as well as of divine presence can be the occasion for the development of a companionable attitude toward others. And there are innumerable ways that advocacy of and partnership with strangers and outsiders can take place; again, Christians have no corner on that market. What they do have, however, is a very powerful model of God as friend to sustain them as they go about the work of sustaining the world. In the model of the church we have sketched, God is present as our friend in all our companionable encounters with the world. For the Christian community, companionship is not necessary because of divine oppression; rather, it is possible because of divine presence. The model of God as friend says that we are not our own, but also that we are not on our own: as friends of the Friend of the world, we do not belong to ourselves nor are we left to ourselves.

It is in this context of God as present with us as we work together to feed, heal, and liberate the world that prayer becomes both natural and necessary. We ask God, as one would a friend, to be present in the joy of our shared meals and in the sufferings of the strangers; to give us courage and stamina for the work we do together; to forgive us for lack of fidelity to the common vision and lack of trust in divine trustfulness. Finally, we ask God the friend to support, forgive, and comfort us as we struggle together to save our beleaguered planet, our beautiful earth, our blue and green marble in a universe of silent rock and fire. Just as betrayal is the sin of friendship in which one hands over the friend to the enemy, so intercessory prayer is the rite of friendship in which one hands over the friend to God.[65] When we pray for our friend the earth, for whose future we fear, we hand it over not to the enemy but to the Friend who is freely, joyfully, and permanently bonded to this, our beloved world. The model of God as friend defies despair.

Conclusion

When we pray, we know we are addressing, not describing, God. When in prayer we add a noun to the Thou, the You, we are addressing, we know it does not define or in any way limit God. When we address God as mother, father, lover, friend, or as judge, healer, liberator, companion, or yet again as sun, ocean, fortress, shield, or even as creator, redeemer, and sustainer, we know that these terms are not descriptions of God. When we speak to God we are most conscious of how inadequate our language is for God, something we more easily forget when we speak about God—that is, when we are doing theology.

And of this profound and permanent inadequacy we need to remind ourselves as we come to the close of our thought experiment with a few models of the relationship between God and the world in an ecological, nuclear age. Even a metaphorical, heuristic theology that believes itself to be skeptical, open-ended, and pluralistic can become enamored of its experiment, finding its new models a sufficient improvement on alternatives that they become subtly elevated to a new trinity with a position of authority. Is it mere coincidence that we dealt principally with *three* models—mother, lover, and friend—and that they conveniently fell into the categories of creator, savior, and sustainer, thus taking the place, as it were, of the most ancient and hallowed names of the trinitarian God—Father, Son, and Holy Spirit?

It was not a coincidence but a deliberate attempt to unseat those names as descriptions of God which will allow no supplements or alternatives.[1] That objective was certainly not the central concern of these pages, but it is an important byproduct of the experiment attempted here. That is to say, if it can be shown that models other than the traditional ones are appropriate and illuminating for expressing the Christian gospel in our time, an important admission will have been made: *God has many names.* The attempt to unseat both monarchical and traditional trinitarian language, however, is not a subterfuge to establish a new trinity using different names. To do so would be to fall into the "tyranny of the absolutizing imagination," which we have all along tried to avoid. There are, however, two moves being made here: one disorienting, the other reorienting. The disorienting move is the introduction of alternative models for God and the world, and the experiment with them to try out their possibilities in relationship to an understanding of the gospel as destabilizing, inclusive, nonhierarchical fulfillment. In this experiment I attempted to see if they could, in their own way, address many of the traditional, formal theological categories of creation, salvation, and preservation; revelation and incarnation; the nature of human existence; sin and evil; the character of Christian life; church and sacraments; and so forth. Part of their power, I believed, was to show how they would do the job that the traditional models have done. So although the stress in these pages has been on an imaginative picture to undergird the new holistic sensibility needed in our time, of substantial importance as well—in order to make this picture persuasive—is its ability to deal with traditional Christian themes. Hence, a reorienting move is also intended. The alternative models we have considered are not a trinity in the old sense of hallowed names for God intended to discourage experimentation and insure orthodoxy; nevertheless, a modest proposal *is* advanced: for our time the new models are illuminating, helpful, and appropriate ways in which to think about the relationship between God and the world. And that is all that is being advanced, inasmuch as metaphorical, heuristic theology says much but means little. It is mostly fiction, mainly fleshing out a few basic metaphors in as deep and comprehensive a fashion as possible to see what their implications might be. Perhaps the imaginative picture that has been painted provides a habitable house in which to live for a while, with doors open and windows ajar, and with the promise that additions and renovations are desired and needed.

One matter of importance remains, however. In one sense the

entire essay has been about God, but the seriatim fashion in which we have considered our models—the world as God's body, and God as mother, lover, and friend—has not allowed us to address in a unified way one of the central issues of the Christian doctrine of God, and what I believe the doctrine of the trinity expresses—namely, the transcendence and immanence of God.[2] I have no intentions of embarking on a historical overview of the myriad ways theologians and church councils have interpreted this doctrine or of the conundrums it has presented, but from the point of view of our models, the doctrine or something like it *is* appropriate. For what it says in light of our models is that God is not a solitary deity distant from and unrelated to the world, nor a God submerged into the world and undifferentiated from it.[3] Rather, God as mother, lover, and friend of the world as God's body is both transcendent to the world (even as we are transcendent to our bodies) and profoundly immanent in the world (even as we are at one with our bodies). We have seen God's transcendence in agapic love that is the source of all life and that wills existence to all; we have seen God's immanence in erotic love that finds the world valuable and that identifies with it in the incarnation— both in the world as the body of God and in paradigmatic individuals, most notably, Jesus of Nazareth. Is more needed? What of the "third" in the trinity?[4] Is there something sacred about three? I do not think so. But the vision of salvation we have attempted to picture, in which an original unity is divided and separated by sin and evil to be healed and made whole again, a unity symbolized by the festive meal of friends where all are included, is, I believe, enriched and filled out by the third. In our understanding of the work of God in relation to the world, it is all of one piece: the creator says that it is good that you exist; the savior, that you are valuable beyond all imagining; the sustainer, that we shall all eat together, even the outsider. Yet in this one piece there are different emphases, providing a picture too rich and varied to be compassed in a single mode of speaking of the way God and the world are related.[5] To be sure, any one of the models of God as mother, lover, and friend of the world as God's body projects an image of God as both transcendent and immanent; moreover, as we have emphasized many times, neither these names nor any others describe, define, or limit the divine nature. In view of the theology presented here, a trinity is not a necessity nor should the divine nature be in any way circumscribed by it. All the same, a trinity fits well with the models of our experiment, and even more important, as other monistic theologians have pointed out, the pattern of three is appropriate for expressing the unity, separation, and reunification that have been the central theme of this experiment.[6] Admittedly, there are other ways besides the trinity to express the transcendence and immanence of God; nonetheless, it is a valuable, rich way. It suggests the profound immanence of God in the world through its dialectical pattern; it underscores the plurality of names for God; it provides a rich context for speaking of the variety of God's activities in relation to the world. In other words, it helps us to talk of God in an economical yet ample way: it is neither too little nor too much, neither the dull limitation of the unitary nor the riotous confusion of uncontrolled numbers. There is, then, a kind of pragmatism in settling for three: it has proved fruitful and illuminating.

But what, more specifically, does our experiment say about the transcendence and immanence of God to and in the world? The central picture we have been developing is of the world as God's body, which God—and we—mother, love, and befriend. God is incarnated or embodied in our world, in both cosmological and anthropological ways.[7] The implication of this picture is that we never meet God unmediated or unembodied. The transcendence of God in our picture, whatever it does mean, cannot be understood apart from the world, or to phrase it more precisely, what we can know of God's transcendence is neither above nor beneath but in and through the world. We meet God in the body of the world. What, then, do we say of God's immanence and transcendence? We have already considered some of the classic theological issues surrounding these themes in our treatment of the world as God's body, but now, in closing, we need to reflect on how we become *aware* of God's immanence and transcendence. If we understand our contact with God always to be a mediated, embodied one—with the body of our world, our universe, as the place where we meet God— what does this imply about divine immanence and transcendence in an ecological, nuclear age? It implies that we perceive or become aware of God not as solitary individuals who meet God in moments of religious ecstasy but as workers—parents, lovers, and friends—in the world. The world is our meeting place with God, and this means that God's immanence will be "universal" and God's transcendence will be "worldly."

To say that God's presence to us, God's immanence, is universal means that it is not limited to special times or places or to particular people or institutions, although special times and places, as well as particular people or institutions, may have paradigmatic importance. If the world, the cosmos, is our point of contact with God, *the* place where we join God to work on a project of mutual importance—the well-being of the body for which we have been given special responsibility—then it is here that we find God, become aware of God. This means we look at the world, all parts and aspects of it, differently: it is the body of God, and hence we revere it, find it special and precious, not as God but as the way God has chosen to be visible, available, to us. In addition, then, to special, paradigmatic individuals and to the church as the fellowship of friends, both of which are illuminating places where God is immanent, there is also the world that belongs to God in so intimate and special a way that we call it God's body. It is not, then, mere earth or dead matter; it is "consecrated," formally dedicated to a divine purpose. We do not know in all ways or even in many ways what this purpose is, but the world is not *ours* to manipulate for *our* purposes. If we see it as God's body, the way God is present to us, we will indeed know we tread on sacred ground. God's immanence, then, being universal, undergirds a sensibility that is open to the world, both to other people and to other forms of life, as the way one meets God. In this picture we do not meet God vis-á-vis, but we meet God only and always as mediated, as embodied.

Such universal immanence is but one side of God's presence: the other is worldly transcendence. We have said much in these pages concerning divine immanence, and in fact the experiment was conducted in part to counter the overly transcendent tradition of historical Christianity, with its emphasis on monarchical, triumphalist models of God. Less has been said about how, in our model, one perceives divine transcendence. What does it mean to call divine transcendence worldly? It means that we look to the universe as God's body for images of transcendence, and not to the political realm with its models of lord, king, and patriarch, as the tradition has done. And in fact, does not the universe provide us with far more awesome images of transcendence than the political arena? An ecological, evolutionary sensibility is aware of what one sees through telescope and microscope: the vast, unending space that is beyond all human comprehension, as well as the intricate pattern on an insect's wing that is likewise beyond our grasp. If one can say that the basic religious apprehension is the wonder at being, wonder that there is something rather than nothing, then the ecological, evolutionary sensibility is in this sense religious, for it avoids the "middle vision" we conventionally use in looking at our world and focuses on the very small and the very large. Both are awesome and wondrous: studying the bark of a tree or reflecting on the eons of geological time brings about the same awareness—that our universe is, in its age and size, its variety and richness, its intricacy and order, its detail and beauty, beyond all comprehension, all imagining. Is this a revival of the old argument from design for the existence of God? Hardly. It is, however, a context for imaging the transcendence of God in a worldly way, not through political images or, like the usual alternative to political models, in abstract terms of infinity, eternality, omniscience, omnipresence, and so forth, but in the mythology or images of our own day that inspire feelings of awe, reverence, wonder. These are the images, and many of them will be naturalistic, springing from the ecological, evolutionary sensibility that sees the universe, the body of God, with eyes of wonder. These as yet unknown, unplumbed metaphors have not been the focus of this essay; we have concentrated on immanental rather than transcendent models, on anthropological rather than naturalistic ones. But much remains for other experiments with alternative models of God, and a rich resource for metaphors of God's worldly transcendence is surely what we perceive through the microscope and the telescope that overturns our conventional middle vision of the world as a comfortable, comprehensible place. As the body of God, it is wondrously, awesomely, divinely mysterious.

We come to perceive our world in this way most immediately and painfully when we think of its end or its desecration. What the ecological, evolutionary sensibility brings to consciousness in a positive way—the wonder of being—awareness of a possible nuclear holocaust does in a negative way. And in this case, it is more effective to "think small." Middle vision, of course, can here also be overcome by thinking big, and that is the direction most consciousness-raising efforts on nuclear war have taken: they have painted a picture of nuclear winter or the extent of death and destruction that will occur after such an event. But it is even more telling in terms of our perception of the world, of how wondrous it is and how much we do in fact care for it, to think small. This demands a new form of meditation in which we call up concrete images of events, people, plants and animals, objects, places, whatever—as long as they are particular, cherished aspects of our world—and dwell upon their specialness, their distinctiveness, their value, until the pain of contemplating their permanent loss, not just to you or me, but to all for all time, becomes unbearable. This is a form of prayer for the world as the body of God which we, as mothers and fathers, lovers, and friends of the world, are summoned to practice. This prayer, though not the only one in an ecological, nuclear age, is a necessary and permanent one. The prayer we *wish* to pray, the prayer of thanksgiving for the joyful feast of all in the presence of God, depends upon accepting responsibility for our beautiful, fragile earth, without which there will be no bread and no wine.

Note to the British Edition

Books mentioned in the Notes are published in British editions as follows:

Barbour, Ian, *Myths, Models and Paradigms*, SCM Press 1974
Bonhoeffer, Dietrich, *Letters and Papers from Prison*, SCM Press 1971
Bornkamm, Günther, *Jesus of Nazareth*, Hodder 1960
Brown, Raymond, *The Gospel according to John*, Geoffrey Chapman 1966
Camus, A., *The Plague*, Penguin Books 1970
Daly, Mary, *Gyn/Ecology*, The Women's Press 1979
—, *Pure Lust*, The Women's Press 1984
D'Arcy, Martin, *The Mind and Heart of Love*, Faber 1945
Fiorenza, Elisabeth Schüssler, *In Memory of Her*, SCM Press 1983
Fletcher, Joseph, *Moral Responsibility*, SCM Press 1967
Hengel, Martin, *The Son of God*, SCM Press 1976
Hick, John, *Evil and the God of Love*, Macmillan 1966
— (ed), *The Myth of God Incarnate*, SCM Press 1977
Hodgson, Peter C. and Robert H. King (eds), *Christian Theology: An Introduction to its Traditions and Tasks*, SPCK 1986
Jantzen, Grace, *God's World, God's Body*, Darton, Longman and Todd 1984
Jeremias, Joachim, *New Testament Theology*, SCM Press 1971
Kelsey, David H., *The Uses of Scripture in Recent Theology*, SCM Press 1975
Lewis, C. S., *The Four Loves*, Fontana Books 1963
McFague, Sallie, *Metaphorical Theology*, SCM Press 1982
Moltmann, Jürgen, *The Trinity and the Kingdom of God*, SCM Press 1981
Nygren, Anders, *Agape and Eros*, SPCK 1953
Perrin, Norman, *Rediscovering the Teaching of Jesus*, SCM Press 1967
—, *The Resurrection according to Matthew, Mark and Luke* was published under the title *The Resurrection Narratives*, SCM Press 1977
Ruether, Rosemary, *Mary. The Feminine Face of the Church*, SCM Press 1979
—, *Sexism and God-Talk*, SCM Press 1983
Teilhard de Chardin, Pierre, *The Divine Milieu*, published as *Le Milieu Divin*, Collins 1960
Tillich, Paul, *Systematic Theology*, reissued SCM Press 1978

Notes

1. A New Sensibility

1. Pierre Teilhard de Chardin, *Writings in Time of War*, trans. René Hague (London: William Collins Sons, 1968), 25.

2. Ibid., 26.

3. Wallace Stevens, *Opus Posthumous*, ed. S. F. Morris (New York: Alfred A. Knopf, 1957), 163.

4. Jonathan Schell, *The Fate of the Earth* (New York: Avon Books, 1982), 117.

5. Ibid., 174.

6. Ibid., 108.

7. Friedrich Nietzsche, "On Truth and Falsity in Their Ultramoral Sense" (1873), in *Works* 2:180.

8. Elisabeth Schüssler Fiorenza, *In Memory of Her: A Feminist Theological Reconstruction of Christian Origins* (New York: Crossroad, 1983), 121.

9. A well-known exception is Rosemary Radford Ruether, who when stating her understanding of the biblical critical principle of renewal, invariably extends it to include a critique of "humanocentrism." "The 'brotherhood' of man needs to be widened to embrace not only women but also the whole community of life" (*Sexism and God-Talk: Toward a Feminist Theology* [Boston: Beacon Press, 1983], 87).

10. See, e.g., Ynestra King, "Making the World Live: Feminism and the Domination of Nature," in *Women's Spirit Bonding*, ed. Janet Kalven and Mary I. Buckley (New York: Pilgrim Press, 1984); Susan Griffin, *Woman and Nature: The Roaring inside Her* (New York: Harper & Row, 1978); Mary Daly, *Pure Lust: Elemental Feminist Theology* (Boston: Beacon Press, 1984); Starhawk, *Dreaming the Dark: Magic, Sex, and Politics* (Boston: Beacon Press, 1982); and idem, *The Spiral Dance: A Rebirth of the Ancient Religion of the Great Goddess* (San Francisco: Harper & Row, 1979).

11. See chap. 4, pp. 99–100.

12. The phrase "the deprivatising of theology" comes from "Editorial Reflections," in *Cosmology and Theology*, ed. David Tracy and Nicholas Lash (New York: Seabury Press; Edinburgh: T. & T. Clark, 1983), 89.

3. Harold K. Schilling, "The Whole Earth Is the Lord's: Toward a Holistic Ethic," in *Earth Might Be Fair: Reflections on Ethics, Religion, and Ecology,* ed. Ian Barbour (Englewood Cliffs, N.J.: Prentice-Hall, 1972), 102. Schilling makes the further and related point that almost everything we value is of a social, relational sort: not only the obvious communities in which we exist, such as family, city, and country, but also education, politics, the arts, science, and language. Moreover, the most basic, precious things we value are profoundly social and relational: friendship, love, parenthood, loyalty, wisdom.

14. Two recent sources (among the many available) that flesh out the implications of this statement for theology are Charles Birch and John B. Cobb, Jr., *The Liberation of Life: From the Cell to the Community* (Cambridge: At the Univ. Press, 1981), and A. R. Peacocke, *Creation and the World of Science* (Oxford: At the Clarendon Press, 1979). Another very interesting treatment by Stephen Toulmin depicts a postmodern cosmology in which human beings, in order to be "at home" in the world, must adopt not just a utilitarian but an appreciative attitude toward the other forms of life with which we are in relationship: "We can do our best to build up a conception of 'the overall scheme of things' which draws as heavily as it can on the results of scientific study, informed by a genuine piety in all its attitudes toward creatures of other kinds: a piety that goes beyond the consideration of their usefulness to Humanity as instruments for the fulfillment of human ends. That is an alternative within which human beings can both *feel*, and also *be*, at home. For to be at home in the world of nature does not just mean finding out how to utilize nature economically and efficiently— home is not a hotel! It means making sense of the relations that human beings and other living things have toward the overall patterns of nature in ways that give us some sense of their proper relations to one another, to ourselves, and to the whole" (*The Return to Cosmology: Postmodern Science and the Theology of Nature* [Berkeley and Los Angeles: Univ. of California Press, 1982], 272). Toulmin claims that postmodern science has more in common with the classical theory of "correspondences" among all aspects of the natural world—the various interlocking relations in creation—than it does with modern (Newtonian) science.

15. Birch and Cobb, *The Liberation of Life*, 42.

16. See George S. Hendry, *Theology of Nature* (Philadelphia: Westminster Press, 1980), for a treatment of what he calls the cosmological, political, and psychological contexts for presenting the saving activity of God.

17. Huston Smith, *The Religions of Man* (New York: Harper & Row, 1965), 209.

18. Peacocke, *Creation and the World of Science*, 54.

19. Ibid., 61–62.

20. One illustration of this point is found in a number of studies with higher mammals, such as apes and dolphins, that reveal complex problem-solving abilities; other studies among a broad range of animals underscore

that what could be called "spirit"—experiences of vitality, joy, and grief—is not limited to human beings. Anyone who has been in a "symbiotic relationship" with a pet for any length of time knows that there is communication across the dividing line of species.

21. Birch and Cobb, *The Liberation of Life*, 123.

22. Carol Gilligan, *In a Different Voice: Psychological Theory and Women's Development* (Cambridge: Harvard Univ. Press, 1982).

23. Ibid., chap. 1.

24. Rosemary Radford Ruether, "Envisioning Our Hopes: Some Models of the Future," in *Women's Spirit Bonding*, ed. Kalven and Buckley, 335.

25. Schell, *The Fate of the Earth*, 113.

26. Ibid., 67.

27. The role of reporters and especially of television in raising consciousness—and in producing subsequent action—in such events as the Vietnam war and more recently the antiapartheid struggle in South Africa is well known.

28. Gordon Kaufman, *Theology for a Nuclear Age* (Philadelphia: Westminster Press, 1985). Kaufman's fine study is almost alone in attempting a serious revision of theology, especially the image-concept of God, for a nuclear age.

29. For an interesting study of the use of political discourse for images of God, see David Nicholls, "Images of God and the State: Political Analogy and Religious Discourse," *Theological Studies* 42 (1981): 195–215. Elsewhere he writes that "our legitimate political concerns should . . . be reflected in the liturgy" but are not; on the contrary, "they [the liturgies] reveal a picture of God as an all-powerful but benevolent administrator whose principal role is to ensure the stability of the *status quo* and in particular to guarantee a quiet life for the church. . . . Almost entirely absent is the idea that Christians are called by God to be 'workers together with him' in the building of his kingdom (or commonwealth) of justice on earth" (*Times* [London], August 16, 1980, p. 14).

30. "Nuclear Eschatology and the Study of Religion," *Journal of the American Academy of Religion* 51 (1983): 7–8.

31. Kaufman, *Theology for a Nuclear Age*, 42.

32. Langdon Gilkey, "God," in *Christian Theology: An Introduction to Its Traditions and Tasks*, rev. ed., ed. Peter C. Hodgson and Robert H. King (Philadelphia: Fortress Press, 1985), 89–90.

33. Kaufman, *Theology for a Nuclear Age*, 56. The closest Kaufman comes to an agential view is in phrases such as "unpredictable grace" and "hidden creativity" as designations for the symbol "God."

34. Ibid., 13.

35. Paul de Man, "The Epistemology of Metaphor," in *On Metaphor*, ed. Sheldon Sacks (Chicago: Univ. of Chicago Press, 1979), 23.

36. The literature on deconstruction and theology is now extensive. The work of Mark Taylor, esp. his *Erring: A Postmodern A/theology* (Chicago:

Univ. of Chicago Press, 1984) is one of the most ambitious works to date. See also Thomas J. J. Altizer et al., *Deconstruction and Theology* (New York: Crossroad, 1982), and Charles E. Winquist, *Epiphanies of Darkness: Deconstruction in Theology* (Philadelphia: Fortress Press, 1986).

37. For a fuller treatment of the relationship between models and their referents, see my book *Metaphorical Theology: Models of God in Religious Language* (Philadelphia: Fortress Press, 1982; 2d printing with new preface, 1985), esp. chaps. 1, 2, and 4. I will, however, attempt a brief reply here. What prevents models of God, such as mother, lover, and friend, from being arbitrary? The most direct answer to that question is that they are not arbitrary, because, along with the father model, they are the deepest and most important expressions of love known to us, rather than because they are necessarily descriptive of the nature of God. But, pressing the ontological issue more sharply, are these loves descriptive of God *as God is?* As I say several times in this essay, it seems to me that to be a Christian is to be persuaded that there is a personal, gracious power who is on the side of life and its fulfillment, a power whom the paradigmatic figure Jesus of Nazareth expresses and illuminates; but when we try to say something more, we turn, necessarily, to the "loves" we know (unless one is a Barthian and believes that God defines love and that all human love only conforms to the divine pattern). That is to say, I do not know whether God (the inner being of God) can be described by the models of mother, lover, and friend; but the only kind of love I know anything about and that matters most to me is the love of these basic relationships, so I have to use these loves to speak of divine love. The metaphors do not illustrate a concept of love (that is basically an allegorical direction); rather, they *project a possibility:* that God's love can be seen through the screen of these human loves. Metaphors and models relate to reality not in imitating it but in being productive of it. There are only versions, hypotheses, or models of reality (or God): the most that one can say of any construct, then, is that it is illuminating, fruitful, can deal with anomalies, has relatively comprehensive explanatory ability, is relatively consistent, has humane consequences, etc. This is largely a functional, pragmatic view of truth, with heavy stress on what the implications of certain ways of seeing things (certain models) are for the quality of both human and nonhuman life (since the initial assumption or belief is that God is on the side of life and its fulfillment). This is obviously something of a circular argument, but I do not see any way out of it: I do not *know* who God is, but I find some models better than others for constructing an image of God commensurate with my trust in a God as on the side of life. God is and remains a mystery. We really do not know: the hints and clues we have of the way things are—whether we call them experiences, revelation, or whatever—are too fragile, too little (and more often than not, too negative) for much more than a hypothesis, a guess, a projection of a possibility that, although it can be comprehensive and illuminating, may not be true. We can believe it is and act as if it were,

but it is, to use Ricoeur's term, a "wager." At the most, I find I can make what Philip Wheelwright calls a "shy ontological claim" with the metaphors and models we use to speak of divine reality (see *Metaphor and Reality* [Bloomington: Indiana Univ. Press, 1971], 162).

38. An excellent entrée into deconstruction and its nineteenth-century background is Christopher Norris, *Deconstruction: Theory and Practice* (London: Methuen & Co., 1982). Another fine essay appears as chap. 5 in Frank Lentricchia, *After the New Criticism* (Chicago: Univ. of Chicago Press, 1980), which traces two directions from the key work of Jacques Derrida, one toward the literary criticism of the "Yale school" and the other toward the social-political historiography of Michel Foucault.

39. See Norris, *Deconstruction*, 64ff., for a discussion of this point.

40. See Derrida's critical essay on metaphor, "White Mythology: Metaphor in the Text of Philosophy," *New Literary History* 6 (1974): 5–74.

41. For two different treatments of this point, see Louis Mackey, "Slouching toward Bethlehem: Deconstructive Strategies in Theology," *Anglican Theological Review* 65 (1983): 255–72; and Carl A. Raschke, "The Deconstruction of God," in Altizer et al., *Deconstruction and Theology*, 1–33.

42. H. Richard Niebuhr, *The Responsible Self: An Essay in Christian Moral Philosophy* (New York: Harper & Row, 1963), 175.

43. This is of course what has been called critical realism, and from some contemporary perspectives it is not fashionable. See, e.g., George Lindbeck's espousal of what he calls a "cultural-linguistic" position, which stresses language over "reality reference." In speaking of Scripture, he writes, "It is the text, so to speak, which absorbs the world, rather than the world the text" (*The Nature of Doctrine: Religion and Theology in a Postliberal Age* [Philadelphia: Westminster Press, 1984], 118). This position gives up the issue of the conflict of interpretations, opting for formation of its own adherents within particular linguistic communities.

44. Michel Foucault's contribution to the demise of the metaphysics of presence is his critique of the illusion of the myth of selves as objective and value-free centers in control of history. He insists that, on the contrary, discourse formation is the product of dominant social and political forces, creating "insiders" and "outsiders." This is a point echoed in the liberation theologies' position on the social context of theology. See esp. "The Discourse on Language," in Foucault's *The Archeology of Knowledge*, trans. A. M. Sheridan Smith (New York: Pantheon Books, 1972), 215–37.

2. Metaphorical Theology

1. The phrase is John Cobb's, and it stands in contrast to attempts to identify the "essence" of Christianity, which he claims represent "essentialist" thinking. The context is worth quoting: "The unity of Christianity is the unity of an historical movement. That unity does not depend on any self-identity of doctrine, vision of reality, structure of existence, or

style of life. It does depend on demonstrable continuities, the appropriateness of creative changes, and the self-identification of people in relation to
a particular history" ("Feminism and Process Thought: A Two-Way Relationship," in *Feminism and Process Thought,* ed. Sheila Greeve Davaney
[New York: Edwin Mellen Press, 1981], 42).

2. John Hick, ed., *The Myth of God Incarnate* (Philadelphia: Westminster
Press, 1977), 201–2.

3. See my book *Metaphorical Theology: Models of God in Religious Language* (Philadelphia: Fortress Press, 1982; 2d printing with new preface,
1985).

4. The literature on metaphor is vast and growing daily. A sampling of
some current titles includes Sheldon Sacks, ed., *On Metaphor* (Chicago:
Univ. of Chicago Press, 1979); Mark Johnson, ed., *Philosophical Perspec-
tives on Metaphor* (St. Paul: Univ. of Minnesota Press, 1981); Paul Ricoeur,
The Rule of Metaphor (Toronto: Univ. of Toronto Press, 1977); Max Black,
Metaphors and Models (Ithaca, N.Y.: Cornell Univ. Press, 1962); Andrew
Ortony, ed., *Metaphor and Thought* (New York and Cambridge: Cambridge
Univ. Press, 1979); Mary Gerhart and Allan Russell, *Metaphoric Process:
The Creation of Scientific and Religious Understanding* (Fort Worth: Texas
Christian Univ. Press, 1984); George Lakoff and Mark Johnson, *Metaphors
We Live By* (Chicago: Univ. of Chicago Press, 1980); Ian Barbour, *Myths,
Models, and Paradigms: A Comparative Study in Science and Religion* (New
York: Harper & Row, 1974); Philip Wheelwright, *Metaphor and Reality*
(Bloomington: Indiana Univ. Press, 1962); Warren A. Shibles, *Metaphor: An
Annotated Bibliography and History* (Whitewater, Wis.: Language Press,
1971); Colin Turbayne, *The Myth of Metaphor* (New Haven: Yale Univ.
Press, 1962); and Frank Burch Brown, *Transfiguration: Poetic Metaphor and
the Languages of Religious Belief* (Chapel Hill and London: Univ. of North
Carolina Press, 1983).

5. The example is from Black, *Models and Metaphors,* 41–42.

6. My position here is very close to that of Ricoeur, as found in his *The
Rule of Metaphor* and elsewhere.

7. For a very helpful introduction to the importance of models in
physics, especially as related to similar as well as different uses in theology, see Barbour, *Myths, Models, and Paradigms.*

8. The role and definition of models in other fields are complex and
beyond our concern here. See chap. 3 of my *Metaphorical Theology* and its
notes, for an introduction to some of this material.

9. Jacques Derrida, "White Mythology: Metaphor in the Text of Philosophy," *New Literary History* 6 (1974): 42.

10. The difference between a traditional, Thomistic view of analogy and
my understanding of metaphor is interesting here. It is sometimes asserted
that the so-called transcendentals can be predicated properly of God
whereas metaphors are always improper. Thus, in the analogy of proper
proportionality, one can assert that human goodness is to human being as

God's goodness is to God's being. To this I would respond with two points:
(1) Since we do not know *what* God's being is, we have no corollary for
asserting "goodness" to God. (2) "Goodness" can *only* be a metaphor when
asserted of God (if it is to mean anything at all); that is, we use the
associations of human goodness as a grid or screen to say something about
God.

11. These comments bear some similarity to interesting research on so-
called dissipative systems by a multidisciplinary group of scholars influenced by the research of Nobel prizewinner Ilya Prigogine in the physical
sciences. In this view, living organisms and sociocultural systems (including the church) may both be regarded as partially open systems that interact with their environments and are in a state of disequilibrium. This
evolutionary paradigm is opposed to equilibrium perfection, permanence,
hierarchical control, and predictability. Rather, imperfection, change, un-
predictability, differentiation, and symbiotic pluralism are major characteristics. Such systems are capable of qualitative change and in fact must
change in order to survive; e.g., the Great Lakes are dying because of a *lack*
of disequilibrium. Disturbance, uncertainty, variability are the sine qua
non of dissipative systems: survival necessitates change and qualitative
transformation. For further reading, see Erich Jantsch, ed., *The Evolutionary Vision: Toward a Unifying Paradigm of Physical, Biological, and Sociocultural Evolution*, AAAS Selected Symposium 61 (Boulder, Colo.: Westview
Press, 1981), and Erich Jantsch and Conrad H. Waddington, eds., *Evolution
and Consciousness: Human Systems in Transition* (Reading, Mass.: Addison-
Wesley Publ. Co., 1976).

12. An outstanding example of theology as hermeneutics is the work of
David Tracy, esp. his *The Analogical Imagination: Christian Theology and the
Culture of Pluralism* (New York: Crossroad; London: SCM Press, 1981). A
fine illustration of theology as construction is the work of Gordon D.
Kaufman, esp. his *The Theological Imagination: Constructing the Concept of
God* (Philadelphia: Westminster Press, 1981).

13. See Paul Tillich, *Systematic Theology*, vol. 1 (Chicago: Univ. of
Chicago Press, 1963), 235ff.; and Gordon Kaufman, *God the Problem* (Cambridge: Harvard Univ. Press, 1972), 82–115. But what is the relationship
between our constructs of God and *God*, or in our postmodern, deconstructionist era is that distinction even appropriate? That is, do our constructions refer to anything, anyone? Is not talk of the "real God" or
"Being-itself" also metaphorical or symbolic? For instance, is not God a
metaphor central for the West, whereas other religious traditions are based
on other foundational metaphors? To the extent that I think that there is
something, someone to which our metaphors refer, my belief falls into
Ricoeur's notion of a wager that, as I phrased it earlier, "the universe is
neither indifferent nor malevolent, but there is a power (and a personal
power at that) which is on the side of life and its fulfillment. . . ." This
God is indeed the central metaphor of the world view of the West, but it is

not *necessarily* only that. Yet, how the metaphor refers we do not know—or indeed, even if it does. At the most one wagers it does and lives as if it does, which means that the main criterion for a "true" theology is pragmatic, preferring those models of God that are most helpful in the praxis of bringing about fulfillment for living beings. The other issue, however, the issue of the referent of the model, not to our world but to God, will not disappear, and here the question arises of whether metaphorical thinking ought to be applied to the idea of God itself. The basic point of metaphorical assertion is that something is there that we do not know how to talk about and which we have no access to except through metaphors. If then, we apply metaphorical thinking to the reality that is the referent of our metaphors, what would, could, that mean? I think it means most basically that we say God both "is" and "is not." Metaphorical theology applied to the "being of God" agrees with the tradition of the *via negativa* and with the deconstructionists in stressing the absence of God over our presumptuous insistence in Western religious thought on the presence of the divine. God *is not*, not just in the sense of being unavailable to us or absent from our experience but as a basic aspect of the being of God. I think something like this is necessary both to include the very different notions of other major religious traditions and to preserve a sense of the mystery of the divine, whatever our hopes, beliefs, or wagers might be. It is a recognition of the "privacy" of God, of the dark side of the divine that the mystics speak of and that a phrase of Robert Scharlemann's points to: "the being of God when God is not being God" (see the essay by that title in Thomas J. J. Altizer et al., *Deconstruction and Theology* [New York: Crossroad, 1982]). To affirm all this, however, does not mean there is not a reality (nor does it mean there is), though the presumption of metaphorical discourse—as evidenced by the conflict of metaphors, the competing "versions" of reality that metaphors project—is that these metaphors, these versions, are of something, or there would be no point in arguing for one rather than another.

14. Examples of theologians who are basically constructive would include Friedrich Schleiermacher, Paul Tillich, and Gordon Kaufman. Though they differ in significant ways, one would not describe their accomplishments with the adjectives I have applied to metaphorical, constructive theology: "experimental," "pluralistic," "imagistic." Rather, more appropriate adjectives would be "systematic," "comprehensive," "conceptual."

15. Robert P. Scharlemann uses this phrase to describe the kind of theology that constructs theological models, and he sees it as an alternative to other kinds of theology: confessional, metaphysical, biblicistic, religious thought. "It is a free theology in the sense that it can make use of any of these materials—confessional, metaphysical, biblical, religious, and secular—without being bound to them" ("Theological Models and Their Construction," *Journal of Religion* 53 [1973]: 82–83).

16. The relationship between image and concept which I support is articulated by Ricoeur, whose well-known phrase "The symbol gives rise to thought" is balanced by an equal emphasis on thought's need to return to its rich base in symbol. See esp. "Biblical Hermeneutics," *Semeia* 4 (1975); and *The Rule of Metaphor,* study 8.

17. For further elucidation of this point, see my *Metaphorical Theology,* chap. 5.

18. David Tracy, "Theological Method," in *Christian Theology: An Introduction to Its Tasks and Traditions,* rev. ed., ed. Peter C. Hodgson and Robert H. King (Philadelphia: Fortress Press, 1985), 52–59.

19. The candidates, needless to say, are many, as Tracy, e.g., notes: "the historical Jesus," "the original apostolic kerygma," "the Christ-kerygma of Paul and John," "canons within the canon," "working canons," and so forth (ibid., 55). Other more concrete, thematic candidates are "justification by grace through faith," "liberation from oppression," "the full humanity of women," etc.

20. This term is used in an essay by Edward Farley and Peter C. Hodgson, "Scripture and Tradition," in *Christian Theology,* ed. Hodgson and King, 81ff. For fuller treatment, see Edward Farley, *Ecclesial Reflection: An Anatomy of Theological Method* (Philadelphia: Fortress Press, 1982).

21. The term "prototype" is suggested by Elisabeth Schüssler Fiorenza as an alternative to "archetype." Scripture is then seen as a "root-model," a resource, not *the* source. See *In Memory of Her: A Feminist Theological Reconstruction of Christian Origins* (New York: Crossroad, 1983), 35. For one treatment of Scripture as a prime Christian classic, see my *Metaphorical Theology,* chap. 2.

22. For a thorough treatment of the collapse of the "house of authority," see Farley, *Ecclesial Reflection.*

23. For a treatment of Jesus of Nazareth as parable of God, see my *Metaphorical Theology,* chap. 2.

24. A frequent comment made in lectures and other public occasions, confirmed in conversation, July 21, 1986.

25. I agree basically with the perspective of Rosemary Radford Ruether on two critical points: (1) that a prophetic, critical principle can be seen, in spite of the androcentric bias, in both the Hebrew Scriptures and the story of Jesus of Nazareth (but like her, I do not find these sources sufficient); (2) that the new vision of inclusive mutuality must be extended to the earth. I am especially indebted to her work on this latter point and recommend the excellent chapter "Woman, Body, and Nature: Sexism and the Theology of Creation," in her *Sexism and God-Talk: Toward a Feminist Theology* (Boston: Beacon Press, 1983).

26. The "hermeneutics of suspicion" presses most liberation theologies to insist that the destabilizing, inclusive, nonhierarchical vision is so embedded in texts distorted by ideologies of power that no "hermeneutics of retrieval" would be possible were the canonical texts (and the tradition

built upon them) taken as the only source. Schüssler Fiorenza in her fine
book *In Memory of Her* and in other writings makes this point eloquently
and persuasively.

27. The theologian's life would be much easier if this were not the case,
especially since it is increasingly difficult for theologians to know how to
use Scripture responsibly and creatively. For a helpful treatment of the
options, see David H. Kelsey, *The Uses of Scripture in Recent Theology*
(Philadelphia: Fortress Press, 1975).

28. The literature on parable interpretation is extensive and growing. For
a more complete treatment of my position, see my *Metaphorical Theology*,
42–54. I am indebted especially to the work of C. H. Dodd, Amos Wilder,
Robert Funk, John Dominic Crossan, Leander Keck, Paul Ricoeur, and John
Donahue.

29. See Ricoeur, "Biblical Hermeneutics," 122–28.

30. John Dominic Crossan, *The Dark Interval: Towards a Theology of Story*
(Niles, Ill.: Argus Communications, 1975), 56–57.

31. See Joachim Jeremias, *New Testament Theology* (New York: Charles
Scribner's Sons, 1971), 1:115–16; Günther Bornkamm, *Jesus of Nazareth*,
trans. Irene and Fraser McLuskey with James Robinson (New York: Harper
& Row, 1960), 80–81; Norman Perrin, *Rediscovering the Teaching of Jesus*
(New York: Harper & Row, 1967), 102, 107; Schüssler Fiorenza, *In Memory
of Her*, 121: "The power of God's *basileia* is realized in Jesus' table community with the poor, the sinners, the tax collectors and prostitutes—with all
those who 'do not belong' to the 'holy people,' who are somehow deficient
in the eyes of the righteous."

32. Jeremias, *New Testament Theology*, 115–16; Bornkamm, *Jesus of
Nazareth*, 81; Perrin, *Rediscovering the Teaching of Jesus*, 107; Schüssler
Fiorenza, *In Memory of Her*, 119.

33. Schüssler Fiorenza, *In Memory of Her*, 120–21.

34. Ruether makes the relationship between ecological and social justice
clear: "There can be no ecological ethic simply as a new relation of 'man to
nature.' Any ecological ethic must always take into account the structures
of social domination and exploitation that mediate domination of nature
and prevent concern for the welfare of the whole community in favor of the
immediate advantage of the dominant class, race, and sex. An ecological
ethic must always be an ethic of eco-justice that recognizes the intercon-
nection of social domination and domination of nature" (*Sexism and God-
Talk*, 91).

35. Ibid., 89–91.

36. See the excellent treatment of this point in Gordon D. Kaufman,
Theology for a Nuclear Age (Philadelphia: Westminster Press, 1985), chap. 4,
as well as in Ruether, *Sexism and God-Talk*: "Perhaps it is this very idea of
God as a great king, ruling nations as His servants, that has been done
away with by Jesus' death on the cross. With Jesus' death, God, the heavenly Ruler, has left the heavens and has been poured out upon the earth

with his blood. A new God is being born in our hearts to teach us to level the heavens and exalt the earth and create a new world without masters and slaves, rulers and subjects" (pp. 10–11).

3. God and the World

1. See, e.g., Norman Perrin, *The Resurrection according to Matthew, Mark, and Luke* (Philadelphia: Fortress Press, 1977), in which he claims that 1 Cor. 15:3–7 predates the Synoptic empty-tomb narratives by twenty to forty years, and that the resurrection in Mark, Matthew, and Luke-Acts should be interpreted in the context of the appearances, not vice versa. Thus, the *continuing empowerment* of God, in light of various interpretations of salvation, is the meaning of the resurrection. "What actually happened on that first Easter morning, according to the evangelists, is that it became possible to know Jesus as ultimacy in the historicality of the everyday (Mark), that it became possible to live the life of a Christian within the church (Matthew), that it became possible to imitate Jesus in the meaningful life in the world (Luke)" (p. 78).

2. To see the resurrection of Jesus as an expression of God's presence in all space and time cannot in any way restrict that presence to the Christian community. The metaphor of the world as God's body is fundamentally linked not to the resurrection of Jesus but to an understanding of creation (see chap. 4, pp. 109–12). For the Christian community, the resurrection is, however, a powerful and concrete expression of this creational reality. Other religious traditions have other particular expressions of it.

3. For a treatment of some of these theological traditions, see Grace Jantzen, *God's World, God's Body* (Philadelphia: Westminster Press, 1984), chap. 3.

4. Gerard Manley Hopkins, "God's Grandeur," in *Poems and Prose of Gerard Manley Hopkins* (London: Penguin Books, 1953), 27; Pierre Teilhard de Chardin, *Writings in Time of War*, trans. René Hague (London: William Collins Sons, 1968), 14.

5. Ian G. Barbour, *Myths, Models and Paradigms: A Comparative Study in Science and Religion* (New York: Harper & Row, 1974), 156. Edward Farley and Peter C. Hodgson agree: ". . . the Christian movement never abandoned the royal metaphor for God and God's relation to the world. The logic of sovereignty, which presumes that God employs whatever means are necessary to ensure the successful accomplishment of the divine will, eventually pervaded the total criteriology of Christendom" ("Scripture and Tradition," in *Christian Theology: An Introduction to Its Traditions and Tasks*, rev. ed., ed. Peter C. Hodgson and Robert H. King (Philadelphia: Fortress Press, 1985), 68.

6. See chap. 1, pp. 16–20, for a discussion of this point.

7. Dorothee Soelle claims that authoritarian religion that images God as dominating power lay behind the "obedience" of Nazism and thus behind the Jewish Holocaust (*The Strength of the Weak: Toward a Christian Feminist*

Identity, trans. Robert and Rita Kimber [Philadelphia: Westminster Press, 1984]). John B. Cobb, Jr., and David R. Griffin view the classic Western God as "the Cosmic Morality," whose main attribute is power over all creatures rather than responsive love that could lead to the fulfillment of all creatures (*Process Theology: An Introductory Exposition* [Philadelphia: Westminster Press, 1976]). Jürgen Moltmann objects to the "monarchical monotheism" of Christianity which supports hierarchalism and individualism, and insists instead that a social, trinitarian doctrine of God is needed (*The Trinity and the Kingdom of God* [San Francisco: Harper & Row, 1981]). Edward Farley claims that the royal metaphors for God have fueled the notion of "salvation history" and its "logic of triumph" (*Ecclesial Reflection: An Anatomy of Theological Method* [Philadelphia: Fortress Press, 1982]).

8. Gerard Manley Hopkins, "God's Grandeur," in *Poems and Prose*, 27.

9. The aural tradition criticized here is obviously only one version of a Logos theology, and one peculiar to Protestantism. I am grateful to Rosemary Radford Ruether for a comment on this point in a letter dated May 16, 1986, in which she writes of "the strong current in neo-Platonism which cultivates a 'cosmos piety' of the visible world as an embodied God, found in Hermetic theology and even in Plotinus and in Plato's *Timaeus*. This tradition flows into a Christian sacramentality which sees the whole cosmos as sacramental, i.e., the bodying forth of the divine Logos. This is a very different understanding of Logos from the 'heard word' that is absent. It is Logos as Ground of Being bodying forth in not only human being, but all visible things. This older cosmos theology needs to be given more credit for a view very similar to yours."

10. See the well-known essay by Lynn White which makes this accusation in its strongest form: "The Historical Roots of Our Ecological Crisis," in *Ecology and Religion in History*, ed. David and Eileen Spring (New York: Harper & Row, 1974). See also a refutation of White's argument in Arthur R. Peacocke, *Creation and the World of Science* (Oxford: At the Clarendon Press, 1979).

11. There is, however, another metaphorical tradition of benevolence that moves in a more positive direction: God as gardener, caretaker, and hence preserver of the world and its life. Here benevolence is not distant good will, as in the royal metaphor, but intimate nurture. Gardeners or caretakers "touch" the earth and the life they care for with the goal of creating conditions in which life other than their own can grow and prosper. Such benevolence promotes human responsibility, not escapism and passivity, and hence these metaphors are helpful ones in our time. For further analysis, see Phyllis Trible, *God and the Rhetoric of Sexuality* (Philadelphia: Fortress Press, 1978), 85ff.

12. The metaphor, especially in its form as an analogy—self:body::God:world—is widespread, particularly among process theologians, as a way of overcoming the externality of God's knowledge of and activity in the

Notes

world. Theologians of nature, who take the evolutionary reality of the
world seriously, also find it attractive as a noninterventionist way of
speaking of God's agency in history and nature. See, e.g., Claude Stewart,
Nature in Grace: A Study in the Theology of Nature (Macon, Ga.: Mercer Univ.
Press, 1983). Even among more traditional theologies, the embodiment of
God is receiving attention. Grace Jantzen's position, e.g., is that, given the
contemporary holistic understanding of personhood, an embodied personal God is more credible than a disembodied one and is commensurate
with traditional attributes of God (*God's World, God's Body*).

13. See Jantzen's fine study on the dualistic, antimatter context of early
Christian theology, in chap. 3 of *God's World, God's Body.*

14. John Cobb makes this point and adds that total identification with
our bodies becomes impossible when they are sick, maimed, aging, enslaved, or dying. We are not our bodies at such times. See his "Feminism
and Process Thought," in *Feminism and Process Thought,* ed. Sheila Greeve
Davaney (New York: Edwin Mellen Press, 1981).

15. Paul Tillich's definition of pantheism is close to Karl Rahner's and
Herbert Vorgrimler's definition of panentheism: "Pantheism is the doctrine that God is the substance or essence of all things, not the meaningless
assertion that God is the totality of all things" (*Systematic Theology,* vol. 1
[Chicago: Univ. of Chicago Press, 1963], 324); "This form of pantheism
does not intend simply to identify the world and God monistically (God =
the 'all') but intends, instead, to conceive of the 'all' of the world 'in' God
as God's inner modification and appearance, even if God is not exhaus-
ted by the 'all'" (*Kleines theologisches Wortenbuchen* [Freiberg: Herder &
Herder, 1961], 275).

16. Most theologians who employ the analogy of self:body::God:world
speak in these terms about God's knowledge of the world. Since God is
internally related to the world, divine knowledge is an immediate, sympathetic awareness. See, e.g., Charles Hartshorne, "Philosophical and Religious Uses of 'God,'" in *Process Theology: Basic Writings,* ed. Ewart H.
Cousins (New York: Newman Press, 1977), 109; Schubert Ogden, "The
Reality of God," in ibid., 123; and Jantzen, *God's World, God's Body,* 81ff.

17. To understand the action of God as interior to the entire evolutionary
process does not mean that some events, aspects, and dimensions cannot
be more important than others. See, e.g., the analysis of "act" of God by
Gordon Kaufman in *God the Problem* ([Cambridge: Harvard Univ. Press,
1979], 140ff.), in which he distinguishes between "master" act (the entire
evolutionary process) and "subordinate" acts (such as Jesus' march to the
cross as an essential constituent of the master act).

18. This position is not unlike that of Boehme, Schelling, and Tillich: that
in some sense evil has its origin in God. In an evolutionary perspective,
however, the issue of what is evil is so complex that to say that evil has its
origin in God means something very different from what saying this
means in nonevolutionary theologians such as the above.

19. Jonathan Schell, *The Fate of the Earth* (New York: Avon Books, 1982), 128. I am indebted to Rosemary Radford Ruether for the import of this paragraph.

20. Gordon Kaufman, *Theology for a Nuclear Age* (Philadelphia: Westminster Press, 1985), 42.

21. Kaufman claims frequently in *Theology for a Nuclear Age* that it is the concrete images of God that influence most deeply our attitudes and behavior, but he fails to suggest what *kinds* of images might support his "formal" concept of God as that which "relativizes" and "humanizes." One must ask whether his concept of God has the kind of empowering attraction of its alternative, the triumphalist, royal model.

22. My evidence here is illustrative, not exhaustive. Karl Barth's position as the most traditional theologian on the contemporary scene serves as a reminder that those who reject a personal God are going counter to the deepest commitment of the Judeo-Christian tradition. That does not in itself mean they are wrong, but it suggests that one should relinquish the idea of a personal God very reluctantly, only when it has been shown to be unable to express God's saving power in our time. Among those who believe a personal God is not only defensible but highly credible are Charles Hartshorne, who sees God as the supreme case of personality, for God is supremely relational and thus "love" is predicated "literally" of God (*The Divine Relativity* [New Haven: Yale Univ. Press, 1948], 36); Schubert Ogden, who claims that the tradition asks how an impersonal God can be conceived in personal terms, whereas God as the one who is related to all others is preeminently agent—a Thou ("The Reality of God," in *Process Theology*, ed. Cousins, 129); Maurice Wiles, who, though believing "father" too individualistic, finds personal reality at the source of things and the language of spirit as the best model for expressing the activity of God as agent (*Faith and the Mystery of God* [London: SCM Press, 1982]); Grace Jantzen, who in *God's World, God's Body* writes, "Theology could hardly be called Christian unless it recognized as fundamental the personal nature of God" (p. 17); and most liberation theologians, who insist on the personal nature of God as the "liberator" of the oppressed or as the "Goddess" (see, e.g., Rosemary Radford Ruether's provocative notion of "God/ess," the Primal Matrix who both creates and transforms reality, in *Sexism and God-Talk* [New York: Crossroad, 1983], chap. 2).

23. Again, the documentation will be illustrative rather than exhaustive. The process theologians are perhaps the leaders here—see the work of John B. Cobb, Jr., Schubert Ogden, Marjorie Suchocki, and many others—but one sees a similar view of divine agency as radically relational and immanental (although the self-body analogy is not always explicit) in theologians as varied as Paul Tillich, Karl Rahner, Pierre Teilhard de Chardin, Gordon Kaufman, Langdon Gilkey, Maurice Wiles, Carter Heyward, and Grace Jantzen.

24. Schubert Ogden, "The Reality of God," 129.

25. To focus on these metaphors is not, of course, to deny the importance of other personal models peculiarly appropriate to our time—such as, e.g., that of God as liberator. That model, however, has received substantial attention, and theologies have been built upon it. The three metaphors I will consider have by comparison been neglected. A basic human relationship with which I do not deal is that of siblings. The "sisterhood" of all women with the Goddess has received some attention, as of course has the relationship of all Christians as brothers and sisters to one another as well as to "Christ as brother." Stress on the sibling model in Christian circles tends to emphasize the dependence of human beings on God as parent, as well as to continue familial imagery as the central model. Much of what I would support as valuable in the models of sister and brother is better dealt with under the model of God as friend.

4. God as Mother

1. Elizabeth Clark and Herbert Richardson, eds., *Women and Religion* (New York: Harper & Row, 1977), 164–65.

2. For a fuller treatment of this point, see my book *Metaphorical Theology: Models of God in Religious Language* (Philadelphia: Fortress Press, 1982; 2d printing with new preface, 1985), chap. 5.

3. Virginia Mollenkott makes this point eloquently, when after quoting Schubert Ogden's statement that God is "the most truly absolute Thou any mind can conceive," continues, "This *Thou*, this Absolute Relatedness, may be referred to as He, She, or It because this *Thou* relates to everyone and everything. . . . This *Thou* is a jealous God . . . jealous . . . that He/She/It be recognized everywhere in everyone and everything. . ." (*The Divine Feminine: The Biblical Imagery of God as Female* [New York: Crossroad, 1983], 113–14).

4. For different but complementary views on this point, see Carolyn Merchant, *The Death of Nature: Women, Ecology, and the Scientific Revolution* (New York: Harper & Row, 1980); Brian Easlea, *Fathering the Unthinkable: Masculinity, Scientists, and the Nuclear Arms Race* (London: Pluto, 1983); Rosemary Radford Ruether, *Sexism and God-Talk: Toward a Feminist Theology* (Boston: Beacon Press, 1983), chap. 2; Mary Daly, *Gyn/Ecology: The Metaphysics of Radical Feminism* (Boston: Beacon Press, 1978); and Rita M. Gross, "Hindu Female Deities as a Resource for the Contemporary Rediscovery of the Goddess," in *The Book of the Goddess Past and Present: An Introduction to Her Religion*, ed. Carl Olson (New York: Crossroad, 1983).

5. One example of the danger inherent in twisted thinking concerning sexuality surfaces in the birth metaphors used by scientists involved in creating the atomic bomb. Brian Easlea in his book *Fathering the Unthinkable* has collected these materials, and I quote a few. Kenneth Bainbridge, the physicist in charge of the Trinity test: "The bomb was [Robert Oppenheimer's] baby" (p. 95). General Farrell: "Atomic fission was almost full grown at birth" (p. 96). Henry Stimson received the following telegram

after the Trinity test: "Doctor has just returned most enthusiastic and confident that the little boy is as husky as his big brother" (p. 96), which meant that the plutonium bomb was as good as the uranium. William Laurence, a reporter at the Trinity test: "The big boom came about a hundred seconds after the great flash—the first cry of a new-born world" (p. 96). Easlea traces the history of science as the conquest of female nature— the taming of Mother Nature—back to Francis Bacon and his call to men to unite and, "turning with united forces against the Nature of things, to storm and occupy her castles and strongholds" (quoted pp. 20–21).

6. Janet Morley, a British theologian, in commenting on the fact that many natural images are used as metaphors of God in the church's hymns (light, sun, sea, rocks, castles, etc.), whereas God is seldom if ever spoken of as mother, wife, sister, midwife, etc., concludes, "Non-human objects may symbolize God's glory, but, by their almost universal absence in this respect, must we conclude that human women cannot?" ("In God's Image?" *Cross Currents* 32 [1982]: 315).

7. Many feminists are concerned to make this distinction. See, e.g., Ruether's rejection of "masculine" and "feminine" characteristics: there is, she says, no evidence that women are caring and nurturing whereas men are not. "We need to affirm . . . that all humans possess a full and equivalent human nature and personhood, *as male and female*" (*Sexism and God-Talk*, 111).

8. There are two ways that the feminine dimension of God can be imagined, as Elizabeth A. Johnson suggests in her excellent article "The Incomprehensibility of God and the Image of God Male and Female," *Theological Studies* 45 (1984): 441–65. Feminine *qualities* can be given to God so that God the father displays motherly qualities and, hence, God becomes a more holistic "person," having integrated the feminine side into a basically male character. But as Johnson points out, "The female can never appear as an icon of God in all divine fullness equivalent to the male" (p. 456). Or a feminine *aspect* can be attributed to God, and this is usually the Holy Spirit. Here, not only do masculine and feminine stereotypes emerge, but as Johnson notes, given the historically indefinite character of the Holy Spirit, we end "with two males and an amorphous third" (p. 458). I would add that even the attempt by process theologians to introduce the feminine dimension of God as God's consequent nature falls into stereotyping, since the qualities associated with God's consequent nature are receptivity, empathy, suffering, and preservation. Two unfortunate examples will illustrate Johnson's main points. Jürgen Moltmann claims that God "is the *motherly Father* of his *only-born Son*, and at the same time *the fatherly Father* of his *only-begotten Son*. . . . The Son was . . . made . . . from the womb of the Father" ("The Motherly Father: Is Trinitarian Patripassionism Replacing Theological Patriarchalism?" in *God As Father?* ed. Johannes-Baptist Metz and Edward Schillebeeckx [New York: Seabury Press, 1981], 53). Nonetheless, Moltmann sees this use of feminine terminology only as

a way to limit the use of masculine terminology; anything more, he says, would be in danger of "changing over to matriarchal conceptions" (ibid.). Donald L. Gelpi in his book *The Divine Mother: A Trinitarian Theology of the Holy Spirit* (Washington, D.C.: Univ. Press of America, 1984) elevates all positive feminine qualities to the Divine Mother as Jungian transformational categories (with none of the negative qualities), thus providing an excellent example of the "eternal feminine" sanctified by the Deity—with the dark side repressed.

9. Rosemary Radford Ruether makes this point tellingly with the comment that those unwilling to give up the male monopoly on God-language often reply to objectors, "God is not male. He is Spirit" (*Sexism and God-Talk*, 67). For the most part, I have avoided using personal pronouns for God in this essay—except for the male pronoun in relationship to the monarchical and patriarchal models—until the issue could be clarified. Henceforth, I shall use both male and female pronouns.

10. For a sampling of this literature, see Judith Ochshorn, *The Female Experience and the Nature of the Divine* (Bloomington: Indiana Univ. Press, 1981); Carol Christ, "Symbols of Goddess and God in Feminist Theology," in *The Book of the Goddess,* ed. Olson; Gross, "Hindu Female Deities"; and Ruether, *Sexism and God-Talk,* chap. 2.

11. This point is made by many feminist theologians and is succinctly summarized by Johnson: ". . . the goddess is not the expression of the feminine dimension of the divine, but the expression of the fullness of divine power and care shown in a female image" ("The Incomprehensibility of God," 461).

12. See, e.g., Rosemary Radford Ruether, *Mary—The Feminine Face of the Church* (Philadelphia: Westminster Press, 1977), and E. Ann Matter, "The Virgin Mary: A Goddess?" in *The Book of the Goddess,* ed. Olson.

13. In Elisabeth Schüssler Fiorenza's study of Sophia in Israelite religion, Sophia is in a symbiotic relationship to God with a variety of appellations (sister, wife, mother, beloved, teacher) and tasks (leading, preaching, teaching, creating, and so on). See *In Memory of Her: A Feminist Theological Reconstruction of Christian Origins* (New York: Crossroad, 1983), 130ff.

14. See Eleanor McLaughlin, "'Christ My Mother': Feminine Naming and Metaphor in Medieval Spirituality," *St. Luke's Journal of Theology* 18 (1975): 356–86; and Caroline Walker Bynum, *Jesus as Mother: Studies in the Spirituality of the High Middle Ages* (Berkeley and Los Angeles: Univ. of California Press, 1982).

15. Paul Tillich, *Systematic Theology,* vol. 3 (Chicago: Univ. of Chicago Press, 1963), 293–94.

16. Anders Nygren, with his much-discussed book *Agape and Eros* (trans. Philip S. Watson [Philadelphia: Westminster Press, 1953]), initiated the twentieth-century conversations on the issue, taking the extreme view that the two kinds of love are totally unrelated and incommensurable, with eros as the corruption of agape—the self-interest that creeps into disinter-

ested love. Gene Outka summarizes the four points in Nygren's position most influential to Protestants: agape is spontaneous and unmotivated; it is indifferent to value; it is creative of value, making the worthless human being worthy; and it is the initiator of fellowship with God (*Agape: An Ethical Analysis* [New Haven: Yale Univ. Press, 1972]). In this picture, God gives all and we take all; moreover, human beings cannot love God but can only serve as a conduit of divine (agapic) love to the neighbors whom we, like God, love in spite of their unlovableness. Nygren's position rests on the worthlessness of human beings; since all worth, all fellowship, must come from God, it is a fellowship based on the pervasiveness of sin, which God overcomes. One of the main critics of Nygren's position is M. C. D'Arcy, a Roman Catholic, according to whom agape and eros exist in balance in human beings (and hence the ideal love relationship is friendship). Were we not capable of giving as well as receiving, says D'Arcy, the human agent would be eliminated and God would be simply loving the divine self through us. See his *The Mind and Heart of Love: Lion and Unicorn—A Study in Eros and Agape* (New York: Henry Holt & Co., 1947).

17. C. S. Lewis, *The Four Loves* (New York: Harcourt Brace & Co., 1960), 176.

18. In Nygren's words, what is critical is to stress the "principle that *any thought of valuation whatsoever* is out of place in connection with fellowship with God. When God's love is directed to the sinner, then the position is clear; all thought of valuation is excluded in advance; for if God, the Holy One, loves the sinner, it cannot be because of his sin, but in spite of his sin" (*Agape and Eros*, 75–80).

19. This phrase comes from Josef Pieper's book *About Love*, trans. Richard and Clara Winston (Chicago: Franciscan Herald Press, 1974), 22.

20. Paul Tillich, *Love, Power, and Justice: Ontological Analyses and Ethical Applications* (New York: Oxford Univ. Press, 1954), 25.

21. Another reason is the Christ-centeredness of the tradition, which overlooks the first birth because it wants to stress the second birth. In promoting Christ's mission of redemption, the tradition has failed to appreciate the gift of creation.

22. The Hebraic-Christian tradition has carried imagery of gestation, giving birth, and lactation as a leitmotif that emerges only now and then over the centuries. For Hebraic use of the "breasts" and "womb" of God as metaphors of divine compassion and care, see Phyllis Trible, *God and the Rhetoric of Sexuality* (Philadelphia: Fortress Press, 1978), chap. 2. Another instance of such imagery emerges in twelfth-century Cistercian mysticism, which according to Caroline Bynum employed three basic stereotypes of maternal images: the female as generative, as loving and tender, and as nurturing. "For a theology that maintained—over against Cathar dualism—the goodness of creation in all its physicality, a God who is mother and womb as well as father and animator could be a more sweeping and convincing image of creation than a father God alone" (Bynum, *Jesus as*

Mother, 134). However, as Bynum points out, this feminization of religious language does not reflect a more positive attitude toward women, nor for the most part was it developed for or by women (with the exception of Julian of Norwich). Much of it is sentimentalized maternal imagery written by cloistered monks who had rejected women and family (see *Jesus as Mother,* 130ff.).

23. Norman Pittenger makes the accompanying theological point: "Thus we wish to speak of God as the everlasting creative agency who works anywhere and everywhere, yet without denying the reality of creaturely freedom—hence we point toward God as Parent" (*The Divine Triunity* [Philadelphia: United Church Press, 1977], 2).

24. The growing worldwide response to starving populations, response beyond anything expected and from all levels of society in all countries, is witness to the basic parental instinct to feed the young, the weak, the vulnerable. It need not (and should not) be named altruism, Christian love, or anything else grand; it is simply what all human beings want to be part of: passing along to others the gift of life.

25. Those who have written in the most balanced way about agape— including Josef Pieper, M. C. D'Arcy, Gene Outka, and Paul Tillich—all insist that although agape is not so completely different that there is nothing that unites the loves, it *is* different: agape qualifies the other loves, guarding against their distortions (as for Tillich), or it provides a base line (as in Outka's notion of agape as "equal regard", the "regard which is independent and unalterable; and which applies to each neighbor qua human existent" [*Agape,* 13]).

26. See Julian N. Hartt's analysis of this consensus in his essay "Creation and Providence," in *Christian Theology: An Introduction to Its Traditions and Tasks,* rev. ed., ed. Peter C. Hodgson and Robert H. King (Philadelphia: Fortress Press, 1985), 144ff.

27. Ian Barbour notes that *ex nihilo* creation was first propounded in the intertestamental period and elaborated by Irenaeus and Augustine in order to counter the idea that matter was the source of evil. This worthy motive, however, does not deflect the criticism that the doctrine of *ex nihilo* creation supports the separation of God and the world. As Barbour notes, "An additional motive in the *ex nihilo* doctrine was the assertion of the total sovereignty and freedom of God" ("Teilhard's Process Metaphysics," in *Process Theology: Basic Writings,* ed. Ewart H. Cousins [New York: Newman Press, 1971], 339).

28. One of the most impressive attempts at such a picture is to be found in Teilhard de Chardin's work, but even he is sufficiently within the main tradition that he avoids (although often narrowly so) "heretical" positions such as, for instance, that the world is God's body or from divine reality, even though his theology would be more consistent had he made such claims.

29. Grace Jantzen, who contrasts the craftsman model with the model of

the universe as God's body, uses language very close to mine but avoids both the birth metaphor and the female pronoun. One wonders why. "God formed it [the world] quite literally 'out of himself'—that is, it is his self-formation—rather than out of nothing" (*God's World, God's Body* [Philadelphia: Westminster Press, 1984], 135).

30. Jürgen Moltmann's position is a good illustration of the point: "If God is love he is at once the lover, the beloved and the love itself. . . . God is love means in *trinitarian* terms: in eternity and out of the very necessity of his being the Father loves the only begotten Son. He loves him with a love that both engenders and brings forth. In eternity and out of the very necessity of his being the Son responds to the Father's love through his obedience and his surrender to the Father" (*The Trinity and the Kingdom of God: The Doctrine of God* [London: SCM Press, 1981], 57, 58). Moltmann calls this a social view of the trinity; in any event, creation in this theology becomes the "tragedy of the divine love" (p. 59), for God must suffer limitation in giving freedom to creatures. It is difficult to see how a real relationship between God and the world can be imagined on this pattern.

31. Elisabeth Schüssler Fiorenza, *In Memory of Her*, 131ff.

32. Ibid., 133.

33. Current research on the relationship of Sophia to the Logos claims that their roles were similar and became eventually competitive, with the female, subordinate one giving over to the male, equal one: Sophia was absorbed by the Logos, the Son who is equal to the Father. Schüssler Fiorenza says of the followers of Jesus, "They are called to one and the same praxis of inclusiveness and equality lived by Jesus-Sophia. Like Jesus, they are sent to announce to everyone in Israel the presence of the *basileia*, as God's gracious future, among the impoverished, the starving, the tax collectors, sinners, and prostitutes" (ibid., 135). Ruether adds, "Theologically, *Logos* plays the same cosmological roles as *Sophia* as ground of creation, revealer of the mind of God, and reconciler of humanity to God" (*Sexism and God-Talk*, 58). According to Hans Conzelman, ". . . as a hypostasis, Logos is analogous to Sophia . . . the historical person Jesus is proclaimed as the cosmic Logos. . . . This is the Christological transformation of wisdom" (*Interpreter's Dictionary of the Bible*, sup. vol., 958). In relation to Paul and Matthew, Martin Hengel writes, "Once the idea of the pre-existence had been introduced, it was obvious that the exalted Son of God would also attract to himself the functions of Jewish Wisdom as a mediator of creation and salvation" (*The Son of God: The Origin of Christology and the History of Jewish-Hellenistic Religion* [Philadelphia: Fortress Press, 1976], 72). Raymond Brown writes that the Gospel of John sees Jesus as the "supreme example of divine Wisdom active in history, and indeed divine Wisdom itself" (*The Gospel according to John*, Anchor Bible 29 [Garden City, N.Y.: Doubleday & Co., 1966], cxxiv).

34. As quoted in McLaughlin, "'Christ My Mother,'" 375.

35. Julian of Norwich, *Showings*, trans. Edmund Colledge and James Walsh (New York: Paulist Press, 1978), 292.

36. Ibid., 298.

37. Ibid., 299.

38. Ruether, *Sexism and God-Talk*, 71.

39. Ibid., 49.

40. Ibid.

41. In the debate between eros and agape, the thought that Christian love is based on self-regard in any form has been anathema to Nygren and his followers. For some it has resulted in a decision to avoid the language of love entirely. Joseph Fletcher, for instance, insists that Christian "love" is a matter of will, not of the emotions, and accuses the Gospel of John of confusing philia (friendship with God and other beings) with agape (justice, with no emotional involvement). *"The best practice is never to use the word 'love'* in Christian ethical discourse. Every time we think 'love' we should say 'justice'" (*Moral Responsibility: Situation Ethics at Work* [Philadelphia: Westminster Press, 1967], 57).

42. The background of this view of God's justice is so evident in the Hebrew Scriptures that it probably does not need mentioning. The emphasis is decidedly on the side of a communal order of well-being in this world, which includes the poor (as well as a concern for animals), rather than on punishment for rebellious individuals, though that is also present.

43. I am indebted to my students Vicki Matson and Doug Gastelum for these thoughts.

44. See chap. 1, pp. 12–13.

45. Jonathan Schell, *The Fate of the Earth* (New York: Avon Books, 1982), 174ff.

46. Needless to say, this is a vast, complex process involving high-level technical knowledge and planning. If one considers the complexity of international business and finance, however, or of current military technology and deployment, it is evident that human beings have the capacity to handle massive problems, when the will is there to do it. The issue before us now is whether we will put human intelligence, resources, and our natural instincts for the preservation of life to work on the side of life.

47. Rita Gross makes the point in regard to God as mother that as a model for human behavior, it should extend beyond what mothers literally do, to include any woman who performs an act that gives positive, creative results. She notes that "father" language is used in this way—"father of the country" or "founding fathers." To call God father, she says, does not mean God is the "cosmic universal inseminator," so why limit God the mother to birth and nurturing ("Hindu Female Deities," 255)?

5. God as Lover

1. Phyllis Trible begins her analysis of the Song of Songs in a way that further counters this tendency of the tradition to ignore passion. "Love is

bone of bone and flesh of flesh. Thus I hear the Song of Songs. It speaks from lover to lover with whispers of intimacy, shouts of ecstasy, and silences of consummation. At the same time, its unnamed voices reach out to include the world in its symphony of eroticism" (*God and the Rhetoric of Sexuality* [Philadelphia: Fortress Press, 1978], 144).

2. The whole passage reads, "Let the mouth that gives the kiss be the Word becoming Flesh. Let the Flesh [Human Nature] which is assumed be the mouth that receives the kiss—a kiss, in truth, perfected equally by Him who gives and Him who receives it,—a single Person subsisting in two natures, the Mediator between God and men, the Man, Christ Jesus. . . . Happy kiss! . . . in which God is united to Man . . ." (Bernard of Clairvaux, *On the Love of God* [London: A. R. Mowbray & Co., 1950], 72).

3. One especially eloquent, as well as nonsexist, example of the lover model occurs in a prayer by the thirteenth-century mystic Gertrude of Helfta. The verse here quoted is preceded and followed by ones that image God as king, prince, protector, craftsman, teacher, counselor, guardian, friend, "burgeoning blossom," brother, "beautiful youth, happiest companion, most munificent host"—with the final image that of "most courteous administrator"! "You are the delicate taste of intimate sweetness. Oh most delicate caresser, Gentlest passion, Most ardent lover, Sweetest spouse, Most pure pursuer" (quoted by Caroline Bynum, *Studies in the Spirituality of the High Middle Ages* [Berkeley and Los Angeles: Univ. of California Press, 1982], 188).

4. I am indebted to Jody Combs, a student at Vanderbilt, for this insight.

5. See the *Shorter English Dictionary on Historical Principles*, 3d ed. (Oxford: At the Clarendon Press, 1973).

6. This passage, from a play on the subject of God as lover, was submitted to my course on the models of God by Sandra Ward-Angell.

7. In his book *Love Looks Deep* (London: A. R. Mowbray & Co., 1969), Norman Pittenger makes the case for God as lover, since God exemplifies all the characteristics associated with human love: commitment, mutuality with tenderness, fidelity, hopefulness, fulfillment, and union. In his *The Divine Triunity* (Philadelphia: United Church Press, 1977) Pittenger says that we should call God not just "love" but "lover," for we are talking about *one who loves*: "God is the cosmic Lover who expresses himself decisively in the human loving which was and is Jesus" (p. 109).

8. From Plato's *Symposium*, as quoted by David L. Norton and Mary F. Kille in *Philosophies of Love* (London: Rowman and Allanheld, 1983), 91; and Paul Tillich, *Love, Power, and Justice: Ontological Analyses and Ethical Applications* (New York: Oxford Univ. Press, 1954), 30–31.

9. The entire passage reads, "In spite of the many kinds of love, which in Greek are designated as *philia* (friendship), *eros* (aspiration toward value), and *epithymia* (desire), in addition to *agape*, which is the creation of the Spirit, there is one point of identity in all these qualities of love, which justifies the translation of them all by 'love'; and that identity is the 'urge

toward the reunion of the separated,' which is the inner dynamics of life. Love in this sense is one and indivisible" (Paul Tillich, *Systematic Theology,* vol. 3 [Chicago: Univ. of Chicago Press, 1963], 145–46).

10. Josef Pieper claims that erotic love is basic, for it reveals the foundation of all love, the tendency toward union (*About Love,* trans. Richard and Clara Winston [Chicago: Franciscan Herald Press, 1974], 98). Tillich puts it this way: "The *appetitus* of every being to fulfil itself through union with other beings is universal. . ." (*Love, Power, and Justice,* 33).

11. Tillich, *Love, Power, and Justice,* 25.

12. Langdon Gilkey makes an interesting summary of this point: "To the Hellenic and Hellenistic epochs the divine was both more real and more good to the extent that it was *not* involved in change and relatedness. In our epoch we tend to reverse the apprehension. . . . Thus the most prominent characteristic of contemporary theologies of all sorts is what may be termed their 'war with the Greeks.' There is hardly a conception of God from Hegel onward that is not dynamic, changing and in some manner intrinsically related to the world of change—and almost the worst thing any school can say of its opponents is that they are in this or that regard 'Greek'" ("God," in *Christian Theology: An Introduction to Its Traditions and Tasks,* rev. ed., ed. Peter C. Hodgson and Robert H. King [Philadelphia: Fortress Press, 1985], 104–5).

13. John B. Cobb, Jr., and David R. Griffin note that one of process theology's major objections to traditional theism is that divine love is portrayed à la Nygren (although also Thomas) as totally outgoing, with no element of responsiveness. They claim that this promotes an idea of love insensitive to the deep needs of others and an ethic that does not respond to the genuine needs of the other. In sum, they claim that if a relationship is going to be real—and this includes the relationship between God and the world—there must be responsiveness on both sides. See their *Process Theology: An Introductory Exposition* (Philadelphia: Westminster Press, 1976), 46–47.

14. Ever since Augustine's victory over Pelagius (even though no council decreed a formula solidifying the victory), the church has been wary of human participation in salvation. The excesses of the Middle Ages' treasury of merits added to Martin Luther's condemnation of human effort, and his notion of justification by grace alone became *the* Protestant dogma. It must be noted, however, that winning one's own salvation through merit of whatever sort is a different matter from participating in God's work of saving the world.

15. Although the imagery—the lover model—may be different, the basic view of salvation here is a very old one, with affinities to contemporary process thought and certainly to Tillich, with echoes from Hegel, Boehme, Augustine, Irenaeus, and John. This tradition prefers the language of "salvation" (making whole, healing) to that of "redemption" (rescuing or reclaiming the sinful), for it sees the problem as a disruption within a

whole that belongs together, rather than as a rebellion that must be punished or made amends for.

16. See chap. 3, p. 77, for another treatment of a revived sacramentalism.

17. Michel Foucault has written a fascinating study of the decline of the complex system of "resemblances" or "signs" between the visible and invisible worlds which until the sixteenth century served as a kind of linguistic sacramentalism, linking all dimensions of reality. "There is no difference between the visible marks that God has stamped upon the surface of the earth, so that we may know its inner secrets, and the legible words that the Scriptures, or the Sages of Antiquity, have set down in the books preserved for us by tradition" (*The Order of Things: An Archeology of the Human Sciences* [New York: Vintage Books, 1973], 33). In all cases, the assumption was that there was an original Text that all the signs pointed to and interpreted, albeit mostly in an oblique fashion. This linguistic "sacramentalism" ended with the loss of faith in an original Text to which the signs referred, and one is left with "mere" words that refer to nothing outside themselves. The sacramentalism I am suggesting—in both its cosmological and personal forms—implies that linguisticality does not exhaust reality: the nonhuman world is nonlinguistic (though admittedly linguistic as *we* apprehend it), and human lives cannot be reduced to linguistic signs (though again, in autobiographies and biographies, we apprehend them linguistically).

18. My position differs substantially from Hegel's, but I have learned much from him. He might, however, have avoided charges of pantheism had his understanding of God as "absolute Person" not been vitiated by his preference for "Spirit" over personal terms such as "love," which he found too emotional. He believed personal metaphors reified God; his impersonal ones, however, tended to blend the finite and infinite. See a fine study by Raymond Keith Williamson that discusses these points: *Introduction to Hegel's Philosophy of Religion* (Albany: State Univ. of New York Press, 1984), 255–85.

19. This understanding of the incarnation bears some resemblance to Karl Rahner's distinction between anthropology as "implicit" christology and christology as "explicit" anthropology. The point is that there is a *continuity* between Jesus Christ and the rest of humanity; otherwise, as Rahner points out, Jesus is a "surd." See, e.g., his essay "Christology within an Evolutionary View of the World," in his *Theological Investigations*, vol. 5 (Baltimore: Helicon Press, 1966).

20. For one helpful summary of the classical position, see Robert R. Williams, "Sin and Evil," in *Christian Theology*, ed. Hodgson and King, 194–221.

21. It is this realization that caused Paul Tillich to equate creation and the fall in vol. 2 of his *Systematic Theology* (Chicago: Univ. of Chicago Press, 1963). The "flaw" is not something that we are entirely responsible

for; "creation" is flawed in some deeply mysterious way. As Tillich noted, the doctrine of original sin (which we owe to Augustine), when understood in its classical form, is riddled with contradictions and absurdities; when interpreted, however, as the sin that is both "there" before us and that we make "our own," it is an expression of our deeply ambivalent situation.

22. One does not have to look far for examples. The current situation of the world's rain forests, which are critical to the continuation of life at its most basic levels, supplying not only untold numbers of species but also oxygen, water, and other necessities of life, are endangered because of the expansion of human populations. How does one proceed in such a complex situation? Another problem that well-intentioned planners are pondering is the best way to deal with increasing world starvation: this problem is so vast and complex that radically different and conflicting policies can be advanced in good faith. The problem is not just one of will; it is also one of knowledge. Nevertheless, theological discussion, though it will want to insist on the great importance of the problem of knowledge, must stay mainly with the problem of will.

23. For somewhat different treatments of this issue, see Pierre Teilhard de Chardin, *The Divine Milieu* (New York: Harper & Row, 1960), and Cobb and Griffin, *Process Theology*, chaps. 4, 9.

24. For analysis of Edwards's notion of "consent to being," see Roland Delattre, *Beauty and Sensibility in the Thought of Jonathan Edwards* (New Haven: Yale Univ. Press, 1968), and Clyde A. Holbrook, *The Ethics of Jonathan Edwards: Morality and Aesthetics* (Ann Arbor: Univ. of Michigan Press, 1973).

25. For a highly perceptive treatment of the Genesis story commensurate with the view presented here, see Paul Ricoeur, *The Symbolism of Evil*, trans. Emerson Buchanan (Boston: Beacon Press, 1967).

26. Augustine's view of sin as an inverse imitation of rightly ordered love lies behind this position. See, e.g., *Confessions* 2.6.

27. See Williams, "Sin and Evil," 198–205.

28. Rosemary Radford Ruether puts it this way: "Evil comes about precisely by the distortion of the self-other relationship into the good-evil, superior-inferior dualism. The good potential of human nature then is to be sought primarily in a conversion to relationality. This means a *metanoia*, or 'change of mind,' in which the dialectics of human existence are converted from opposites into mutual interdependence" (*Sexism and God-Talk: Toward a Feminist Theology* [Boston: Beacon Press, 1983], 163).

29. See John Hick's fine study on the two major classical theodicies, the Augustinian and the Irenaean: *Evil and the God of Love* (New York: Harper & Row, 1966).

30. Maurice Wiles makes this point in a persuasive way with an example: "In 1940 a far greater proportion of the British Expeditionary Force succeeded in getting away from the Dunkirk beaches than had at one time

looked likely thanks in no small measure to a spell of exceptionally fine weather. Many people at the time attributed that fine weather to the intervention of God. But if such is a conceivable form of God's action in the world, we cannot but wonder at God's apparent inaction in other comparable cases of human need" (*Faith and the Mystery of God* [London: SCM Press, 1982], 14).

31. This statement is, of course, very close to the position of some process theologians that God "feels" the joys and sufferings of all creatures in what is called the consequent side of the divine nature.

32. One version of the classical model of atonement can be found in Walter Lowe, "Christ and Salvation," in *Christian Theology*, ed. Hodgson and King, 222–48.

33. This position is close to what is usually called the Abelardian view of salvation, which Lowe describes: "Abelard held that Christ's work is best understood as a manifestation of God's love, which has the purpose of awakening a corresponding love in the hearts of humankind" (ibid., 231).

34. Throughout this essay we have used the term "salvation" rather than "redemption" for the work of God as lover. Redemption implies a recovering by effort or payment, a ransom or rescue—all of which fit the classical sacrificial, substitutionary atonement theories—but salvation implies the healing of divisions, making whole what has been torn apart.

35. The literature on the model of healing is extensive; a few important sources are William Clebsch and Charles Jaekle, *Pastoral Care in Historic Perspective* (Englewood Cliffs, N.J.: Prentice-Hall, 1964), chap. 3; Thomas A. Droege, "The Religious Roots of Wholistic Health Care," in *Theological Roots of Wholistic Health Care*, ed. Granger E. Westberg (Hinsdale, Ill.: Wholistic Health Centers, 1979), 5–47; R. K. Harrison, "Health and Healing," in *Interpreter's Dictionary of the Bible*; James N. Lapsley, *Salvation and Health: The Inter-locking Processes of Life* (Philadelphia: Westminster Press, 1972); Roland E. Miller, "Christ the Healer," in *Health and Healing*, ed. Henry L. Letterman (Chicago: What Ridge Foundation, 1980), 15–40; William F. May, *The Physician's Covenant: Images of the Healer in Medical Ethics* (Philadelphia: Westminster Press, 1983); Henri Nouwen, *The Wounded Healer* (New York: Image Books, 1979); Paul Tillich, "The Relation of Religion and Health," in *Healing: Human and Divine*, ed. Simon Doniger (New York: Association Press, 1957); and "The Meaning of Health," in *Religion and Medicine*, ed. David R. Belgum (Iowa State Univ. Press, 1967).

36. See esp. Droege, "The Religious Roots of Wholistic Health Care," and Tillich, "The Relation of Religion and Health."

37. Needless to say, this power over life and death can be misused by the medical profession. Thus, doctors appear as "gods" who can perform miracles, usually on essential parts of individuals, often elderly and wealthy ones. Less often, however, is the connection made between the health of the body and the rest of the person, or of even greater importance, rarely are basic nutritional and medical needs of the population,

especially the young, given comparable attention as aspects of the healing profession.

38. Elisabeth Schüssler Fiorenza puts it directly when she says that just as oppressive ideologies are not abstract but concrete in being social-economic-political systems, so liberation from these systems must be equally concrete: "Being human and being Christian is essentially a social, historical, and cultural process" (*In Memory of Her: A Feminist Theological Reconstruction of Christian Origins* [New York: Crossroad, 1983], 30).

39. See Harrison, "Health and Healing."

40. Albert Camus's novel *The Plague* deals with the issue of evil as "the plague" in an allegorical and highly complex way. The plague cannot be "cured," for "it can lie dormant for years and years in furniture and linen-chests," only one day to "rouse up its rats again and send them forth to die in a happy city" (trans. Stuart Gilbert [New York: Alfred A. Knopf, 1964], 278).

41. Camus notes that no one is innocent; all persons participate actively or passively in passing death sentences on others, being indifferent to the suffering of others. As one character remarks, "There are pestilences and there are victims, and it is up to us, so far as possible, not to join forces with the pestilences" (ibid., 229).

42. I owe this insight to a paper by Nancy Victorin, a Vanderbilt student.

43. The treatment here of the active and passive phases owes much to Teilhard de Chardin's *The Divine Milieu*.

44. Norman Pittenger expresses it in the following way: "Very likely [Jesus] came to the conviction that only in this way, through obedience to the point of death, could he disclose and impart the reality which evidently possessed him completely: the reality of God as loving Parent, we might even say as cosmic Lover, whose care for his people would go to any lengths and would accept suffering, anguish, even death, if this would bring to his children a full and abundant life, *shalom* or harmonious and truly human existence in and under his loving yet demanding care" (*The Divine Triunity*, 26).

45. See Nouwen, *The Wounded Healer*, for expansion of this point.

46. One impressive example is Black Elk of the Sioux nation, who reports a vision of inclusive love: "And while I stood there I saw more than I can tell and understood more than I saw; for I was seeing in a sacred manner the shape of all shapes as they must live together like one being. And I saw that the sacred hoop of my people was one of many hoops that made one circle, wide as daylight and as starlight, and in the center grew one mighty flowering tree to shelter all the children of one mother and one father. And I saw that it was holy" (*Black Elk Speaks*, ed. John Neihardt [Lincoln: Univ. of Nebraska Press, 1961], 43).

47. In teaching a course on religious autobiography for some years, I have noted a number of characteristics shared by a type of religious autobiography that I call vocational; that is, a type that links the personal and

public in such a way that the personal life is in the service of a commitment to public issues, such as issues of peace, abolitionism, women's rights, and poverty, within a religious context. Some of these characteristics are a profound, ongoing practice of meditation and prayer; a concern with the uses of money and often the adoption of a very simple lifestyle, combined with a monetary discipline; a relinquishment of the nuclear family or at least an enlargement of it to include many others in a communal family; a wrestling with sexuality, either as a problem to conquer or as a freedom to achieve a more inclusive kind of love; and a gradual movement toward a more and more inclusive love, as barrier after barrier of race, creed, sex, class, and religion falls.

48. See *The Journal of John Woolman* (New York: Corinth Books, 1961).

49. See Dietrich Bonhoeffer, *Letters and Papers from Prison*, rev. ed. (New York: Macmillan Co., 1967).

50. See *Narrative of Sojourner Truth* (Battle Creek, Mich., 1878).

51. See Dorothy Day's autobiography, *The Long Loneliness* (New York: Harper & Bros., 1952).

52. See Mohandas K. Gandhi, *An Autobiography: The Story of My Experiments with Truth* (Boston: Beacon Press, 1957).

53. This notion of fellow feeling is expanded in Norton and Kille, *Philosophies of Love*, 263, though the authors restrict it to human beings. Max Scheler, however, in *The Nature of Sympathy* (trans. Peter Heath [London: Routledge & Kegan Paul, 1954]), extends it to other species.

54. Scheler, *The Nature of Sympathy*, 281.

6. God as Friend

1. C. S. Lewis, *The Four Loves* (New York: Harcourt, Brace & Co., 1960), 103.

2. Daniel J. Levinson, *The Seasons of a Man's Life* (New York: Alfred A. Knopf, 1978), 335. The seeming indifference to friendship here is deepened to cynicism in a remark such as the novelist Gore Vidal's: "Every time a friend succeeds, I die a little" (quoted in Martin Marty, "Friendship Tested," *The Christian Century* 97 (1980): 1261.

3. *Nicomachean Ethics*, ed. and trans. John Warrington (London: J. M. Dent & Sons, 1963), 1155a.

4. *The Tennessean*, January 7, 1985, p. 4D.

5. Michel de Montaigne, *Essays*, vol. 1, trans. Jacob Zeitlin (New York: Alfred A. Knopf, 1934), 168.

6. In the search for a definition, friendship is often sorted out into different *types*. Thus, Aristotle speaks of friendships of utility, pleasure, and value (*Ethics* 1156a–1158a), with only the last being true friendship; he also speaks of unequal friendships (1158b) between, for instance, ruler and subjects, or parents and children. A contemporary writer, John M. Reisman, mentions three types of friendship: reciprocity, where the ideal instance is Damon and Pythias; receptivity, Jonathan and David; and

association, Brutus and Cassius. See his *Anatomy of Friendship* (New York: Irvington Pubs., 1979).

7. *Ethics* 1155a.

8. For one treatment of this controversy, see Robert Brain, *Friends and Lovers* (New York: Basic Books, 1976). The Oxford zoologist Richard Dawkins, whose book *The Selfish Gene* was widely interpreted as arguing for the competitive, nonfriendly nature of all animals, including humans, recently clarified his position, claiming it encourages "mutual reciprocity," or as the title of the BBC-TV documentary on his work puts it, (shown April 1986) "Nice guys finish first." Another similar view is Robert Axelrod's, in *The Evolution of Cooperation* (New York: Basic Books, 1985).

9. Brain claims that democracies, unlike communities built on the organic model, are based on the rights and responsibilities of individuals, not on affectional ties: "Democrats owe nothing to any man and expect nothing from any man. . . . It is only in a democratic, individualistic universe—and the capitalist West is the best example—that one can afford to ignore one's neighbour, cousin, and the rest of the world" (*Friends and Lovers*, 121).

10. *Ethics* 1158b.

11. In an essay on Christian discipleship, David Burrell opens with the Johannine invitation, commenting, "An invitation to friendship with divinity taxes our credulity, so much so that to accept it *is* to believe Christianly. That seemingly impossible barrier being breached, it is a relatively small step to speak of intimacy with God—both as individuals and as a people, for this God has already acknowledged delight in being with us" ("The Spirit and the Christian Life," in *Christian Theology: An Introduction to Its Traditions and Tasks*, rev. ed., ed. Peter C. Hodgson and Robert H. King [Philadelphia: Fortress Press, 1985], 302).

12. Lewis, *Four Loves*, 88.

13. Dietrich Bonhoeffer, *Letters and Papers from Prison*, rev. ed. (New York: Macmillan Co., 1967), 192–93.

14. For a somewhat different treatment of the model from the one presented in these pages, see my book *Metaphorical Theology: Models of God in Religious Language* (Philadelphia: Fortress Press, 1982; 2d printing with new preface, 1985), 177–92.

15. Immanuel Kant, "The Metaphysical Principles of Virtue," in his *The Metaphysics of Morals*, part 2, para. 46f. (Indianapolis: Bobbs-Merrill, 1964), 135ff.

16. In this regard, C. S. Lewis's reluctance to use the image of friend in relationship to God is interesting. He finds the image *too* close to the mark, and hence he claims that one might be tempted to forget it is an image! "God can safely represent Himself to us as Father and Husband because only a lunatic would think He is physically our sire or that His marriage with the Church is other than mystical. But if Friendship were used for this purpose we might mistake the symbol for the thing symbolized" (*Four Loves*, 124).

17. Dante's vision in the *Divine Comedy* is a classic example; in that vision and in similar ones, the notes of delight, reciprocity, mutual attraction, and play are evident.

18. Thus, C. S. Lewis says of friendship, "This love, free from instinct, free from all duties but those which love has freely assumed, almost wholly free from jealousy, and free without qualification from the need to be needed, is eminently spiritual. It is the sort of love one can imagine between angels" (*Four Loves*, 111).

19. The ethicist Joseph Fletcher takes this view: "Only in the Fourth Gospel is love often rendered *philia* instead of *agape*. . . . This nonsocial or selective-exclusive meaning of 'love' in the Fourth Gospel (for the 'brother' or fellow-believer but not for the 'neighbor') is in contrast to the wider and more general reference of *agape* in the Synoptics and Paul" (*Moral Responsibility: Situation Ethics at Work* [Philadelphia: Westminster Press, 1967], 53). Fletcher finds the friendship relationship to be in direct contrast to justice.

20. See *Ethics* 1169b–1170a.

21. See ibid., 1168b. Aristotle claims that "the extreme of friendship is likened to one's love for oneself," and that the same intentions apply in friendship, for a man "is related to his friend as to himself (his friend being another self)."

22. In addition to the classic studies by Aristotle, Cicero, Kant, and Hegel, and the books by Brain and Lewis, other works of interest on friendship include Aelred of Rievaulx, *Spiritual Friendship*, trans. Mary E. Laker (Washington, D.C.: Consortium Press, 1974); Robert R. Bell, *Worlds of Friendship* (Beverly Hills, Calif.: Sage Pubs., 1981); John M. Cooper, "Aristotle on the Forms of Friendship," *Review of Metaphysics* 30 (1977): 618–48; Mary Daly, *Pure Lust: Elemental Feminist Philosophy* (Boston: Beacon Press, 1984), chap. 11; Adele M. Fiske, *Friends and Friendship in the Monastic Tradition* (Cuernavaca: Centro Intercultural de Documentacion, 1970); Mary E. Hunt, *Fierce Tenderness: Toward a Feminist Theology of Friendship* (New York: Seabury Press, 1987); Horst Hutter, *Politics as Friendship: The Origins of Classical Notions of Politics in the Theory and Practice of Friendship* (Waterloo, Ont.: Wilfrid Laurier Univ. Press, 1978, microfiche); Ignace Lepp, *The Ways of Friendship*, trans. Bernard Murchland (New York: Macmillan Co., 1966); William F. May, "The Sin against the Friend: Betrayal," *Cross Currents* 17 (1967): 159–70; Gilbert Meilaender, *Friendship: A Study in Theological Ethics* (Notre Dame, Ind.: Univ. of Notre Dame Press, 1981); Jürgen Moltmann, "Open Friendship," in *The Passion for Life: A Messianic Lifestyle*, trans. M. Douglas Meeks (Philadelphia: Fortress Press, 1977); Ruth Page, "The Companionship of God," in *Ambiguity and the Presence of God* (London: SCM Press, 1985), 188–216; Rosemary Rader, *Breaking Boundaries: Male/Female Friendship in Early Christianity* (New York: Paulist Press, 1983); Janice Raymond, *A Passion for Friends* (Boston: Beacon Press, 1986); John M. Reisman, *Anatomy of Friendship*

(New York: Irvington Pubs., 1979); Letty M. Russell, *The Future of Partnership* (Philadelphia: Westminster Press, 1979); and idem, *Growth in Partnership* (Philadelphia: Westminster Press, 1981).

23. See, e.g., Brain, *Friends and Lovers*.

24. This connection in Greek society is well known, but even in the twentieth century a writer such as C. S. Lewis finds friendship suspect for the same reason. See *Four Loves*, 88–89.

25. In addition to what is mentioned by the studies listed in nn. 2 and 4, one might observe that in a society such as contemporary North America, where women outlive men and are often left living alone apart from children and other relatives, friends—usually other elderly women—become very important. In housing complexes for the elderly, they often form "families" of friends who cook and eat together, care for one another, and become one another's primary partners.

26. See the fine study by May, "The Sin against the Friend."

27. As May puts it, betrayal, though usually seen as a separate act, can become a way of life: "One no longer makes a discrete decision to betray a particular person; betrayal has become a pattern of behavior in which one is disloyal to others almost aimlessly and continuously. The secrets and weaknesses of friends are readily surrendered in social chatter wholly undisciplined by loyalty" (ibid., 164). It is to counter these and other acts of betrayal that children, for instance, want "best friends."

28. Lewis, *Four Loves*, 91.

29. As quoted in ibid., 97.

30. This is certainly Aristotle's view in the *Ethics*, and it carried over into many of the other well-known treatments of friendship down the ages.

31. One of the startling insights of an ecological age is that the "others" can be of a different sort from what most Westerners are accustomed to. While Eastern and more nature-based religions have always known that friendly relations with flora and fauna were possible, Martin Buber's distinction between I-It and I-Thou relationships—especially when the latter are extended to, say, trees—opened many eyes. One commonplace way that even our culture has acknowledged the appropriateness of nonhuman friendly relations and even inorganic ones (!) is in the existence of such groups as "Friends of the Botanical Gardens" and "Friends of the Library."

32. One is reminded here of the Johannine passage in which Jesus makes a similar transition from dependency to interdependency with his statement to the disciples that they are no longer servants but friends (John 15:12–17). Moltmann elaborates this point in the following way: ". . . the disciples are no longer called 'pupils' or 'servants,' but 'friends.' The relationship of men and women to God is no longer the dependent, obedient relation of servants to their master. Nor is it anymore the relation of human children to a heavenly Father. In the fellowship of Jesus they no longer experience God as Lord, nor only as Father; rather they experience him in his innermost nature as Friend" ("Open Friendship," 57).

33. *Ethics* 1155a.

34. There are many impressive authorities one could quote to document this point, including Hegel and process theologians, but I have chosen a contemporary British hymn writer who uses nontraditional models of God: "One function of trinitarian theology is to express and guard the truth that God is not a Oneness of uniformity, self-absorption, or isolation. In our human experience we know an incredible variety of relationships: female-male, father-son, sister-sister, sister-brother, colleague–fellow worker, team and group relationships, community, communion, grandparent-grandchild, and others too numerous to list. If we, with all our multifaceted relationships, are made in God's image and likeness, *it follows that the creative Godhead is, contains, and moves in, an incredible richness and reciprocity, in which all our varieties of relationship find their source*" (Brian Wren, "Sexism in Hymn Language," *News of Hymnody Quarterly* 7 [July 1983]: 8).

35. Lewis, *Four Loves*, 103.

36. See chap. 2, pp. 51–53.

37. The separatist view of friendship, the exclusive fellowship of the like-minded, also has as its central ritual the shared feast, but here who is invited (and not invited) is critical, as is evident in the parable of the wedding feast or great banquet (Matt. 22:1–10; Luke 14:16–24), where the "insider" guest list is traded for an "outsider" list. Secret societies, fraternities and sororities, country clubs, etc., survive by limiting table fellowship to the like-minded—however that term may be defined.

38. See chap. 3, pp. 59ff.

39. The Spirit model has much support from impressive quarters: both Hegel and Tillich, for instance, find "Spirit" the most adequate term for God. Hegel claims it expresses divine presence to or permeation of all creation, especially rational human beings, and Tillich says it is the "most inclusive symbol for the divine life" because it emphasizes God as living (see Raymond K. Williamson, *Introduction to Hegel's Philosophy of Religion* [Albany: State Univ. of New York Press, 1983], 275; and Paul Tillich, *Systematic Theology*, vol. 1 [Chicago: Univ. of Chicago Press, 1963], 277). British theologians of the twentieth century have been especially interested in the model, and works of note include C. F. D. Moule, *The Holy Spirit* (Oxford: A. R. Mowbray & Co., 1978); G. W. H. Lampe, *God as Spirit* (Oxford: At the Clarendon Press, 1977); Ian T. Ramsey, *Models of Divine Activity* (London: SCM Press, 1973); and Maurice Wiles, *Faith and the Mystery of God* (London: SCM Press, 1982), chap. 7.

40. Hegel, and especially Tillich, have a somewhat more cosmological bent, but most supporters of Spirit as a primary designation for God do not. See, e.g., Moule, *The Holy Spirit*, 19, where he claims that whereas Wisdom/Logos had cosmological functions in Christianity, Spirit did not, inasmuch as it was specialized to speak of God's immanence in human life. Lampe agrees: "To speak of 'the Spirit of God' or 'Holy Spirit' is to speak of the transcendent God becoming immanent in human personality. . . ." (ibid., 61).

41. See Grace Jantzen, *God's World, God's Body* (Philadelphia: Westminster Press, 1984), 22–23, for her treatment of this point.

42. Tillich, for instance, claims that Spirit is not in contrast to body or mind; when the term "Spirit" is used of God it refers not to a part but to the "all-embracing function in which all the elements of the structure of being participate" (*Systematic Theology* 1:277). That may well be, *as defined by Tillich*, but defining it as inclusive will not change the perception of it in a dualistic culture such as ours.

43. When "Spirit" language is used in relationship to the church, as in Schleiermacher's designation of the Holy Spirit as the "common Spirit of the new corporate life founded by Christ" or Hegel's identification of the Spirit of God with the "common Spirit" of the church—a tradition that is continued in Tillich's understanding of the church—corporateness and interdependence among *human* beings are emphasized: the cosmos is not explicitly included. For an analysis of this material, see Peter C. Hodgson, *The Church in the New Paradigm: A Theological Exploration* (Philadelphia: Fortress Press, forthcoming).

44. See Lampe, *God as Spirit*, 16; and Ramsey, *Models of Divine Activity*, 13.

45. The literature on this subject is large and interesting. For a brief but excellent introduction to Greek hospitality to the stranger, see Robert Meagher, ed., *Albert Camus: The Essential Writings* (New York: Harper & Row, 1979), intro. For a good bibliography for New Testament and other Christian sources, see John Koenig, *New Testament Hospitality: Partnership with Strangers as Promise and Mission* (Philadelphia: Fortress Press, 1985).

46. Euripides claimed that "he needs no friends who has the love of gods. For when god helps a man he has help enough" (quoted in Meagher's introduction to *Albert Camus*, 20). But the characteristic Greek attitude was that one could in no way count on such help.

47. Ibid., 21–22.

48. Koenig, *New Testament Hospitality*, 8–9.

49. The fluidity between these categories is suggested by the Greek noun *xenos* which means both "host" and "guest" or "stranger." In the New Testament, *philoxenia* means not simply "love to the stranger" but a delight in the reversals and gains in the hospitality situation. See ibid., 8.

50. Ibid., 125.

51. Quoted in Meagher's introduction to *Albert Camus*, 21.

52. See treatment of this image and others in Peter C. Hodgson and Robert C. Williams, "The Church," in *Christian Theology*, ed. Hodgson and King, 249–73.

53. See Moltmann, "Open Friendship," 60.

54. My understanding of the church is similar to the following definition but differs from it mainly in its inclusion of nonhuman life: "Ecclesia is a transfigured mode of human community, comprised of a plurality of peoples and cultural traditions, founded upon the life, death, and resurrection of

Christ, constituted by the redemptive presence of God as Spirit, in which privatistic, provincial, and hierarchical modes of existence are overcome, and in which is actualized a universal reconciling love that liberates from sin, alienation, and oppression" (Hodgson and Williams, "The Church," 271).

55. Hodgson and Williams note, ". . . the characteristic perversion of ecclesia in our time is no longer institutionalism but individualism; that is, the notion that Christian faith exists for the sake of the salvation of individuals" (ibid., 264).

56. See the fine work by Thomas W. Ogletree, *Hospitality to the Stranger: Dimensions of Moral Understanding* (Philadelphia: Fortress Press, 1985), esp. 41–43.

57. This very complex issue is dealt with by Charles Birch and John B. Cobb, Jr., in a way compatible with the view presented in these pages, namely, that an ecological, evolutionary model of living demands a "symbiosis of desirable goals" rather than one species or individual's winning out over others. See their *The Liberation of Life: From the Cell to the Community* (Cambridge: At the Univ. Press, 1981), 273–75.

58. It is interesting to note that human beings—at least in the popular media, such as the television series "Star Trek" or the film *Close Encounters of the Third Kind*—seem more interested in meeting aliens than mere (human) strangers. The alien from outer space appears fascinating, but the foreigner (from Russia?) is *dangerous*. Hence, the value in retaining reversal of roles is that we keep the stranger "close to home."

59. See the fine analysis of this concept in Aristotle by Cooper, "Aristotle on the Forms of Friendship," 645ff.

60. Ibid., 646–47. One sees this clearly in a number of democratic nations that have achieved a "compassionate society" based on both justice and care or friendship. These societies, such as England and the Scandinavian countries, insist from a sense of justice on narrowing the distance between the wealthy and the poor in order to provide basic medical, educational, and nutritional assistance to all.

61. Moltmann, "Open Friendship," 53.

62. Meagher's introduction to *Albert Camus*, 22.

63. Moltmann, e.g., regrets the split that keeps "enemy" as a public term while relegating "friend" to the private realm ("Open Friendship," 61–62). On the other hand, Meilaender finds obligation, and hence justice, alone appropriate for the public sphere, fearing sentimentality should philia be allowed into matters of governance (*Friendship*, chap. 4).

64. See Letty M. Russell's development of the concepts of advocate and partner in her books *The Future of Partnership* and *Growth in Partnership*.

65. May makes this point in his essay "The Sin against the Friend," 169.

Conclusion

1. There are many, especially those influenced by Karl Barth, who wish to insist that Father, Son, and Holy Spirit are the "names" of God whereas

other appellations such as creator, redeemer, reconciler and so forth are "activities." Claude Welch, e.g., says that *"Fatherhood is an eternal mode of existence of the divine essence"* (*In This Name: The Doctrine of the Trinity in Contemporary Theology* [New York: Charles Scribner's Sons, 1952], 183). Robert W. Jenson is even more insistent, claiming that "Father, Son, and Holy Spirit" is "God's proper name," allowing no substitutes, not even Creator, Redeemer, or Sanctifier, and most especially not Mother, against which he advances a special case (*The Triune Identity: God according to the Gospel* [Philadelphia: Fortress Press, 1982], esp. 1–24).

2. There are many other reasons theologians find for supporting a trinitarian view. The original one, if we take Athanasius's view, was that unless Jesus is one with God, unless the second person is of one substance (*homoousios*) with the first person, we are not saved, for only God can save. On the contemporary scene, to oversimplify somewhat, one could say there are two main camps: those who deal with the trinity *first*, as the foundation of theology (Karl Barth, Claude Welch, Jürgen Moltmann, Robert Jenson), and those who deal with it *last*, as a summation of their ontology or of the Christian experience of God (Schleiermacher, Paul Tillich, and various process theologians). The former group tend to identify the trinity with revelation and to see it focused on God's nature, whereas the latter group are more flexible in their trinitarian claims, understanding the trinity as a form of dialectic that underscores both the relational quality of divine existence and human experience of divine transcendence and immanence. The comments in these pages obviously identify with the latter group.

3. Although the trinity is often seen as a way of insuring God's relational character, there are, as I have pointed out earlier (chap. 6, pp. 166–67), difficulties with this function of the trinity, if stress is put on the immanent trinity as distinct from the economic. That is, the point of the trinity becomes protecting God from any dependence on the world. Jenson, e.g., writes that "God could have been also *communal* without us, that in his eschatological immanence he would finally be 'we' with or without creatures" (*The Triune Identity*, 146). Quite apart from how theologians or anyone else can know this about the internal nature of the divine being, it creates a picture of the God-world relationship totally opposed to the interdependent, communal, reciprocal one needed today. Moltmann does somewhat better, attempting to overcome what he calls monarchical monotheism, which he believes supports hierarchicalism and individualism, with a social doctrine of God, but again, his stress on the immanent trinity, since he is afraid to allow God any dependency on the world, gives a picture of the divine nature as self-absorbed and narcissistic (*The Trinity and the Kingdom of God* [San Francisco: Harper & Row, 1981]).

4. The question of the "third" has interested many. The Holy Spirit was something of a tag-along in the Nicene discussions, with the first two persons of the trinity getting most of the attention. Tillich discusses the

issue but dismisses it, claiming that "it seems most probably that the three corresponds to the intrinsic dialectics of experienced life and is, therefore, most adequate to symbolize the Divine Life. Life has been described as the process of going out from itself and returning to itself. The number 'three' is implicit in this description, as the dialectical philosophers knew" (*Systematic Theology*, vol. 3 [Chicago: Univ. of Chicago Press, 1963], 293). But Cyril Richardson disagrees, finding that the Father and Son are adequate for expressing the absolute and yet related nature of God, and the Spirit is an unnecessary additional way of talking about God in relation to the world (*The Doctrine of the Trinity* [Nashville: Abingdon Press, 1958]).

5. It should be obvious that the trinitarian view I am supporting is a functional one, focused on God's activity in relationship to the world and our talk about that activity. It makes no claims about the so-called immanent or intrinsic trinity, for I see no way that assumptions concerning the inner nature of God are possible. My interest centers on the economic trinity, on the experience of God's activity in relation to the world. This experience, in the models we have considered, of a Thou who both transcends the world and is radically immanent to it, is well expressed by the sort of trinitarianism I am sketching.

6. The similarities of my position with those of Hegel and Tillich are obvious, though my reasons are less grandiose than theirs, especially Hegel's. For Hegel, the idea of the trinity—the process of differentiation and return—is the heart of his philosophy and Christianity illustrates it magnificently (see Peter C. Hodgson, ed., *Hegel's Lectures on the Philosophy of Religion* [Berkeley: Univ. of California Press, 1984]). Tillich places the trinity at the end of his theology and sees it, as he does other theological symbols, as a response to questions implied in human existence (*Systematic Theology* 3:296). My reasons are more modest.

7. See chap. 5, pp. 135–36.